CASE STUDIES
IN PSYCHOTHERAPY

CASE STUDIES
IN PSYCHOTHERAPY
FIFTH EDITION

Editors

Danny Wedding
Raymond J. Corsini

THOMSON

BROOKS/COLE

Australia • Brazil • Canada • Mexico • Singapore • Spain
United Kingdom • United States

THOMSON ™
BROOKS/COLE

Case Studies in Psychotherapy, Fifth Edition
Edited by Danny Wedding and Raymond J. Corsini

Senior Acquisitions Editor: Marquita Flemming
Assistant Editor: Samantha Shook
Editorial Assistant: Meaghan Banks
Technology Project Manager: Julie Aguilar
Marketing Manager: Meghan McCullough
Marketing Communications Manager: Shemika Britt
Project Manager, Editorial Production:
    Christy Krueger
Creative Director: Rob Hugel
Art Director: Vernon Boes
Print Buyer: Nora Massuda
Permissions Editor: Margaret Chamberlain-Gaston

Production Service: Aaron Downey/Matrix
    Productions Inc.
Copy Editor: Frank Hubert
Cover Designer: Denise Davidson
Cover Image: Diana Ong/Superstock. "Blue, Red
    and Yellow Faces 1998"
Cover Printer: Thomson West
Compositor: International Typesetting and
    Composition
Printer: Thomson West

Printed in the United States of America
1 2 3 4 5 6 7 11 10 09 08 07

Library of Congress Control Number: 2006939110

ISBN-13: 978-0-495-10025-6
ISBN-10: 0-495-10025-0

Thomson Higher Education
10 Davis Drive
Belmont, CA 94002-3098
USA

For more information about our products,
contact us at:
Thomson Learning Academic Resource Center
1-800-423-0563

For permission to use material from this text or
product, submit a request online at
http://www.thomsonrights.com.

Any additional questions about permissions
can be submitted by e-mail to
thomsonrights@thomson.com.

In Memory of

Carl Rogers
(1902–1987)

Rollo May
(1909–1994)

and

Joseph Wolpe
(1915–1997)

CONTENTS

CONTRIBUTORS

Edna Adelson

David H. Barlow

Aaron T. Beck

Larry E. Beutler

Sally Denham-Vaughan

Claire Douglas

Albert Ellis

Selma Fraiberg

Arnold A. Lazarus

Michael Maniacci

Ed Mendelowitz

Harold H. Mosak

Peggy Papp

Carl R. Rogers

Deane H. Shapiro, Jr.

Vivian Shapiro

FOREWORD

Observing an expert perform a skills-based task has always been the most effective way for an apprentice to learn a complex procedure. For this reason, witnessing and studying the work of those who have mastered their craft have always been at the heart of the apprenticeship system. This method of training is more effective when it has been preceded by instruction that allows novices to place their observations into a meaningful conceptual context. This book, which presents case studies conducted and written by experts in specific therapeutic modalities, corresponds to the apprenticeship aspect of a training program. The primary text, *Current Psychotherapies,* parallels these case studies chapter by chapter. Although a reading of that text is not necessary for a fruitful reading of these case studies, it can heighten understanding of what the therapists are doing by presenting the theoretical and applied underpinnings of their systems.

All clinicians personalize the systems that they have studied and chosen to use. Their therapy reflects their personal life histories, the scripts, values, attitudes, and dispositions that form (mostly at a tacit or implicit level) the weft of that elusive fabric we call the psyche. None of us can entirely escape the conditions that have made us who we are, and our experiences inevitably get enmeshed in the treatment plan and the procedures that we use with our clients. For this reason, the therapist, as a person, becomes the primary instrument of therapy. The techniques become secondary.

Most of you who will read these case studies are motivated by an interest in improving your clinical skills. A first reading will excite a sense of profound admiration for the clinicians who worked the marvels of "therapeutic outcome" described in the studies. Their virtuosity should not discourage you from aspiring to their level of expertise. One must keep in mind that these cases are not examples of their least accomplished performances. The editors chose them precisely because they are instructive of the highly evolved clinical skills these therapists possessed at an advanced point in their careers. Although these clients challenged their resources to the utmost, they were clients who were apt, and suitable, for the treatments these therapists were prepared to provide.

Becoming a skilled clinician is like becoming skilled at any other complex human activity. It is the work of the "long-distance runner." It is building a repertoire of techniques and broad strategies that fit a consistent theoretical paradigm, honing various clinical skills, and learning to recognize the appropriate moments to use them. It is the work of fashioning coherent treatment plans for particular individuals who will be facing us filled with hope and anxiety. It is becoming a therapist with a therapeutic personality—the privileged instrument of every successful therapy, polished by the inevitable stresses, frustrations, and failures of life and of our profession—for not every therapeutic relationship turns out as we had hoped it would.

This book raises questions that go far beyond the boundaries of psychotherapy as that discipline is generally construed. The concerns and the personages that are depicted in these cases implicitly evoke issues of cultural anthropology, social psychology, hermeneutics, psychopedagogy, developmental psychology, and cognitive science.

Psychotherapeutics has borrowed the terms *etic* and *emic* from cultural anthropology. The former, etic, characterizes a nomothetic or universal approach to framing theories of personality development; the latter refers to principles that are more culture sensitive and culture bound. An emic approach refrains from generalizing principles beyond the group in which they have been found to be valid. In the limiting case, it treats each individual as possessing his or her own "culture."

Inclusion of the case on meditation reflects the editors' recognition of the richness that non-Occidental philosophies and approaches to healing can bring to the Western therapist. Of course, this East-West conceptualization of the culture specificity of any therapy is not a true dichotomy. Like any other psychological, anthropological, or sociological variable, culture specificity lies on a continuum. All the case studies in this book can be placed somewhere on that continuum.

Readers of this book will no doubt experience an approach-avoidance dilemma with several, if not most, of the therapies described here, for there are drawbacks and benefits for each system. The editors make no apology for that and expect both the practitioner and the trainee to struggle with the issue of choice. The decisions you make about therapy will be quite personal. Some prefer a predominantly intrapsychic approach to therapy; others a more contextual, social engineering approach. Some like the freedom of a time-unlimited model; others a time-limited, even very brief, model. Some will prefer didactic and directive methods; others will be inclined to the Socratic, client-centered approaches. Some will veer to etiological and history-focused exploration; others will prefer teleological, motivational, or even exclusively present-focused perspectives. Some will prefer a reductionistic model; others a holistic model that involves exercise, nutrition, physical fitness, medical exams, and heavy social penetration of clients' ambient worlds. Some of you will prefer the highly cognitive; others the principally affect-centered. You will find examples of all of these among the 13 case studies of this volume.

The following case studies will be rich ore to exploit, but in mining them, you will inevitably transform them. These studies are like rushing streams, of which the Greek philosopher Heraclitus spoke, into which you can dip your foot (or even plunge). You cannot, however, do the same thing twice, not because the case history will change, but because *you* will have changed at a second reading. Be that as it may, you have a banquet table set before you. The chapters were a pleasurable and useful read for me. I have no doubt they will also be for you.

Frank Dumont
McGill University

ACKNOWLEDGMENTS

We are grateful to dozens of colleagues and friends who have taken time to discuss psychotherapy with us and to share their ideas about how it can best be taught. Sometimes, these conversations took hours and went on late into the evening; at other times, a friend would make a casual comment that would later shape our decisions about which cases to include in *Case Studies in Psychotherapy.* Although *Current Psychotherapies* chapter authors usually selected the case study used to supplement their chapters in *Case Studies in Psychotherapy*, we sometimes solicited outside advice and opinions, and we are indebted to the following individuals who helped in a variety of ways with the preparation of this book.

Bernard Beitman
University of Missouri–Columbia
Juris Draguns
Pennsylvania State University
Vicki Eichhorn
University of Missouri–Columbia
Ken Freedland
Washington University
Glenn Good
University of Missouri–Columbia
James Hennessy
Fordham University
Lockie Johnson
American University of the Caribbean
Judy Kuriansky
Columbia University
Tony Marsella
University of Hawaii
Lisa Marty
Milliken Publishing Company
Richard Nelson-Jones
Cognitive Humanistic Institute, Chiang Mai, Thailand
Tom Oltmanns
Washington University
Paul Pedersen
University of Hawaii
Paul Priester
University of Wisconsin–Milwaukee
Sombat Tapanya
Chiang Mai University
Robert Woody
University of Nebraska–Omaha

PREFACE

Psychotherapy is a difficult calling. Its practice requires creativity as well as intelligence, ingenuity as well as training, and hard work as well as good intentions. It is easy to do badly but exceedingly difficult to do well. Its ranks include both charlatans and grand masters. Psychotherapy involves skills that are almost never completely mastered, and it provides opportunities for, and indeed demands, lifelong learning.

Unfortunately, the very features that make psychotherapy so fascinating also make it difficult to teach or explain. Those of us who presume to instruct others in this arcane craft realize that modeling is our most powerful tool, and it is often more heuristic to *show* students what we do rather than *tell* them what we do. However, all of us realize the limits of our own training: There are myriad clients with multiple problems, and their needs are protean.

One way to deal with the limits of our own experience and training is to expose students to role models through case histories such as those collected in this volume. Each case in *Case Studies in Psychotherapy* is written by an experienced psychotherapist, and each parallels a chapter in the eighth edition of the companion volume, *Current Psychotherapies.*

More than half a million students have used *Current Psychotherapies* to learn about the theoretical underpinnings and fundamental methods of a dozen or so therapeutic systems. The cases in the current volume were carefully selected to expand and supplement the information in the parent text. This fifth edition includes new cases to illustrate psychoanalysis, analytical psychotherapy, existential psychotherapy, Gestalt therapy, multimodal therapy, and integrative psychotherapy.

The serious student of psychotherapy can benefit greatly by reading *Case Studies in Psychotherapy* in tandem with the core chapters in *Current Psychotherapies.* We're convinced students who make this investment will appreciate more fully both the beauty and the art of psychotherapy.

Danny Wedding
danny.wedding@mimh.edu

Raymond J. Corsini
rjcor@hawaii.rr.com

CASE STUDIES
IN PSYCHOTHERAPY

Editors' Introduction

This is an intriguing case study that demonstrates how a psychoanalytic approach can be applied in a nontraditional setting and in somewhat nontraditional ways. This case illustrates the work of staff from the Infant Mental Health Program at the University of Michigan with a very impaired mother whose history of childhood trauma and abuse severely impeded her ability to properly mother her own infant. The team treating this family recognizes that the mother is oblivious to the cries of her baby, and they surmise that she will not be able to mother adequately until she confronts her own pain and learns to hear herself cry. The case illustrates transference, interpretation, and the key psychoanalytic concept of the repetition of the past in the present. In addition, we see the therapists incorporating their knowledge of child development to plan the treatment for the mother, and contrary to the popular stereotype of psychoanalytic treatment, we see the treatment team actively educating the mother and teaching her how to respond to her baby. It will be useful for you to consider what recommendation you would make if you were a claims reviewer asked to justify the need for 2 years of treatment for this mother. How often do psychotherapy patients present with a history of childhood sexual abuse? How would the other therapists included in this book have handled the case?

1 | GHOSTS IN THE NURSERY: A PSYCHOANALYTIC APPROACH TO THE PROBLEM OF IMPAIRED INFANT-MOTHER RELATIONSHIPS

Selma Fraiberg, Edna Adelson, and Vivian Shapiro

THE CASE OF MARY

Mary, who came to us at $5^1/_2$ months, was the first baby referred to our new Infant Mental Health Program. Her mother, Mrs. March, had appeared at an adoption agency some weeks earlier. She wanted to surrender her baby for adoption. But adoption plans could not proceed because Mr. March would not give his consent. Mary's mother was described as "a rejecting mother."

Now, of course, nobody loves a rejecting mother, in our community or any other, and Mary and her family might at this point have disappeared into the anonymity of a metropolitan community, perhaps to surface once again when tragedy struck. But chance brought the family to one of the psychiatric clinics of our university. The psychiatric evaluation of Mrs. March revealed a severe depression, an attempted suicide through aspirin, a woman so tormented that she could barely go about the ordinary tasks of living. The "rejecting mother" was now seen as a depressed mother. Psychiatric treatment was recommended at a clinical staffing. And then one of the clinical team members said, "But what about the baby?" Our new Infant Mental Health Program had been announced and scheduled for opening the following day. There was a phone call to us, and we agreed to provide immediate evaluation of the baby and to consider treatment.

Early Observations

From the time we first saw Mary, we had reason for grave concern. At $5^1/_2$ months, she bore all the stigmata of the child who has spent the better part of her life in a crib with little more than obligatory care. She was adequately nourished and physically cared for, but the back of her head was bald. She showed little interest in her surround; she was listless and too quiet. She seemed to have only a tenuous connection with her mother. She rarely smiled. She did not spontaneously approach her mother through eye contact or gestures of reach. There were few spontaneous vocalizations. In moments of discomfort or anxiety, she did not turn to her mother. In our developmental testing, she failed nearly all the personal-social items on the Bayley scale. At one point in the testing, an unexpected sound (the Bayley test bell) shattered her threshold of tolerance, and she collapsed in terror.

S. Fraiberg, E. Adelson, V. Shapiro, "Ghosts in the Nursery: A Psychoanalytic Approach to Problems with Impaired Infant-Mother Relationships" in *Journal of the American Academy of Child Psychiatry,* vol. 14, no. 3, pp. 387–402. Copyright © 1975 Lippincott Williams & Wilkins. Reproduced with permission of the publisher.

The mother herself seemed locked in some private terror, remote, removed, yet giving us rare glimpses of a capacity for caring. For weeks we held onto one tiny vignette captured on videotape in which the baby made an awkward reach for her mother and the mother's hand spontaneously reached toward the baby. The hands never met each other, but the gesture symbolized for the therapists a reaching out toward each other, and we clung to this symbolic hope.

There is a moment at the beginning of every case when something is revealed that speaks for the essence of the conflict. This moment appeared in the second session of the work when Mrs. Adelson invited Mary and her mother to our office. By chance it was a moment captured on videotape because we were taping the developmental testing session as we customarily do. Mary and her mother, Mrs. Adelson, and Mrs. Evelyn Atreya, as tester, were present.

Mary begins to cry. It is a hoarse, eerie cry in a baby. Mrs. Atreya discontinues the testing. On tape we see the baby in her mother's arms screaming hopelessly; she does not turn to her mother for comfort. The mother looks distant, self-absorbed. She makes an absent gesture to comfort the baby and then gives up. She looks away. The screaming continues for 5 dreadful minutes on tape. In the background, we hear Mrs. Adelson's voice, gently encouraging the mother. "What do you do to comfort Mary when she cries like this?" Mrs. March murmurs something inaudible. Mrs. Adelson and Mrs. Atreya are struggling with their own feelings. They are restraining their own wishes to pick up the baby and hold her, to murmur comforting things to her. If they should yield to their own wish, they would do the one thing they feel must not be done. For Mrs. March would then see that another woman could comfort the baby, and she would be confirmed in her own conviction that she was a bad mother. It is a dreadful 5 minutes for the baby, the mother, and the two psychologists. Mrs. Adelson maintains her composure and speaks sympathetically to Mrs. March. Finally, the visit comes to an end when Mrs. Adelson suggests that the baby is fatigued and probably would welcome her own home and her crib. Mother and baby are helped to close the visit with plans for a third visit very soon.

As we watched this tape later in a staff session, we said to each other incredulously, "It's as if this mother doesn't *hear* her baby's cries!" This led us to the key diagnostic question: "*Why doesn't this mother hear her baby's cries?*"

The Mother's Story

Mrs. March was herself an abandoned child. Her mother suffered a postpartum psychosis shortly after the birth of Mrs. March and her twin brother. In an attempted suicide, her mother had shattered part of her face with a gun and was horribly mutilated for life. She had then spent nearly all of the rest of her life in a hospital and was barely known to her children. For 5 years, an aunt cared for Mrs. March. When the aunt could no longer care for her, she was shifted to the house of the maternal grandmother, where she received grudging care from the burdened, impoverished old woman. Mrs. March's father was in and out of the family picture. We did not hear much about him until later in treatment.

It was a story of bleak rural poverty, sinister family secrets, psychosis, crime, a tradition of promiscuity in the women, of filth and disorder in the home, and of police and protective agencies in the background making futile uplifting gestures. Mrs. March was the cast-out child of a cast-out family. In late adolescence, Mrs. March met and married her husband, who came from poverty and family disorder not unlike her own. But he wanted something better for himself than his family had. He became the first member of his family to fight his way out of the cycle of futility, to find steady work, and to establish a decent home. When these two neglected and solitary young people found each other, there was mutual consent that they wanted something better than what they had known. But now, after several years of effort, the downward spiral had begun.

There was a very high likelihood that Mary was not her father's child. Mrs. March had had a brief affair with another man. Her guilt over the affair and her doubts about Mary's paternity became an obsessive theme in her story. In a kind of litany of griefs that we were to hear repeatedly, there was one theme: "People stared at Mary," she thought. "They stared at her and knew that her father was not her father. They knew that her mother had ruined her life."

Mr. March, who began to appear to us as the stronger parent, was not obsessed with Mary's paternity. He was convinced that he was Mary's father. And anyway, he loved Mary and he wanted her. His wife's obsession with paternity brought about shouting quarrels in the home. "Forget it!" said Mr. March. "Stop talking about it! And take care of Mary!"

In the families of both mother and father, illegitimacy carried no stigma. In the case of Mrs. March's clan, the promiscuity of their women over at least three or four generations cast doubt over the paternity of many of the children. Why was Mrs. March obsessed? Why the sense of tormenting sin? This pervasive, consuming sense of sin we thought belonged to childhood, to buried sins, quite possibly to crimes of the imagination. On several occasions in reading the clinical reports, we had the strong impression that Mary was the sinful child of an incestuous fantasy. But if we were right, we thought to ourselves, how could we possibly reach this in our once-a-week psychotherapy?

Treatment: The Emergency Phase

How shall we begin? Mary and Mrs. March were our first patients. There were no treatment models available to us. In fact, our task in this first Infant Mental Health Program was to develop methods in the course of the work. It made sense, of course, to begin with a familiar model in which our resident in psychiatry, Dr. Zinn, works with the mother in weekly or twice-weekly psychotherapy, and the psychologist, Mrs. Adelson, provides support and developmental guidance on behalf of the baby through home visits. But within the first sessions, we saw that Mrs. March was taking flight from Dr. Zinn and psychiatric treatment. The situation in which she was alone with a man brought forth a phobic dread, and she was reduced to nearly inarticulate hours or to speaking of trivial concerns. All efforts to reach Mrs. March, or to touch upon her anxieties or discomfort in this relationship, led to an impasse. One theme was uttered repeatedly. She did not trust men. But in addition, we caught glimpses in her oblique communications of a terrible secret that she would never reveal to anyone. She broke appointments more frequently than she kept them. With much difficulty, Dr. Zinn sustained a relationship with her. It was nearly a year before we finally heard the secret and understood the phobic dread that led to this formidable resistance.

There are no generalizations to be drawn from this experience. We have been asked sometimes if women therapists are more advantaged in working with mothers who have suffered severe maternal deprivation themselves. Our answer, after nearly 2 years of work, is "not necessarily; sometimes not at all." We have examples in our work in which the male therapist was specially advantaged in working with mothers. We tend to assign cases without overconcern about the sex of the therapist. Mrs. March must be regarded as an exceptional case.

But now we were faced with a therapeutic dilemma. Mrs. Adelson's work was to center in the infant-mother relationship through home visits. Mrs. March needed her own therapist, Dr. Zinn, but a morbid dread of men, aroused in the transference, prevented her from using the psychiatric help available to her. With much time and patient work in the psychiatric treatment, we would hope to uncover the secret that reduced her to silence and flight in the transference to Dr. Zinn.

But the baby was in great peril. And the baby could not wait for the resolution of the mother's neurosis. Mrs. Adelson, we soon saw, did not arouse the same morbid anxieties in Mrs. March, but her role as the baby-mother therapist, the home-based psychologist, did not lend itself easily to uncovering the conflictual elements in the mother's relationship to the child and the treatment of the mother's depression.

Because we had no alternatives, we decided we would use the home visits for our emergency treatment.

What emerged, then, was a form of "psychotherapy in the kitchen," so to speak, which will strike you as both familiar in its methods and unfamiliar in its setting. The method, a variant of psychoanalytic psychotherapy, made use of transference, the repetition of the past in the present, and interpretation. Equally important, the method included continuous developmental observations of the baby and a tactful, nondidactic education of the mother in recognition of her baby's needs and her signals.

The setting was the family kitchen or the living room. The patient who couldn't talk was always present at the interviews if she wasn't napping. The patient who could talk went about her domestic tasks or diapered or fed the baby. The therapist's eyes and ears were attuned to both the nonverbal communications of the baby and the substance of the mother's verbal and nonverbal communications. Everything that transpired between mother and baby was in the purview of the therapist and in the center of the therapy. The dialogue between the mother and the therapist centered upon present concerns and moved back and forth between the past and the present, between this mother and child and another child and her family, in the mother's past. The method proved itself and led us, in later cases, to explore the possibilities of the single therapist in home-based treatment.

We shall now summarize the treatment of Mary and her mother and examine the methods that were employed.

In the early hours of treatment, Mrs. March's own story emerged, haltingly, narrated in a distant, sad voice. It was the story we sketched earlier. As the mother told her story, Mary, our second patient, sat propped on the couch or lay stretched out on a blanket, and the sad and distant face of the mother was mirrored in the sad and distant face of the baby. It was a room crowded with ghosts. The mother's story of abandonment and neglect was now being psychologically reenacted with her own baby. The problem, in the emergency phase of the treatment, was to get the ghosts out of the baby's nursery. To do this, we would need to help the mother see the repetition of the past in the present, which we all know how to do in an office that is furnished with a desk and a chair or couch, but we had not yet learned how to do this in a family living room or a kitchen. We decided the therapeutic principles would need to be the same. But in this emergency phase of the treatment, on behalf of a baby, we would have to find a path into the conflictual elements of the mother's neurosis, which had a direct bearing on her capacity to mother. The baby would need to be at the center of treatment for the emergency period.

We began with the question to ourselves: "Why can't this mother hear her baby's cries?"

The answer to the clinical question is already suggested in the mother's story. This is a mother whose own cries have not been heard. There were, we thought, two crying children in the living room. We saw the mother's distant voice, her remoteness, and remove as defenses against grief and intolerable pain. Her terrible story had been first given factually, without visible suffering, without tears. All that was visible was the sad, empty, hopeless look upon her face. She had closed the door on the weeping child within herself as surely as she had closed the door on her crying baby.

This led to our first clinical hypothesis: *When this mother's own cries are heard, she will hear her child's cries.*

Mrs. Adelson's work, then, centered upon the development of a treatment relationship in which trust could be given by a young woman who had not known trust and in which trust could lead to the revelation of the old feelings that closed her off from her child. As Mrs. March's story moved back and forth between her baby, "I can't love Mary," and her own childhood, which can be summarized, "Nobody wanted me," the therapist opened up pathways of feeling. Mrs. Adelson listened and put into words the feelings of Mrs. March as a child. "How hard this must have been. . . . This must have hurt deeply. . . . Of course, you needed your mother. There was no one to turn to. . . . Yes. Sometimes grownups don't understand what all this means to a child. You must have needed to cry. . . . There was no one to hear you."

The therapist was giving Mrs. March permission to feel and to remember feelings. It may have been the first time in Mrs. March's life that someone had given her this permission. And gradually, as we should expect—but within only a few sessions—grief, tears, and unspeakable anguish for herself as a cast-off child began to emerge. It was finally a relief to be able to cry, a comfort to feel the understanding of her therapist. And now, with each session, Mrs. Adelson witnessed something unbelievable happening between mother and baby.

You remember that the baby was nearly always in the room in the midst of this living room-kitchen therapy of ours. If Mary demanded attention, the mother would rise in the midst of the interview to diaper her or get her a bottle. More often, the baby was ignored if she did not demand attention. But now, as Mrs. March began to take the permission to remember her feelings, to cry, and to feel the comfort and sympathy of Mrs. Adelson, we saw her make approaches to her baby in the midst of her own outpourings. She would pick up Mary and hold her, at first distant and self-absorbed, but holding her. And then, one day, still within the first month of treatment, Mrs. March, in the midst of an outpouring of grief, picked up Mary, held her very close, and crooned to her in a heartbroken voice. And then it happened again and several times in the next sessions. An outpouring of old griefs and a gathering of the baby into her arms. The ghosts in the baby's nursery were beginning to leave.

These were more than transitory gestures toward rapprochement with the baby. From all evidence to Mrs. Adelson's observing eyes, the mother and the baby were beginning to find each other. And now that they were coming in touch with each other, Mrs. Adelson did everything within her capacity as therapist and developmental psychologist to promote the emerging attachment. When Mary rewarded her mother with a beautiful and special smile, Mrs. Adelson commented on it and observed that she, Mrs. Adelson, did not get such a smile, which was just the way it should be. That smile belonged to her mother. When a crying Mary began to seek her mother's comfort and found relief in her mother's arms, Mrs. Adelson spoke for Mary. "It feels so good when mother knows what you want." And Mrs. March herself smiled shyly but with pride.

These sessions with mother and baby soon took on their own rhythm. Mr. March was often present for a short time before leaving for work. (Special sessions for him were also worked out on evenings and Saturdays.) The sessions typically began with Mary in the room and Mary as the topic of discussion. In a natural, informal, nondidactic way, Mrs. Adelson would comment with pleasure on Mary's development and weave into her comments useful information about the needs of babies at 6 months or 7 months, and how Mary was learning about her world, and how her mother and father were leading her into these discoveries. Together, the parents and Mrs. Adelson would watch Mary experiment with a new toy or a new posture, and with close watching, one could see how she was finding solutions and moving steadily forward. The delights of baby watching, which Mrs. Adelson knew, were shared with Mr. and Mrs. March, and to our great pleasure, both parents began to share these delights and bring in their own observations of Mary and of her new accomplishments.

During the same session, after Mr. March had left for work, the talk would move at one point or another back to Mrs. March herself, to her present griefs and her childhood griefs. More and more frequently now, Mrs. Adelson could help Mrs. March see the connections between the past and the present and show Mrs. March how "without realizing it," she had brought her sufferings of the past into her relationship with her own baby.

Within 4 months, Mary became a healthy, more responsive, often joyful baby. At our 10-month testing, objective assessment showed her to be age-appropriate in her focused attachment to her mother, in her preferential smiling and vocalization to mother and father, and in seeking her mother for comfort and safety. She was at age level on the Bayley mental scale. She was still slow in motor performance but within the normal range.

Mrs. March had become a responsive and proud mother. Yet our cautious rating of the mother's own psychological state remained: "depressed." It was true that Mrs. March was progressing, and we saw many signs that the depression was no longer pervasive and constricting, but depression was still there and, we thought, still ominous. Much work remained.

What we had achieved, then, in our first 4 months of work was not yet a cure of the mother's illness but a form of control of the disease, in which the pathology that had spread to embrace the baby was now largely withdrawn from the child. The conflictual elements of the mother's neurosis were now identified by the mother as well as ourselves as "belonging to the past" and "not belonging to Mary." The bond between mother and baby had emerged. And the baby herself was ensuring those bonds. For every gesture of love from her mother, she gave generous rewards of love. Mrs. March, we thought, may have felt cherished by someone for the first time in her life.

All this constitutes what we would call "the emergency phase of the treatment." Now, in retrospect, we see that it took a full year beyond this point to bring some resolution to Mrs. March's very severe internal conflicts, and there were a number of problems in the mother-child relationships which emerged during that year, but Mary was out of danger, and even the baby conflicts of the second year of life were not extraordinary or morbid. Once the bond had been formed, nearly everything else could find solutions.

Other Conflictual Areas

Now we summarize the following months of treatment. Mary remained the focus of our work. Following the pattern already established, the therapeutic work moved freely between the baby and her developmental needs and problems and the mother's conflicted past.

One poignant example comes to mind. Mrs. March, in spite of newfound pleasure and pride in motherhood, could still make casual and unfeeling plans for baby-sitting. The meaning of separation and temporary loss to a 1-year-old child did not register with Mrs. March. When she took part-time work at one point (and the family's poverty gave some justification for additional income), Mrs. March made hasty and ill-thought-out sitting arrangements for Mary and then was surprised, as was Mr. March, to find that Mary was sometimes "cranky" and "spoiled" and "mean."

Mrs. Adelson tried in all tactful ways to help the Marches think about the meaning to Mary of her love for mother and her temporary loss of mother during the day. She met a blank wall. Both parents had known shifting and casual relationships with parents and parent substitutes from their earliest years. The meaning of separation and loss was buried in memory. Their family style of coping with separation, desertion, or death was, "Forget about it. You get used to it." Mrs. March could not remember grief or pain at the loss of important persons.

Somehow, once again, we were going to have to find the affective links between loss and denial of loss, for the baby in the present, and loss in the mother's past.

The moment came one morning when Mrs. Adelson arrived to find family disorder: Mary was crying at the approach of an old visitor, and the parents were angry at a baby who was being "just plain stubborn." Thoughtful inquiries from Mrs. Adelson brought the new information that Mary had just lost one sitter and started with another. Mrs. Adelson wondered out loud what this might mean to Mary. Yesterday, she had been left, unexpectedly, in a totally new place with a strange woman. She felt alone and frightened without her mother and did not know what was going to happen. No one could explain things to her; she was only a baby, with no words to express her serious problem. Somehow, we would have to find a way to understand and help her with her fears and worries.

Mr. March, on his way to work, stopped long enough to listen attentively. Mrs. March was listening too, and before her husband left, she asked him to try to get home earlier today so that Mary would not be too long at the sitter's.

There followed a moving session in which the mother cried, and the baby cried, and something very important was put into words. In a circular and tentative way, Mrs. March began to talk about Aunt Jane, with whom she had lived during her first 5 years. There had not been a letter from Aunt Jane for some months. She thought Aunt Jane was angry with her. She switched to her mother-in-law, to thoughts of her coldness and rejection of Mrs. March. There were complaints about the sitters, with the theme that one sitter was angry because Mary cried when her mother left. The theme was "rejection" and "loss," and Mrs. March was searching for it everywhere in the contemporary scene. She cried throughout, but somehow, even with Mrs. Adelson's gentle hints, she could not put this together.

Then, at one point, Mrs. March left the room, still in tears, and returned with a family photograph album. She identified the pictures for Mrs. Adelson. Mother, father, Aunt Jane, Aunt Jane's son who had been killed in the war. Sorrow for Aunt Jane. Nobody in the family would let her grieve for her son. "Forget about it" is what they said. She spoke about her father's death and her grandfather's death in the recent past.

She said there were many losses, many shocks, just before Mary's birth. And the family always said, "Forget about it." Then Mrs. Adelson, listening sympathetically, reminded her that there had been many other losses, many other shocks for Mrs. March long ago in her infancy and childhood. The loss of her mother, which she could not remember, and the loss of Aunt Jane when she was 5 years old. Mrs. Adelson wondered how Mrs. March had felt then, when she was too young to understand what was happening. Looking at Mary sitting on her mother's lap, Mrs. Adelson said, "I wonder if we could understand how Mary would feel right now if she suddenly found herself in a new house, not just for an hour or two with a sitter, but permanently, never to see her mother or father again. Mary wouldn't have any way to understand this; it would leave her very worried, very upset. I wonder what it was like for you when you were a little girl."

Mrs. March listened, deep in thought. A moment later she said, in an angry and assertive voice, "You can't just replace one person with another. . . . You can't stop loving them and thinking about them. You can't just replace somebody." She was speaking of herself now. Mrs. Adelson agreed and then gently brought the insight back on behalf of Mary.

This was the beginning of new insights for Mrs. March. As she was helped to reexperience loss, grief, the feelings of rejection in childhood, she could no longer inflict this pain upon her own child. "I would never want my baby to feel that," she said with profound feeling. She was beginning to understand loss and grief. With Mrs. Adelson's help, she now began to work out a stable sitter plan for Mary, with full understanding of the meaning to her child. Mary's anxieties began to diminish, and she settled into her new regimen.

Finally, too, we learned the dreaded secret that had invaded the transference to Dr. Zinn and caused Mrs. March to take flight from psychiatric treatment. The morbid fear of being alone in the same room with the doctor, the obsessive sense of sin that had attached itself to Mary's doubtful paternity, had given us the strong clinical impression that Mary was "an incestuous baby," conceived long ago in childhood fantasy, made real through the illicit relationship with an out-of-wedlock lover. By this, we meant nothing more than "an incestuous fantasy," of course. We were not prepared for the story that finally emerged. With great shame and suffering, Mrs. March told Mrs. Adelson in the second year of treatment of her childhood secrets. Her own father had exhibited himself to her when she was a child and had approached her and her grandmother in the bed they shared. Her grandmother had accused her of seducing her elderly grandfather. Mrs. March denied this. And her first intercourse at the age of 11 took place with her cousin, who stood in the relationship of brother to her, since they shared the same house in the early years of life. Incest was not fantasy for Mrs. March. And now we understood the obsessive sense of sin that had attached itself to Mary and her uncertain paternity.

Mary at 2 Years of Age

During the second year of treatment, Mrs. Adelson continued as the therapist for Mrs. March. Dr. Zinn had completed his residency, and Mrs. March's transference to Mrs. Adelson favored continuity in the work with the mother. William Schafer of our staff became the guidance worker for Mary. (We no longer have separate therapists for parent and child, but in this first case, we were still experimenting.)

It is of some considerable interest that in the initial meetings with Mr. Schafer, Mrs. March was again in mute terror as her morbid fear of a man was revived in transference. But this time, Mrs. March had made large advances in her therapeutic work. The anxiety was handled in transference by Mr. Schafer and brought back to Mrs. Adelson, where it could be placed within the context of the incestuous material that had emerged in treatment. The anxiety diminished, and Mrs. March was able to make a strong alliance with Mr. Schafer. The developmental guidance of the second year brought further strength and stability to the mother-child relationship, and we saw Mary continuing her developmental progress through her second year, even as her mother was working through very painful material in her own therapy.

Are there residues in Mary's personality from the early months of neglect? At the time of this writing, Mary is 2 years old. She is an attractive child, adequate in all ways for her age, and presents no extraordinary problems in development. There may be residues that we cannot detect, or cannot yet detect. But at the present time, they are not discernible to us. Are there depressive tendencies? None that we can discern. When frustrated, for example, she does not withdraw; she becomes very assertive, which we consider a favorable sign. What does remain is a shyness and inhibition of play, which seems related to temporary increases in mother's own social discomfort, as in new settings or with strangers.

Mary's attachment to her mother and father appears appropriate for her age. In spontaneous doll play, we see a strong positive identification with her mother and with acts of mothering. She is a solicitous mother to her dolls, feeding, dressing them with evident pleasure, and murmuring comforting things to them. In her recent Bayley testing, she threw the test procedures into disorder when she fell in love with the Bayley doll and could not be persuaded to do the next items on the test. She wanted to play with the doll; she spurned the block items that were next presented for tower building and finally compromised on her own terms by using the blocks to make "a chair" for the doll. It was in doll play at 1 year, 10 months that Mr. Schafer heard her speak her first sentence. Her doll was accidentally trapped behind a door with a spring catch, and Mary could not recover it. "I want my baby. I want my baby!" she called out in an imperative voice. It was a very good sentence for a 2-year-old. It was also a moving statement to all of us who knew Mary's story.

For us the story must end here. The family has moved on. Mr. March begins a new career with very good prospects in a new community that provides comfortable housing and a warm welcome. The external circumstances look promising. More important, the family has grown closer; abandonment is not a central concern. One of the most hopeful signs was Mrs. March's steady ability to handle the stress of the uncertainty that preceded the job choice. And as termination approached, she could openly acknowledge her sadness. Looking ahead, she expressed her wish for Mary: "I hope that she'll grow up to be happier than me. I hope that she will have a better marriage and children who she'll love." For herself, she asked that we remember her as "someone who had changed."

Editors' Introduction

This is a teaching case in the best sense: An example of Adlerian therapy conducted in the context of a graduate course in psychotherapy. Dr. Harold Mosak, a skilled Adlerian therapist, accepts the risks involved in permitting public scrutiny of his work, and in relatively few sessions he provides for new insights and behavioral change in a troubled young man.

This case involves a gay man struggling, in part, with issues of sexual identity. Mosak, like many Adlerians, unquestioningly sees this as a matter of choice: "Homosexuality is a choice, not a biological condition." Do you agree? Is it ever ethical for a therapist or counselor to attempt to change sexual orientation in a client, or even to support a client who desires to change? Does Mosak subtly try to shape his client's sexual values? Questions of sexual orientation and behavior inevitably arise with some clients, and you need to come to terms with your own feelings and beliefs about sexuality if you are going to be effective in helping others understand and respond to their feelings about these sometimes vexing issues.

We believe this is a good teaching case because it provides a meaningful springboard for class discussions of the ethical and professional issues associated with treating clients who may be dealing with sexual or gender identity concerns. In addition, the case illustrates the hands-on application of dozens of Adlerian techniques.

Mosak is more direct and focused, therapy is time-limited, and his style is didactic. This is a form of cognitive therapy that focuses on the values, beliefs, and attitudes of the client. Mosak and Maniacci do a masterful job in illustrating the core elements of individual psychotherapy.

2 | THE CASE OF ROGER

Harold H. Mosak and Michael Maniacci

Alfred Adler developed a theory and strategy of psychology and psychotherapy which have proven to be quite relevant to contemporary clinical and counseling practice. *Individual Psychology,* the name Adler gave his system, derives from the Latin *individuum,* and means "indivisible," emphasizing the holistic perspective that Adlerian psychology is built upon. Distinctions such as conscious and unconscious, mind and body, or approach and avoidance are subjective experiences; in reality, they are a part of a unified relational system. Individuals are viewed as being in movement towards subjectively determined goals which, though influenced by heredity and environment, are in the final analysis the result of choices made according to biased apperceptions. These biased apperceptions about self, others, and the world form a self-consistent cognitive and attitudinal set which organizes and directs movement towards the goal, and is called by Adlerians the *style of life.* The goal, though idiographic and individualized for specific people depending upon the particular circumstances in which they grew up and based upon certain choices they made, in general, is always designed to move individuals from a subjective sense of inferiority towards a sense of superiority, perfection, competence, or completion, from a felt minus situation towards a plus situation. Movement can take place in either of two directions: useful or useless. Useful, as defined by Adlerians, is that which moves with others in prosocial, egalitarian ways; useless is that which moves against others in self-centered, uncooperative ways. All behavior, both adaptive and maladaptive, is conceptualized as taking place within a social field. Behavior that is useful is that which is in line with social interest, a potentiality which requires development and encouragement.

Individuals who move in useless ways are not considered sick, but rather discouraged; they have underdeveloped social interest. They have selected goals which they attempt to move towards in self-centered rather than cooperative ways. Cognitively, they have a private logic which construes events and situations according to biased apperceptions that generally are distorted, overgeneralized, or exaggerated perceptions and are not in line with the less dogmatic common sense followed by most others. The main tasks of life are conceptualized as social tasks which require cooperation, not competition. Adler delineated three of these life tasks: work, friendship, and love. Later Adlerians delineated a fourth and a fifth implied in Adler's writings: a self task and a spiritual task. Maladjustment is characterized by increased inferiority feelings, underdeveloped social interest, and an exaggerated, uncooperative goal of personal superiority.

Adler conceptualized psychotherapy as the awakening of the client's innate social interest. By explaining the client's subjective distress not as sickness but as discouragement due to the erroneous meaning given to life, Adler attempted to encourage the client

---

"The Case of Roger" was written specifically to complement Dr. Mosak's chapter in *Current Psychotherapies.*

to move towards a more useful, adaptive style of life. Such a change took place by examining how the client grew up and what choices he or she made. The client's family constellation, family atmosphere, family values and earliest recollections were explored in order to understand what particular goals towards which the individual was striving.

Rudolf Dreikurs described Adlerian psychotherapy as consisting of four processes: (a) forming a relationship; (b) investigating the client's life style; (c) interpreting it to the client; and (d) helping the client to reorient towards a more prosocial stance by modifying certain convictions held by the client and putting into practice more cooperative attitudes and behaviors. Though heuristically valuable, these should not be regarded as "phases" or "stages" in actual clinical practice. Interpretation may occur during every phase of the process, and the establishment and maintenance of a positive relationship will require ongoing effort. New material can be investigated throughout the course of treatment, and reorientation is encouraged beginning with the initial interview.

BACKGROUND AND REFERRAL

The case presented here was selected from the audio recordings of an eleven-week graduate psychotherapy course taught by the senior author at the Alfred Adler Institute of Chicago. "Roger" came to the counseling center at the Institute requesting services. After an intake interview, he agreed to participate in front of a class for a pre-established period of ten weeks at no charge.

Coming in shortly after his thirty-sixth birthday, Roger's major complaint was agoraphobia which had grown progressively worse for the past twelve years. Along with the agoraphobia, his intake sheet noted that he drank heavily, was overweight, was dissatisfied with his job (which he had managed to keep only at the expense of considerable anxiety), had multiple specific phobias, and was actively homosexual. Roger requested no treatment for his sexual orientation which he claimed was not a problem, except for the fact that his agoraphobia interfered with making contact with other gay men.

SESSION 1
FORMING A RELATIONSHIP
AND DEFINING THE PROBLEM

The session began with Mosak attempting to clarify the problem.

Therapist: O.K. What brings you to the Institute?
Client: I have a problem. I guess they call it agoraphobia, a fear of going out in the open. It's been getting steadily worse for the past ten or twelve years. Now it's getting to the point where I can hardly exist.
T: Is that why you brought a friend?
C: Yeah, somebody to go with me. . . .

The friend made it possible for Roger to move about outside. Roger went on to explain that his anxiety was not so acute if he knew where he was going; then at least he would know where he could "run and hide" along the way should he start to panic. He dealt with his anxiety by drinking "a fifth of wine" before his trips outside of his house.

C: . . . I think it's basically insecurity. In the past year I've had three different jobs, and I started a new job last week. I was a wreck for about a week before time, worrying about going to this place. I was frightened to death driving there . . . I had my brother take me and pick me up. But now that I've been there about a week I did it myself the past couple of days. But still, I worry all day about leaving work . . . If I hit traffic, I sit there and worry about getting into an accident. I might panic. It scares me.

T: You've said something twice now, and that is your symptom permits you to put other people into your service. You have to get somebody to accompany you down here, and for a week, you had to get your brother to drive you to work. It almost sounds like you feel pretty helpless and have to count on "the big boys" to take care of you.

The therapist is offering a tentative interpretation. Adlerian psychology is a psychology of use, not possession. For example, Adlerians do not say that someone has a bad temper, but rather that someone uses temper to intimidate others. The bad temper serves the individual's purpose. In Roger's case, Mosak reframes the symptom to show how it is used: Roger is putting others into his service and though he may not totally be aware (conscious) of it, he is responsible for it.

T: What have you done about it [*the agoraphobia*] for the past twelve years?
C: Well, try to cope with it the best I can . . . avoid certain things, avoid certain areas, don't go into the woods or take vacations or do things you normally would do.

Adler considered a neurosis an evasion of the tasks of life. Roger has constricted life to the point where it is manageable. He is saying, in effect, that he will only operate where he feels secure.

T: Yeah, but that doesn't overcome it. That's living within the confines of your symptom . . . Have you done anything about trying to overcome the symptom?
C: Yeah, I went to a psychiatrist downtown for a while. He gave me Thorazine and it made me sick. I never went back to him. In fact, he made me nervous . . . He really didn't seem to care about the problem that much. He made a comment, he said: "You seem mainly interested in yourself . . . I think you're an egotist." That kind of bothered me . . . He was flippant with me too—we just didn't hit it off.

The message is clear. Roger is warning his new therapist: Take me and my problems seriously or else I will not return. In effect, he is saying he wants someone to care about him. If he feels others do not care, his mode of action is consistent with his style of life—he becomes "nervous" and avoids them (in this case his former psychiatrist). Roger did not feel understood by his last therapist.

T: If I had a magic wand and could wave it over your head and get rid of this agoraphobia . . . what would be different in your life?

This is known as *The Question*. Adlerians use it to determine the purpose of the symptom and to differentiate somatic from psychogenic disorders. It is also usually indicative of what is being avoided—that is, for what purpose the symptom is generated.

C: It would take away a lot of the fears, frustrations of planning ahead. You see, I have to plan my week . . . I've got to make arrangements with friends to pick me up and drive me back . . . I could just float and enjoy life . . . I had to give up several good [job] positions because I'm afraid to fly.
T: Suppose I could get you to take a plane ride with me to Los Angeles? Suppose I would take care of whatever would happen at the other end?
C: You're on.

Without realizing it, Roger has told Mosak the purpose of his agoraphobia: he wants to be in control. Without his symptoms, he would not have to "plan ahead" and get others to look after him. The symptoms provide him with the excuse to dictate to others and have them in his service.

The rest of the session involved an exploration of the tasks of life. The extent to which individuals function adequately in each of these areas is a barometer of their level of social interest. Roger rated himself in this way:

Work: Poor. He had to arrange for others to be with him. His symptoms were beginning to interfere with his role as a manager in the trucking business. He had to drink every morning to get to the office.

Friendship: His friendships came mostly through his homosexual contacts, which were being affected by his agoraphobia.

Love: He was engaged once, but she broke it off. He had never had intercourse with a woman but he had frequent sexual relations with men. Roger claimed this area was not a problem.

Self: Basically, Roger thought he was a good person, but he was dissatisfied with his weight. He added that he didn't like himself—he felt "ugly inside." He was also worried about becoming alcoholic.

Spiritual: Roger was raised a devout Catholic. He still prayed and lit candles but avoided confession due to his sexual orientation. When he claimed, "*I* don't need confession," Mosak noted that "Even the Pope has a confessor." Roger replied without a hint of humor, "He needs it more than *I* do."

In conclusion, Roger was offered encouragement. He felt that at thirty-six, it was "too late in life" to continue with much else. He expressed openly his discouragement with himself and his inability to move ahead with his life. Mosak mentioned a former colleague who did not start medical school until he was forty-seven. However, Roger only wanted to work on his agoraphobia, and he seriously doubted his ability to overcome it.

The interview concluded with the therapist structuring the next two sessions, a technique especially effective with controllers. Roger would be meeting with a co-therapist who would be gathering the data for a *Life Style Assessment,* a form of investigation which Adlerians use to understand the goals, intentions, and biased apperceptions of clients. While Mosak implicitly made it clear that he was in control of the process, he respected Roger's desire to be in control.

In summary, Roger is a controller who uses passive means of controlling others. At thirty-six, his passive means of controlling (via his agoraphobia) has begun to exact a toll that even Roger can no longer tolerate, and he has begun therapy. He has strong inferiority feelings and underdeveloped social interest, as indicated by his poor overall functioning in the life tasks. Despite his poor self-concept, he still considers himself somewhat superior (he has higher standards than the Pope). The therapist has shown that he understands Roger's problems, that he takes them seriously, and that he is willing to align his goals with the client's, therefore reducing resistance. Most importantly, he has encouraged Roger, who is seriously discouraged, and he has given him hope.

SESSIONS 2–3
THE LIFE STYLE INTERVIEW

The next two sessions were spent with the co-therapist gathering Life Style Assessment data. Adlerians frequently practice *multiple psychotherapy* and have documented its benefits.

The Life Style Assessment is a diagnostic procedure which investigates the client's past and present situation in order to come to an understanding of the particular person's way of construing the world, other people, and ideas about self. Understanding the premises upon which a client operates helps to tailor treatment to the particular client and brings idiographic relevance to the nomothetic principles of Individual Psychology. The primary areas of investigation are the client's family constellation, which includes sibling descriptions, ratings, and an investigation of parental guiding lines and the family atmosphere, and the client's earliest recollections, the earliest memories the client can visualize and report to the therapist. Through this investigation, the therapist and client can arrive at an understanding of the particular client's personal history and current beliefs.

SESSION 4
THE LIFE STYLE SUMMARY

Mosak and the co-therapist spent the fourth session discussing the Life Style Summary with Roger. First the co-therapist read the recorded data to Mosak. Some highlights follow:

> Roger, age thirty-six, is the oldest in his family. He has a sister, Ginger, minus two (i.e., two years younger), a brother Evan, minus six, a brother, Arthur, minus nine and another brother died in childhood after Arthur. Roger described himself as a dreamer who fantasized a lot, had delusions of grandeur, looked at the world through rose-colored glasses, and who was happy through the age of six/seven. He was sexually promiscuous with boys and girls; they played show and tell. He was overweight as were his siblings. He had the usual arguments/fights with his sister— she is described as dumb and slovenly.
>
> Evan was described as being very precocious, very personable. He loved everyone, everyone loved him, both adults and kids . . . He was more masculine than Roger. Arthur was born handicapped and was always overprotected. He was allowed to have his own way.
>
> Evan was most different—more outgoing and more gregarious. Ginger was most like Roger. She was feminine and he could relate to her more.
>
> As a youngster Roger was afraid of his father, who seemed like a tyrant. Roger was the most intelligent and the most industrious and he had higher standards of achievement. Evan was more athletic, rebellious, better looking, more masculine, and made more mischief. Roger was always overweight and he was the last to be picked for sports.
>
> Roger originally hated school and his mother had to keep taking him out of school. He hated other kids and felt inferior. There were no problems with behavior and Roger was smart enough to keep his mouth shut. He was a patrol boy in the fourth and fifth grades and he enjoyed the role. He was "the captain" who liked having other people under him.
>
> Roger's father would have been fifty-seven but he died in 1965. He was a truck driver and Roger didn't like him. The father used to beat Roger's mother and he chased them out of the house with a gun when he was drunk. He was seldom sober and he was always in a rotten mood. He was filthy and he took family possessions and sold them for booze.
>
> The mother is fifty-nine years old and a housewife. She held the family together; she did the cooking and baking. She was always complaining about her ill health and how close she was to dying. She tried to play on everyone's sympathy and she was usually successful. Roger was most like her.

The co-therapist went on to describe the stormy and troubled marriage of Roger's parents. The mother saw herself as a "martyred saint." They had violent fights. Two other paternal uncles lived with them. Both were ex-convicts and one had five marriages, all ending in divorce; the other was an alcoholic. Mosak dictated the following summary.

SUMMARY OF FAMILY CONSTELLATION

Roger is the oldest of four, in a 2-2 family, which makes him the older of two and the only boy in his group. He grew up in a family characterized by poverty and ethnic and marital discord, a family in which all the men acted as arms of the devil. The father was an alcoholic, a tyrant, abusive, and a squanderer of the family's money. Both uncles were thieves. One was moody in the negative sense, and the other was a playboy with five wives. The only positive model was Roger's mother, but she overdid a good thing. She was not only the standard bearer of good; she was also a martyr and a saint. Nevertheless, Mother was also a fearful person who, in spite of her religious faith, didn't believe that God would preserve her. Roger grew up hating his father, and determined that if all men were like his father and uncles, he wasn't going to be like that. He adopted his mother's standards of rightness and like her, opted for sainthood. Nevertheless, he fell short, but even though he acknowledged at times that he was wrong, he was still "righter" than others. He sat in judgment upon the whole world and himself—they were beneath him and he looked down upon them or expressed temper when he had too much of their wrong. He also looked down upon himself since he too was not all he felt he should be. He was fat in a family where being fat was bad. He was sexually active and this was bad. He was having negative feelings and for an observant Catholic, the thought was as sinful as the deed. He rested his feeling of belonging upon his intelligence, trying to be good, trying to be right, and staying out of trouble because that would make him like the men. He wanted to be a real man, and his sexual promiscuity was evidence of his pursuit. But somewhere along the line, Roger became discouraged, because (a) he misdefined masculinity (e.g., Evan was more masculine because he was more athletic), (b) he could not identify with the male role models in his family, and (c) he couldn't resolve the conflict between "goodness" and masculinity. In Roger's mind, one couldn't be good *and* a man simultaneously. He grew up unhappy partly because of the climate in which he grew up, partly because of his exalted standards for himself and others, partly because of his disdain for other people, and partly because of his disdain for himself.

T: Roger, how does that sound as a summary of the way you grew up?
C: Yeah—very much [*noticeably shaken*]. I think you hit it on the head.

They then went on to review the early recollections. The co-therapist read them aloud.

1. I went to first grade, I didn't go to kindergarten. The teacher asked me to do something—I told her to go to hell . . . [Age 5.]
2. I remember sitting in church. I stared at the statue of Christ on the cross. I was told that if you stared at it long enough, you could see Christ come off the cross. I got very excited and agitated—only saints were supposed to be able to do that. I imagined Christ coming towards me . . . [Age 7; Feeling excited.]
3. I remember an aunt of mine. She had come over with presents. I loved her . . . Everybody loved her. She was a very joyful woman. I was in total awe of her . . . [Age 5–6; Feeling awe.]
4. My mother got pregnant. My father was swearing at her and saying something about getting rid of it. He was going to stick his hand up her and pull it out. [Age 7; Feeling scared.]
5. They [the parents] had a couple that used to come over every weekend—a Polish couple. They started fighting. I remember specifically this woman talking about her sex life, that she wanted it, he didn't. The woman was crying in the kitchen . . . The husband telling her that she's a lousy lay anyway . . . [Age 8; Feeling "something I didn't understand—why was it so important."]

Early recollections are those memories which individuals store and use to assist them in moving through life. They reflect how people perceive life currently, and are quite effective as projective techniques. Mosak proceeded to dictate a note about Roger's view of life, self, and others, and noted Roger's "Basic Mistakes" and "Assets."

SUMMARY OF EARLY RECOLLECTIONS

"Nobody should tell me what to do; otherwise I balk. Men and women get along poorly and the conflict generally has to do with sex. I just can't understand what the conflict's all about. Men brutalize women and all women can do is suffer. Women, independent of men, can radiate warmth and joy. I stand in awe of them but I keep my distance and do not get involved with them. If I did want to get involved, it would be too late anyway. I want to be purged of all sin and be in union with God."

BASIC MISTAKES

1. He doesn't see the possibility of good man/woman relationships. Put a man and a woman in a cage and the blood is going to start to flow.
2. Roger idealizes women, feels he can't have them, and distances himself from them.
3. Roger wants to do it his way. "No one has the right to tell me what to do."
4. Roger tries too hard to be perfect because he regards himself as so much less than perfect.

ASSETS

1. He has positive feelings for women.
2. He does try to be better.
3. He uses religion for sanctification rather than downgrading himself.
4. Even though he is confused, he tries to figure things out.
5. He has a vivid fantasy life. He's had excellent training in it.
6. In many ways he comes close (though not in terms of birth order) to Joseph in the Bible: the one who can read omens in dreams, who has great dreams about the sun, moon, and planets.

T: O.K. Roger, that's our summary. [*Roger gets up to leave.*] No—don't get up yet.
C: I thought we were through.
T: No, just with the summary. Now that's how it looks to us. How do you feel about it?
C: I think it's pretty interesting about the women.
T: About the women?
C: Yeah . . . about not really relating to them—putting them on a pedestal. In my life I have a lot of women friends and they're all looked at this way—and none of them are really with men.
T: Yeah, that comes out in your recollection . . .
C: In fact any woman who's close to me doesn't have a relationship with men . . .
T: Yeah, well men are all bastards anyway.
C: Then why am I sleeping with them?
T: Maybe that's so you can look down on them and look down on yourself?

C: [*Sighing—noticeably shaken*] Maybe it's just too much for me to comprehend right now.

T: O.K. We'll talk about that some more later. You said that the reading of the material was getting to you. What was getting to you?

C: . . . Just thinking about things I've tried to avoid thinking about for a long time.

T: Do you feel understood?

C: Right now—more so than I have in a long time.

T: You see, while what we wrote may not be 100% accurate, it's our first guess about you—

C: I'd say it's a good 95%.

T: And on that basis we have some things that we can already start talking about. If something is wrong, we'll modify it. Now next week we're going to talk a little about this, but we're also going to start talking about your present situation, because basically, that's the thing you've got to change. We may refer to some things in your childhood, but basically we're going to be talking about your fears . . . your job, and all those kinds of things you told us about in the first interview.

C: Very good—I'm looking forward to it.

T: Good. See you next week.

C: Thank you. Goodnight. [*Addressing the class*] Goodnight.

Roger, from wanting to talk only about his symptoms, is now examining his way of relating to the world and other people. Through the use of the Life Style Assessment, he is examining his view of life. Even the previously taboo subject of his homosexuality is now open for discussion and was raised by Roger himself. What was once unconscious and never clearly formulated has now been brought to light and presented to him in a way he can grasp and in his own language, using his own metaphors and imagery. He is told before he leaves that he is to be prepared at the next session to discuss his present situation since that is what he has to change.

SESSIONS 5–9
MODIFYING CONVICTIONS

The fifth session opened with Mosak asking Roger what he remembered from the previous session, two weeks ago (Roger had been sick and missed a week).

C: Well, let's see. I think I remember the fact that there were more good points than bad points about myself. Also, the tendency to put women on a shrine . . . and feel that they're untouchable. I also made a comment that I never have women who have anything to do with men totally as friends. . . .

Roger was obviously struck by the fact that the therapist included more "good points" (i.e., assets) than "bad points." Roger is discouraged, and hearing assets included in his Life Style Assessment encouraged him and helped strengthen the therapeutic relationship. He reports that he was impressed by his new understanding of his attitude towards women. Mosak reread the entire Life Style Assessment summaries and discussed some of the points with him.

T: Now, as you hear it a second time today, Roger, what does it sound like?

C: It doesn't sound like anybody I know.

T: It doesn't?

C: No.

T: And yet two weeks ago you gave me a grade of "95." So what's happened in the two weeks?

C: I feel like a different person now.

T: You feel like you've changed.

C: Yeah.

T: Would you identify for me what the change is like or maybe how or what happened?

C: I don't know what happened. First of all I feel a little more sure of myself today. I feel less emotional today, not as embarrassed.

T: What was wrong with the emotional feeling you had?

C: I don't like to show emotion.

T: Why?

C: It's a sign of weakness.

T: Is it?

C: I think so. I try to be rather cold and calculating most of the time.

T: Where did you learn that emotion was a sign of weakness?

C: Well, I don't like to put up with anybody who shows emotion. I don't have the patience for anybody who starts crying in front of me or starts pouring out their heart to me—I don't like it at all.

T: I see. So if you don't show emotion or other people are not permitted to show emotion to you, then you can keep your distance from them?

C: Yeah. It's like somebody saying that they love you—to me it's a negative word. I don't ever use it because it's stupid. Nobody ever really loves anybody.

Mosak raised the issue of Roger's style of relating to people. Hearing one's style of life summarized can have a disorienting effect upon one's self-image and perspective of others and life. Roger grew emotional upon hearing it, and that bothered him. The therapist interpreted Roger's dampening of emotions as a method for keeping distance from others. As Roger went on to point out, getting close to people meant getting hurt, and he wanted no more pain in his life. By "cutting off" his emotions, he attempted to protect himself.

Roger sees life *vertically* rather than *horizontally*—that is, he is concerned with who is better than or on top of whom. People are not equals cooperating for a common cause and working together; they are "out to get you." This is evident in Roger's agoraphobia: if he does not get too far out of his house, people will not get too close to him.

T: So for you the important goal is to be dominant in every relationship. There's a master and a slave and by golly—

C: I like to call the shots.

T: You better be the master.

C: Um hmm, yeah. I'm the leader too . . .

T: Will you do something for me, Roger? While there's no way for us to predict what's going to happen, I'd like you to compose, since you have a great fantasy life, a future autobiography . . . Ten years from now you'll be forty-five years old. What do you think your life will be like?

C: It could go either way. If this therapy-thing works out, I might be quite a fantastic individual . . . have a lover, a beautiful home somewhere, travel a lot . . .

T: Supposing therapy doesn't take, as it were?

C: Well, I think ten years from now I would just be a bum . . . I would just sell everything, have long hair, and look like Jesus Christ walking down the street . . . It might be rather interesting.

T: No problems, but what meaning?

C: It's better to be a king of derelicts than not a king at all.

T: As you just put it, in ten years, if therapy takes you'll be doing something fantastic . . . and if not, you'll be the king of the derelicts.

C: One way or another I'm going to make it.

Roger is exhibiting what Adler called *antithetical modes of apperception*. He'll either be the best or the worst. The strong sense of inferiority and superiority are two sides of the same coin and the basic problem is the meaning Roger has given to life: He must be the best. With that as a prerequisite for relating, he runs into considerable difficulty in life. The goal at this point in treatment is to encourage Roger to begin relating horizontally to others.

T: Roger, you're counting on your mentality [*Roger's term for "intellect"*] to dominate people . . . What if you met your match?

C: . . . Maybe you're my match.

T: What if somebody gets to you through feelings? What then? . . . You see, two weeks ago, we got to you through feeling.

C: I know—that bothered me all the way home.

T: You see, I didn't see you as submissive [*Roger earlier had referred to himself as "submissive" for showing feelings*]. I saw you as feeling. You're the one who attached "feeling equals weakness." I attached to it "feeling equals humanity." By golly, the guy's human.

C: Yeah, but that phase is over.

T: Oh, I don't know—Isn't it possible I might get you again?

C: It's possible.

T: How hard are you going to defend yourself against it?

Roger claimed he did not have to defend himself in therapy, and Mosak pointed out that no, he did not have to but that in fact he *did*. Roger pointed out that he would be "mortified" if he ran into any of the class on the street—he is afraid to look any of them in the face. The therapist drew a parallel between that and his behavior toward others in general: He keeps his distance from others. When asked if anyone in the room really cared about him, Roger flatly, and sincerely, replied, "No."

C: If I threw myself out the window right now, nobody would shed a tear.

T: Do you think any of them would try and stop you?

C: No. Why would they? They might get their names in the paper tomorrow. That's why they would stop me . . . [*They'd be famous.*]

T: Supposing somebody grabbed you [before you jumped out]? What would you feel?

C: Maybe they'd want to go to bed with me, I don't know.

T: But that's the only reason?

C: They'd probably push me out after one night.

T: So it's inconceivable that anybody would really care?

C: People really don't care about people that much. They put on a good front, but basically—

T: Are you speaking about people or are you speaking about Roger?

C: Just in general.

T: Roger—Do I care? [*Mosak is introducing the issue of "love."*]

C: I'd like to think you care. I'm not sure though.

T: What makes me the exception?

C: Financial gain.

T: I don't get one penny for seeing you.

C: I know that—I appreciate that. But, you get [money] from these people in here [the class].

T: I don't get one penny from them.

C: [*Surprised*] I apologize, I didn't know that. [*Apologizes repeatedly.*]

T: So the best you can do is accuse me of being interested in you as a case study . . .

C: [*Still apologizing sheepishly.*]

T: You've got to find some other reason [than financial gain]—that ain't it. What makes me different? Why might I possibly care for you? Because I'll tell you—You try and go out that window and I'm going to grab you.

C: Maybe you don't want the notoriety—bad for business.

T: Yeah, you're right. But on the other hand, maybe I want the fame? . . . My name would get in the paper. [*Long pause*] Why might I possibly care?

C: I was thinking about that—I'm really rather confused . . . I mentioned it to a friend as a matter of fact—I asked "Why is this man even bothering?"

T: That's my question . . .

C: Feelings of being a great humanitarian?

T: Not really. Not by seeing one patient for free . . .

C: Yeah, that's true.

T: What's my game?

C: Maybe you thought it was an interesting case? . . .

T: You know, Roger, after thirty years—

C: Nothing is new—

T: Yeah . . . [I've dealt with about everything.] Why am I bothering?

C: [*Subdued*] Give me a week to think about it.

T: I will. I hope you will.

C: I am going to think about it.

T: Good, because that's a crucial issue . . . it is not only important in terms of your therapy, but it's important for your life. Because if one person can care for you, then you'll have to ask another question, and that is, maybe two can.

C: [*Somewhat choked up*] It's very difficult for me to believe it.

The interview concluded on that note. Roger added that he does listen to what his therapist talks about. He came to the therapy session alone, and has found it easier and easier to move about unescorted outside. He has also been driving to work with greater ease. Roger commented, "I just wanted you to know that." The drinking had decreased noticeably as well. Asked how he accounted for it, Roger replied, "It's an awakening to reality, finding out I am a somebody."

This session, along with the previous one (the Life Style Assessment interview), was a turning point in treatment. Roger, having begun to accept himself as "a somebody," was losing his feelings of inferiority. The less inferior he felt, the easier time he had with healthy, consensual interaction. He no longer had to *safeguard* himself against what he feared would be a horrible fate if he exposed himself and his imperfections to others.

The sixth session began with Roger claiming to have been doing a lot of thinking. "I haven't wasted so much time in my life as I thought," he reported. His gains, from a behavioral standpoint, continued to grow as he attempted more activities independently. Mosak encouraged even more, and used task-setting (i.e., homework) to continue the growth.

T: So my question, Roger, is what can we do—since apparently you do want to live a happier life—to help you live a happier life? . . .

Mosak is using the pronoun "we." He is communicating to Roger that therapy is a collaborative enterprise, and that human interaction can be one of mutual respect and cooperation.

C: Well, can the people here [the class] make suggestions?

T: No, they're only permitted to be observers.

C: Well, can you make suggestions?

T: I can, but I don't think I want to, Roger, because I don't think that would do you any good. And being committed to your welfare I don't think I would want to do anything that wasn't for your good . . .

The responsibility for therapy is squarely on Roger's shoulders. The message being communicated is this: We may be in this together, but *you* are in charge of your life and are ultimately responsible for it, for better or worse. Should any action or homework assignment "backfire," Roger will not be able to blame anybody. He will be responsible.

Roger decided to attend the opera—provided that he could sit in the back row. Roger also agreed to go to the Art Institute. Mosak readily agreed and showed "faith" in Roger's ability to do it. Roger wondered why things had become so hard for him to do. "When I was twenty-one, it was easier," he commented.

T: Because at twenty-one, you apparently got discouraged about yourself and at twenty-one you "came out."

C: Yeah, at twenty-one, exactly.

T: Somewhere along that period, you apparently became discouraged.

C: Well, what happened? What caused the total disintegration . . . ?

T: Well, my guess is, that as time went on your confidence in yourself eroded because you weren't going anywhere in life. And then you have a few bad experiences tossed in [*Roger was deeply hurt by his first lover*], and you weave all of those things together, and you say, "Well, what's the use?" And that's the point I would like to turn around. Because I think people function better when they are encouraged than when they're discouraged.

C: I found out an important thing this week . . . I can't stand disappointments or anybody rejecting me. I never realized how deep rooted it was . . . It goes deeper than just lovers, even people, friends—as a consequence I really go overboard with people as far as being overly generous with gifts, entertaining, so forth.

T: You mean you try to buy their approval?

C: Yeah, a little too much so.

T: Why do you think you need their approval so badly?

C: I don't know, I just don't think I could exist without it.

Roger is overcompensating for his perceived inferiority in the eyes of others. His low opinion of himself, combined with his high standards, convinced him that no one would be able to "truly" care for him, therefore, he bought their approval. Mosak placed Roger's goal into perspective.

T: . . . I don't think any of us could exist, Roger, if we didn't have some approval—but do we *have* to have everybody's approval, and do we *have* to have everybody's approval constantly?

C: That's my problem. I need it constantly. I've got to be constantly wanted, constantly sought after . . .

T: Roger, your desire to please and to buy people—that kind of thing—and your fearing their rejection or disapproval of you is really a very ambitious kind of goal. You see, as a Catholic you believe in God, and here is God, the most perfect Being, right? Does everybody love God?

C: [*Very softly*] No.

T: Some people even reject Him?

C: [*Again, very softly*] Definitely.

T: And even the people who love God—do they love God constantly? So here is God, the most perfect Being, willing to take his chances with human beings—but you're not willing to take the same chances that even God takes.

C: Good point.

T: Do you think you might want to take the same chances with humanity God does? . . . And if somebody rejects you . . . there are always atheists!

C: Doesn't make them an atheist if they reject me, does it? [*Laughing.*]

T: Well, in a sense, it does.

C: In my mind it would—Saint Roger is not being venerated. True—[*laughing again*] very true.

T: . . . Perhaps, Roger, you have a place, even if somebody does reject you?

Roger, needing caring and approval, is afraid of rejection, and Mosak confronts him with the unrealistic and unattainable nature of his goals. He even gets Roger to joke about it. If he gets too intimate with people, they have some control over him, and if he gives up control, they are liable to hurt him—and the surest way to hurt Roger is to reject him. Therefore Roger will attempt to control ("dominate," to use Roger's language) his relationships. What he cannot control, he does not want. If he does it too actively, he is afraid of being too much like his father; therefore he will do it passively, like his mother, through fears and suffering (i.e., agoraphobia). Roger assumes that in order for him to be "relaxed" he must be in control. Mosak is attempting to convince him that maybe he can be *more* in control by being *less* in control.

Roger raised the issue of his engagement when he was nineteen. The discussion which followed highlighted the above issues.

C: I was engaged to a young woman . . . we got along beautifully. She would get me aroused—to a point—but not to actual intercourse, and I broke it off with her . . . Her closing statement to me was "You're queer." Now evidently she picked something up. In the two years I was with her there was no rejection. This is before I even came out and knew what a homosexual was.

T: Well, first of all, her calling you a queer, when you had not come out, was certainly rejection. She was telling you that she was plenty mad at you . . . But secondly, my feeling is that she called you a queer not because she sensed anything, but having tried to arouse you over and over and over again and your not responding, she just had to rub your nose in it. She was just plain mad at you because here she is having gone to all that trouble and you're not going to respond. I don't think she sensed anything.

C: Yeah, it does seem to fall into place.

They continued to explore Roger's relationship to men and women. Roger moved back to the topic of his homosexuality. Of the many possible reasons they discussed for it, three were meaningful to Roger: (a) He had a very low opinion of men and rejected the masculine role while growing up; (b) It was easier to be homosexual than heterosexual. There were no commitments, fewer responsibilities, and less intimacy; and (c) Roger was very concerned that a woman would control him, whereas he could control a man more easily. The interview concluded with a discussion about a woman who had been trying to seduce Roger for the past few weeks.

T: What would happen if you succumb to this girl who is out to seduce you?

C: I would be afraid that I would get involved emotionally.

T: And?

C: I don't know what would happen. It just goes against my mentality or grain. I just can't accept it, that's all.

T: So, you apparently are not willing to rule out that it could ever happen?

C: [*Laughing*] You really know how to get to me.

T: [*Laughing with him*] I hope so.

C: I don't believe you. You're right, I didn't say "No." So maybe I'm not ruling out the idea of it ever happening.

T: Apparently not.

The session ended with one additional point about Roger's homosexuality: Homosexuality is a choice, not a biological condition. If Roger is to choose it, he needs to choose it for "good" reasons, and not out of fear and insecurity.

The seventh session opened with Roger in very good spirits. He had spent a half hour standing on a busy downtown street watching people go by and enjoyed it. The discussion led to him asking about the nature of fears.

T: You see, the only people who have difficulties with fears are those that have to be in control. If you feel you have to be in control, there's so much you have to be afraid of because there are so many things that can go wrong.

C: Well why does somebody get that way? . . .

T: They lose their courage . . . You see, courage is the willingness to take a risk, even if you don't know what's going to happen . . . or even if there's a chance it might go against you.

C: I'm not a coward. I mean I'd fight if I had to or defend myself if I had to . . .

T: You're talking about a total coward, in some areas you think of yourself as a coward. When you're afraid to leave your house, alone, you're a coward. Aren't you?

C: Yeah, but I don't want to think of myself as a coward . . .

T: Well, what is a coward?

C: Someone who's afraid of something.

T: [*Laughing*] By that definition, I guess, in some areas, you're a coward.

C: [*Somewhat taken aback*] No one's ever called me that before.

T: Well, I haven't called you that—

C: Well, you're intimating it.

T: No, I haven't called you that—I'm saying *you think* of yourself as a coward.

C: [*Very softly*] A tough front.

T: Did you hear what you just said? A "tough front" implies that that's not what you are. Strip the front away and you've got somebody who's afraid.

C: I come on very strong with people though, I suppose.

T: A lot of cowards do. They hope that nobody will pick them out . . .

C: But I deal with dockmen, you know, truck drivers. Now I can really buffalo them . . .

T: But in intimate relationships—and I'm not talking about sexual relationships—

C: No, no—

T: Between people, you're scared.

C: Well, I don't have any intimate relationships with people . . .

T: Sure, you see yourself as a coward. You're unwilling to risk it.

C: Why does it have to be cowardly because you're unwilling to risk an intimate relationship? Why do you have to have an intimate relationship?

T: You don't have to, but there's a difference between "I choose not to have any," and "I'm afraid to have any."

C: I'll buy that.

The therapist is working in two directions here. First, he is working to assure that the gains made with the agoraphobia will last. By reframing the symptoms as indicative of a loss of *courage,* Roger's ability to rationalize was greatly diminished. Adlerians call this technique "spitting in the soup." He may still choose to do it, but it will certainly not "taste" as good. With the therapeutic relationship well established, Mosak became more *confrontive* in his interpretive style.

The other direction the therapist was taking involved motivating Roger to engage others meaningfully. Given the limited number of sessions, Mosak was working on Roger's attitude of being "tough" with others. He may be tough when he is in control (e.g., at work with subordinates), but intimately, one-to-one, he is a "coward." Again, the distinction is made between *having* to choose something out of fear and *choosing* to do something due to preference: Roger is choosing out of fear. The discussion rapidly turned to Roger's overall distaste for people in general.

T: You told me that you did all kinds of things to sort of buy people's favor. Why would you want to do that for people who are basically stinkers? . . .

C: I think it's more interesting inviting [over to his home] people you dislike . . . you can prove your superiority to them, put them down . . .

T: Yeah, but then, at least I've been taught—and I happen to think there's a large element of truth in it—that people that have to buy their superiority by pushing other people down don't think very much of themselves in the first place.

C: That may be true but it still is a nice feeling—

T: And that, as you say—

C: [*Bitterly*] Revenge is sweet . . .

T: Instead of having to talk about *them* [the people Roger looks down upon], let's talk about your inferiority feelings . . . What makes you inferior?

C: A combination of things—the area I was born in, the environment, family, we were a bunch of fat slobs. I didn't want anybody to even see them—I'd be ashamed.

T: What's that got to do with you? . . .

C: I always felt I was cheated because I never really had a good family life . . .

T: Well, I'd say to that perhaps, tough. I feel regret that you didn't have a better family life, but, what's that got to do with today, feeling inferior? A lot of people have transcended their early, unhappy family life. . . .

C: It's my perfection again . . . I won't even go out of the house if . . .

T: In other words, to be equal to the rest of us you have to be perfect, without blemish.

C: Well, I have to be above—I like admiration . . . [*Emotionally*] All my life I've been put down, with people making fun of me—calling me a fat slob, a pig . . . Now I want people to look at me and I want to be wanted, I want them to eat their hearts out to get at me—male or female. I want them to really just lust after me . . .

T: You said something which just threw me there for a moment.

C: What's that?

T: Male or female to lust over me. Why both?

C: Why both? I enjoy a woman who adores me or wants to go to bed with me, especially when I say no. It turns me on . . .

T: It turns you on to turn them on?

C: [*Sheepishly*]Yeah, sexually.

T: So basically, you want to get revenge on the world for giving you a bad time growing up?

C: It didn't end at growing up. It continued on and on.

T: So you want to hurt the world back?

C: [*Remorsefully*] People know how to hurt. They know how to stick a knife in you. Nobody knows the private misery people go through because somebody will just say, "My God—you've gained weight. You look like hell," or whatever the case may be . . .

T: So you plan to continue with your fight against the world?

C: No, I'm tired of fighting . . .

T: It sounds like you're preparing to fight for the rest of your life.

C: If need be . . .

They continued to discuss Roger's stance towards others. Adler described neurotics as going through life as if they were in hostile territory, and that is Roger's movement through life exactly. Mosak encouraged him to change his attitude—about himself, especially.

T: Maybe you want to stop fighting?

C: I'm willing, but—

T: But they aren't?

C: But they aren't exactly. I'm more than willing [*passionately*], I'm tired of fighting. I've been fighting for a long time.

T: There's only one way to tell you're tired—not if your mouth says so, but if you put your fists down.

Mosak encouraged him to choose different friends, ones that would not find so many faults and who would not be so ready to "fight." "I would much rather have friends who are going to treat me well," his therapist added.

C: You know what—you're right. This week I went through a whole list of people I know—mentally, and I started cutting them out. And I must agree with you, some of them are real assholes. They always have been assholes and why I've been bothering with them ten, fourteen years I don't know.

T: Good . . . Is it possible you might want to choose someone who isn't an asshole?

Roger agreed to make the effort. Mosak invited him to have an "easier life": Life, as Roger had been living it, must have been awfully tough. Roger conceded he has a "chip" on his shoulder when he meets people. He expects them to be hostile. Mosak *created an image* for Roger to keep in mind when he met new people.

C: Now I'm going to have to think they're a nice person.

T: Why do you have to think that? Just look them over . . . Why don't you just experience them, just get to know them without any preconceptions about whether they're nice or lousy? . . . Have you ever seen two dogs engaged in sniffing behavior? [*Both laugh.*] They look each other over, you know? . . .

C: [*Laughing*] So you want me to go "sniffing"?

T: Yeah, sniffing around, exactly . . .

C: Then I'll have my fear of rejection again . . .

T: So what—you mean everybody has to love you? Remember, even God doesn't have that privilege. If you know you're good enough, you don't have to worry about what they think.

C: It's time to start taking my shrine apart, right? Someone told me that, about my house. He says you're building a shrine to yourself. And at the time I was really upset. Now I realize he was right. [*Long pause*] Completely. That's something I noticed a long time ago, but I was never ready to admit it . . .

T: So even your house reflects your god-like standards.

Mosak and Roger discussed issues which Roger knew all too well but had never clearly formulated or examined. He was confronted with his "god-like" standards, his strong feelings of inferiority, hypersensitivity, and hostile attitude towards others. While sympathetic to Roger's history, the therapist powerfully confronted Roger with his responsibility for *continuing* to feel and act inferior. Roger cannot keep blaming his past. The other crucial issue worth commenting upon is the Adlerian's emphasis upon behavior—if Roger is truly tired of fighting, then he must "put down his fists." Adlerians emphasize the primacy of behavior; individuals must do more than simply "talk a good game." They must make movement.

Roger raised the issue of his relationship with his mother during the eighth session. He was by then functioning with virtually no agoraphobic symptoms. He had attended a play and enjoyed it; he had ceased having a problem with his drinking.

T: Now, Roger, it would seem to me that nobody could make a person feel guilty unless he chooses to feel guilty himself . . . Why do you choose to feel guilty with respect to your mother?

C: Primarily because she's blind and crippled. She uses this as kind of a crutch against me. It's not like she's alone, she has company all the time—people living with her.

T: How does she make you feel guilty? . . . Give me the words.

C: "You left me—you don't care about me" . . . It just goes on and on.

T: . . . What are your lines?

C: I usually don't say anything because I don't want to hurt her feelings.

After clarifying the problem a bit more, Mosak came to the point.

T: I would like to ask a couple of things, Roger. First of all, when your mother says, "You left me, you don't care for me, etc., etc.," do you think she's trying to get you to feel guilty? . . .

C: She loves it.

T: I got a hunch she wants something else.

C: You do?

T: Yeah—and I got a hunch that that's what you're not delivering. Not because you don't want to deliver it, but because you don't even know that that's what she's asking. My guess is she's inviting you to tell her that you love her . . . Maybe she's just looking for some kind of reassurance that you care? . . .

C: That's true, I never say that to her. I'll have to give that a try. This may be exactly it. I think you hit it pretty well.

They went on to discuss why Roger should choose to feel guilty. The primary purpose seemed to be his desire to be perfect. It was related to his god-like goals. Roger felt that there was so much he should do, he felt guilty for doing anything less than would be ideal. This, combined with the fact that Roger was afraid of getting too close to people and showing/expressing his feelings, created a distance which his mother attempted to close by using her suffering and complaining.

Adlerians believe that you cannot change other people's behavior, but you can change your own, and in that way, possibly the situation. Roger could not change his mother's behavior, but he could change his response to it. When he did, something happened which amazed him. Roger told her he loved her and showed some genuine concern, and his mother became "much more liberal," according to Roger. He reported that after one afternoon conversation, their relationship improved.

The interview then turned to Roger's opinion of the way others perceive him. Roger, while admitting he had come a long way, expressed concern over the fact that he was still afraid of opening himself up too much to others. They just would not like him if they knew the "real Roger." Mosak then "broke" one of his own rules: He allowed the class to participate and say what they thought of Roger. Roger was stunned and waited anxiously. The response was overwhelmingly one of interest and genuine concern. Unlike Roger's (admitted) expectations, no one was bored and no one found him in any way disagreeable. When the class was done, Mosak asked Roger what he thought.

C: [*Very subdued*] I'm very impressed . . . They make me feel very, very good—I feel great . . . They do take me seriously. I never dreamed that I was worth concern . . .

Roger went on with Mosak to discuss why Roger was so surprised. People had seen all his weaknesses, flaws, and imperfections, and still they cared about him. Roger was sincerely moved. The issue the therapist raised was that now Roger might want to do something about his newly discovered knowledge and take a chance with people. Almost immediately Roger stated, "I've met someone who I think cares and I'm trying."

Roger admitted that he really wanted somebody to love him, and he thought he had found somebody to love, a young man. They had spent an entire week living together (it had been two weeks since the last therapy session) and despite Roger's attempts to "buy" the man's affections, the man had refused to be "bought." He seemed to genuinely care. The session ended with Roger stating, "I do care about people." Mosak gave Roger a homework assignment.

T: What would we see if the real you came out of hiding?

C: [*Laughing*] Probably one hell of a mess . . . an emotional wreck, someone who can't really cope . . .

T: [*Speaking of Roger's tendency to secretly become emotional and occasionally cry when alone*] Crying . . . has nothing to do with masculinity—or to make a pun, mess-culinity, since you said you were a mess.

C: That's a good term—I like that.

T: It only has to do with being human. I would like to set you a task. Do you know any people who aren't messes?

C: Yeah.

T: Good. For the next week, I would like you to act as if you were one of those adequate people. Now it's going to be an act, no doubt about it, but it's not phony any more than a person that plays Hamlet is phony even though he's playing a role. I would just like you to try out that role. I would like you to act, for one week, as if you were not a mess. And if you don't know what that means concretely, then when you get into a certain kind of situation where you feel in doubt, you say "How would so-and-so who is adequate behave in this kind of situation?" And then, act that way.

Roger is moving in a healthy, prosocial direction. Social interest is being fostered. As his attitude changes and his motivation is modified, Mosak is including the behavioral component. Roger is accustomed to thinking of himself as a "mess." His strivings for perfection have usually met with feelings of inferiority; hence, subjectively, he feels like a "wreck"—a mess. Though motivation may change rapidly, the behavioral component requires practice and self-training and quite often lags behind the motivational change. The task to act *as if* he were an adequate person introduces modeling principles, especially when Roger is asked to act as if he were someone adequate that he knows. If Roger follows through with the task, he will incorporate the behavioral component more rapidly into his modified life style. In time, it will be difficult to differentiate acting adequate from being adequate.

Roger came into the ninth session and told of a situation that occurred at work. He had been "ranting and raving" about how life is so "rotten" and how "everybody is out to hurt you and nobody cares," when a woman came up to him and said, "I care." He said all he could think about were the therapy sessions. He said he felt "great." He said he smiled, and it changed the whole course of the evening.

The interview moved to a discussion of Roger's *dreams*. Adlerians view dreams as rehearsal for possible solutions to the problems of living. They are teleologic and serve to generate emotions which carry through to the next day and help motivate individuals to behave in certain ways which are consistent with their styles of life. Roger related this dream:

C: I was laying in bed . . . and I opened my eyes and I looked at the end of my bed. There was kind of a cocktail party going on with everybody dressed in 1800s garb. Out of this crowd came a woman—fantastically beautiful—who sat on the edge of my bed and said, "Well, can I help you with your problem—we're going to talk about it." I said, "Go away—this is the result of too many martinis or something." But we talked and she said, "Tell me what's wrong?" and I went on about things we [Mosak and Roger] had talked about. I really felt much better.

T: Much better about what?

C: About myself and life . . .

T: O.K. It [the dream] is your creation: Why did you put a woman at the foot of your bed?

C: I thought about that. [*Laughing*] I don't know why . . .

T: Why a beautiful woman? You could have put an ugly woman there. Roger, are you toying with the notion of becoming heterosexual? Or at least giving it a whirl?

C: [*Sheepishly*] Ah—yeah, I have been thinking about it.

They went on to discuss Roger's surprising admission. He was afraid that if he got involved with a woman, he would be tied down. It never occurred to Roger that he could get involved with a woman without being committed. It related back to Roger's idealizing women: He believed that women would not just "sleep around."

T: Roger, suppose I went down to see my bookie this afternoon and bet on whether in the next six months you would wind up in bed with a woman, should I give or take odds?

C: You should take them.

T: O.K. What odds should I take?

C: Ninety to one [that he won't sleep with a woman].

T: Ninety to one hardly leaves any room, and your [dream] would sort of indicate to me that your odds are better than ninety to one . . .

Mosak and Roger played the "Game of Probabilities." It is a way of investigating the potential movement of an individual in the future. Though Roger is preparing himself psychologically and emotionally for a heterosexual encounter, behaviorally he is hesitant. Mosak and Roger explored different situations in which Roger might be more comfortable being with a woman.

The session ended with Roger summarizing what he learned in therapy: He was less fearful and accepted himself more. He learned to say "no" to people, to stop feeling sorry for himself, and to "function better." Most importantly, Roger said he learned that he was a human being, and that was the most meaningful thing for him. Before he left, he said that his performance at work had improved so much that he was getting a "major promotion." As he left, he warmly said goodbye to the class and the therapist.

Roger never made it back for the last interview. Unexpectedly, his mother became very ill. Roger decided he wanted to be there for her. She died soon after he arrived. The quarter ended at the Institute and Roger decided to attempt to manage on his own.

SUMMARY AND CONCLUSION

Adlerian psychology is a holistic, teleoanalytic theory that stresses the unity of the person and the examination of the individual's goals and movement through life. Behavior that is useful—that is, conducive to healthy, cooperative functioning—is viewed as the ultimate goal of therapy. Such behavior, with its component emotional and psychological factors, is called social interest.

During the course of psychotherapy, Roger moved from a position of viewing others as his enemies, the world as hostile, and himself as inferior, to a position of genuine concern for others and acceptance of himself. His unrealistically high goals of personal superiority, most prominently evident in his choice of agoraphobic symptoms to control and dominate those around him, gave way to a more accepting, caring, and mutually respectful stance as he gained more confidence in himself and as his feelings of inferiority were put to rest. In nine therapy sessions, he reappraised his orientation to life, others, and himself, and emerged a happier, more productive individual. In short, he developed social interest.

Mosak utilized a number of techniques to move Roger towards social interest. He encouraged him and gave him hope. By utilizing a Life Style Assessment, the therapist worked on modifying the client's mistaken attitudes, and not just eliminating symptoms. At various times, the therapist used such tactics as Confrontation, Future Autobiography, Humor, the Game of Probabilities, Acting "As If," Tasksetting, Dreams, Multiple Psychotherapy, Interpretation, "Spitting in the Client's Soup," Placing in Perspective, Creating Images, and The Question.

As Roger's convictions became more adaptive and flexible, his private logic came more in line with common sense. He became more motivated to meet the challenges of life in a useful, cooperative way. Individual Psychology provides the psychotherapist and client with a system and philosophy to encourage such change.

Editors' Introduction

Dr. Claire Douglas, author of the chapter on analytical psychotherapy in the 8th edition of Current Psychotherapies, *selected one of her own cases to illustrate the Jungian approach to therapy. The case comes from her recent book,* The Old Woman's Daughter.

Bruce is similar to many of the patients one sees in therapy. He has had a reasonably successful career, but he feels somehow incomplete and senses that something is missing from his life. He had been reading Jung's work, and he deliberately sought out a Jungian therapist. When he began therapy, he was already conversant with the vocabulary used in analytical psychotherapy, and he appreciated and valued the rich symbolism typically uncovered by Jungian therapists.

This case illustrates the importance of archetypes, the client's need to understand and confront his feminine side, the integration of the shadow and its relationship to sexuality, the ways in which sexuality presents in the therapy hour, the Jungian approach to dream analysis, projection, regression, transference and countertransference, termination issues, and the ways in which a skilled therapist deals with a patient's anger during therapy sessions.

How important is it for a patient to come to therapy already prepared to accept the theoretical model used by the therapist? Would most patients feel comfortable with Jung's ideas, or would analytical psychotherapy be seen as simply too esoteric and arcane for ordinary people? What mental health problems are most conducive to treatment using Jungian approaches?

3 | THE CASE OF BRUCE

Claire Douglas

BRUCE

Bruce was an intense, compact man of Greek heritage with a Taurus-like energy and natural physicality that he disguised behind an almost priestly attitude. He was a self-made man who came to see me when he was near retirement. Like many perceptive and sensitive people in their middle years, he had successfully negotiated job, marriage, and children, yet he felt that he was missing something. His dreams propelled him to go over his life and look at all he had neglected or let pass. His relation to the feminine was damaged as he had been brought up in a faith and culture that considered women inferior, unreliable, and divided into Holy Virgins, to be worshipped from afar, and the majority, who were untrustworthy, false-hearted, and seductive. Yet he had a profound sadness underlying his cavalier energy and yearned for connection and depth. He felt he lacked mothering because his own mother, seemingly constantly pregnant, had little time for him. Bruce felt she was also sometimes inappropriate with her boy children in what he took to be a coarse and belittling manner. He tended to idealize unobtainable women and to reject and demean the women around him. He had started to read Jung and was very taken by Jung's and Joseph Campbell's work on archetypes, especially the Mother Archetype. Its manifestations in nature infused him with profound longing and yet also, again, with distrust. He had a very good heart but suspected it and his "unmanly" feelings. He did some of his best introspective work on the long runs he took for exercise.

I will follow the changes in Bruce's relationship with the Mother Archetype and with the feminine by following a few of the dreams through which his psyche instructed him. Most are exactly as he dreamed them, but I have shortened some longer ones. Bruce was a big dreamer and demonstrated what Jung called "an ethical responsibility" toward them. By that I mean he scrupulously recorded them, made notes about them, and also, after bringing them to analysis, often did Active Imagination with some aspects of them and then attempted to incorporate what they taught him into his daily life. Over the 5 years of our work together, I have more than 1,000 pages of his effort. His dedication and hard work got us over some very rough places.

Bruce's first dream after making an appointment but before seeing me is in three parts:

Part One: I [Bruce] am standing in a yogic balance pose. A short, uncoordinated young girl tries to do this also. Everyone in the room is laughing at her. I get angry and order them to respect her.

Part Two: I am a baby and an unknown woman is holding me and gently rocking me when my childhood friend breaks in and says "No! You have to take turns."

From *The Old Woman's Daughter* (Claire Douglas, 2006, College Station: Texas A&M University Press). Reprinted by permission.

Part Three: I go to a friend's house and see kittens and cats running and tumbling and having a great time. I get uneasy and angry and say they have to behave or else!

So, here his psyche, as indicated in his first dream, gave me images of the work we needed to do together: First, help Bruce bring out his now unconscious respect for the feminine in this initial form of the gawky girl. To help it become conscious, we need to investigate the split between his psyche asking for respect for the feminine and his consciously mocking and disparaging it in its present form. Second, allow him to have the experience of a cherishing analyst who would tend his young self by holding him and gently caring for him. This would help repair his early infantile deprivation. Third, help Bruce change his distrust of the feminine (the cats' animal nature), especially feminine physicality, exuberance, and play.

A month later, Bruce did an Active Imagination:

X was receptive to my desire. She lay down nude spreading her legs to receive me. Her head appeared to me like the sun and her huge breasts like twin mountains. Her legs—she had the soles of her feet on the earth with her knees bent—seemed like two large trees as a gateway into the deep dark forest. As I entered, I felt like I was going into the depths of the Earth. I felt an immense desire to plunge in, yet this desire was accompanied by a fearful reservation.

This shows Bruce in relationship to the Animal, now Earth Goddess, aspect of the archetypal feminine. He wanted to stress the sexuality of the feeling and its power. He resented and fought my attempt to explore his "fearful reservation" and its possible link with his anger at the cats of his first dream.

Bruce's psyche, however, also wanted to deal with the "fearful reservation" as he soon dreamed:

I follow a woman out of a store onto a busy street. Her skirt was caught way up behind. I'm interested. She smoothes the skirt out and walks on, then hurries down some subway stairs. When I got to the top I asked the subway attendant if "these stairs went down?" She said "Yes." I went down into the bottom of a dead end. A loathsome, disfigured, decrepit man in a dirty black robe walked toward me with his arms outstretched. I thought he was a bum and started to turn away. But he grinned as if he were waiting for me and put his arms around me. His burning eyes looked deeply into mine. I sprung free and raced up the stairs. It felt like a chilling confrontation with death.

This dream initiated a long and major part of Bruce's work on reclaiming and owning his shadow's creepily misshapen relationship to sexuality. This was not only his personal shadow but a collective one we, in this culture, all share in the dead-end passages and back alleys of our internal night towns. My respect for Bruce and my holding him analytically as he struggled with the disfigured, deformed, and decrepit parts of his own sexuality and sexual fantasies helped him negotiate some very rough passages, as did his courageous acceptance of the "death of the ego" experience he had to undergo to confront and claim this shadow. We struggled, as he was continually tempted to split off from, and disclaim, the shadow or else project it onto me. One of the hardest things in analysis is to look at these creatures within us and see the immense damage they can wreak, yet at the same time not turn away from them or suppress or bury them. Integration of the shadow is such an easy thing to say—almost a Jungian cliché—but so very difficult in practice. I needed all my skill and more to help Bruce confront his shadow without making him feel shamed, inferior, or judged. One of the most valuable ways I did this, unknown to him, was sharing some of his shadow work by revisiting my own night towns and the shadow side of my own sexuality in both my training analysis and in my supervision. I felt I had a clear responsibility to do my own share of this confusing work. However, it made me really aware of the truth of Jung's (1929) statement: "It is sometimes exceedingly painful to live up to everything one expects of one's patient" (p. 73).

It was a difficult period of shadow work, as Bruce was often caught either in guilt for his past behavior and current thoughts or in a negative transference that blamed me for all his or his anima's failings. Jung's alchemical model helped us both find our way:

> Alchemy describes, not merely in general outline but often in the most astonishing detail, the same psychological phenomenology which can be observed in the analysis of unconscious processes. The individual's specious unity that emphatically says "I want, I think" breaks down under the impact of the unconscious. So long as a patient can think that somebody else . . . is responsible for his difficulties, he can save some semblance of unity . . . But once he realizes that he himself has a shadow, that his enemy is his own heart, then the conflict begins. (Jung, 1946, p. 198)

Every time Bruce left his own struggle with the shadow and projected it onto me so that I became the person responsible for his difficulties, his psyche came to our rescue with dreams. For instance:

> A young bikini-clad woman and Bruce search under a stadium for a golf ball and a wet photo of a famous [and womanizing] singer. He keeps warning her to be careful or they would literally step into crap. They find the golf ball and the photo but then begin to sink into the muck.

Or Bruce dreams:

> He is on a construction job. He walks over the lawn and realizes the cesspool has overflowed. He tries to keep his shoes clean by jumping on its cover but it tips and almost tips him in. Bruce realizes he had the responsibility of fixing the cesspool. An irritating blatty-mouthed old woman [whom he associated to me] keeps reminding him of this. Bruce simply planned to raise the level of the lawn.

Both dreams again required him to take back his projections and deal with all the crap and the mucky aspects of his male–female relationships as well as with material he needs to process and digest rather than just cover over. "Raising the level of the lawn" seems, at first, and to many people, so much easier and simpler than examining what one wants to suppress. Here, Bruce's alliance with the bikini-clad woman and her involvement with his womanizing shadow are shown to be associated with shit and cesspools. These are collective as well as personal problems. We spent many painful months of exploration of bad habits, vices, and how our culture teaches us to make a game out of sexuality instead of seeing it as a way to connect. We also examined our own and our culture's objectification of the feminine and all our fascinations with pornography and the seamy side of life. I tried to help Bruce with this again through my own analysis but also by struggling to be neither "a blatty-mouthed" nag nor getting my kicks from his fantasies.

At this time, a new aspect of the feminine started to appear in his dreams. She was a forthright and loving little girl whom Bruce described as a tomboy. She was quite irrepressible and started to frequent his dreams. He found out her name was Joy. At first she was about 5 or 6 and told him she was his daughter but had to live far away because his wife (his own conventionally feminine part) neither understand nor liked Joy. Bruce, in the dreams, felt very happy to have found her and wanted her to live with them. She couldn't quite yet, as Bruce still needed to do more outer work on his inherited attitudes toward the feminine. Joy helped him in his inner work and became more and more important to him as she continued to appear in his dreams.

About 6 months into the analysis, one of Bruce's most important dreams occurred; it was archetypal in its intensity. It was as if the psyche wasn't content with digging up personal cesspools but wanted to go even deeper, possibly into the collective, so that his new feminine child could be securely held in a safe home with firm foundations. He described the dream this way:

> A guide, a younger woman, and Bruce were in a huge mansion. The guide [whom he associated to his analyst and to whom I now associate the Old Woman] carried a light. We turned left down a long corridor and the guide says "Okay, tonight we are going into the pits, the bowels of the universe." She led the way down through a trap-door in the bottom floor to a set of stairs. When we reached the bottom, we stood in a vast place that seemed without walls. The floor wasn't solid. There was a mist and all sorts of prehistoric antediluvian creatures crept or lumbered their way slowly through the mud and ooze. Bruce was frightened thinking that his guide [his analyst] was insisting he go with her back to the beginning of time. Bruce described his stomach knotting up and he felt great fear and awe, as well as distrust of his analyst/guide.

Because of his fear, Bruce continued the dream later, alone, in an Active Imagination where he then saw a ray of light, and his spiritual guide (a man) led him away and up through the water to a sort of Garden of Eden lagoon where I, no longer in the role of analyst or guide, frolicked about and swam in the water, and then we danced and the three walked toward the sun.

I, frankly, had a very hard time with this because I valued his descent far more than his, to me, too idealistic escape. I bridled at the change of my role as guide and analyst into a romantic anima figure. However, I respected Bruce's feeling that he had journeyed bravely and ventured into the bowels of the universe, and I kept quiet about what he consciously concluded was the aim of his journey: his reclamation of his anima—his hidden inner Aphrodite—the swimming woman. He noted, "I, through my anima, can either serve as the creator of life or serve as the waste disposal (the cesspool). Both creator and waste disposal are in fact very close to being in the same place in my psyche. Hence, it is like being on the razor's edge."

I didn't crush what Bruce was struggling with at this level, but it was an effort to keep my peace and I rued his valuing his Eden more than the depths. His imagining me frolicking and dancing like the bikini-clad woman also felt like an attack on my role as analyst. I resented being made into a sort of erotic anima figure. This was yet more work that I had to undergo to keep my own house in order. I needed neither to reject Bruce's Active Imagination nor become too stiff—even puritanical—nor too diminished. Part of me told me to lighten up and experience the joy of frolicking, swimming, and dancing. But when I tried it in my own Active Imagination, it felt all wrong. I realized, finally, that it felt as if I would be breaking an incest taboo imagining a scene with my patient. I wondered if that may not have been part of what Bruce was after to defeat his analysis. Getting back to Bruce's psyche, it seemed to me that he had had a invaluable opportunity to witness the primordial roots of his and all our essences and that he'd turned aside from it. However, I trusted his unconscious to go at the pace he needed, and I kept my silence.

I feel that the psyche may have agreed with my assessment because more shit and cesspool dreams followed as he explored both Aphrodite and the women in his life (including me) and his mostly very negative, distrustful attitude toward them. A month into this process, Bruce dreamed, "Now the cesspool is really clogged. I decide the only thing to do is dig the whole thing up and start again." He then had a dream that both shocked him and shook him up in a way that any number of interpretations from me could never have done. Bruce dreamed of a sexual scene from which he tries unsuccessfully to shield his new little girl, Joy (the one who wasn't ready to live with him quite yet). He knew it was an inappropriate, even traumatic, scene for her to watch. In it an attractive, adult, "sexy" woman both lures and teases him. He tries to seduce her as a sort of Eros figure, and when that doesn't work, he rides in like a "blind bull" and seizes her with the intention of bending her to his will. He notes, "Why am I beating the hell out of my feminine part? And what does it mean for the little girl to witness this?"

This is shadow work at its hardest, where one is confronted by what one so often buries, projects, or disclaims. And so we engaged in ever deeper consideration of a certain aspect of both men's and women's sexuality and the negative games each play with and on the other. We explored the role-playing in which Bruce had been engaged; we also explored how much more difficult it was for him to be open to, and accepting of, the dance of sexuality. Bruce was most upset that his inner little girl had witnessed the scene. This gave us a chance to explore his early childhood and to investigate the ramifications of our oversexualized culture on its children—here on Bruce's new feminine energy, the little girl Joy. (While I, in my analysis and supervision, did equally heavy work investigating where I, like Bruce's Joy, brought an unprocessed, too young, and too early sexualized part of myself into our work.)

About a year into the analysis, Bruce started to feel less hostile and suspicious of me and more needy and dependent, hating the seemingly endless time between sessions. My countertransference turned from sometimes being hostile and on guard to a very positive, caring, and maternal one. I had kept quiet about my suspicion of his Garden of Eden fantasy, letting his own dreams lead and instruct him. However, at the end of the year, as he kept returning to it, I suggested he do an Active Imagination to explore why he found himself in that particular earthly paradise. (While I privately explored my huge aversion to representing, or being a carrier for, his "beautiful anima figure." Especially since I knew that the anima, as well as the analyst, can serve as the one who understands and that the anima's true role bridges the way to greater consciousness.) Bruce's answer at the next session was very revealing:

> It is a shelter, not an end but a means to an end, my shelter from the pull of life. It's the center between heaven and earth [Bruce thought of his analyst as the shelter]. I [Bruce] am here in this particular lagoon/paradise to learn the connection between heaven and earth and the unity of it all. I am here now as a result of being born in my family, to have suffered poverty and deprivation, to feel distanced from heaven, to be stretched out beyond remembering, to feel/understand the utmost sense of estrangement. My task is to find my way through this maze, like Theseus connected to Ariadne's thread, to travel deep down into the center but with my cord connected to both you, Claire, and my spiritual mentor. My task, though, is the opposite of Theseus'. He goes to liberate the maidens; the maidens have imprisoned me. I see that my Minotaur (the half bull, half man who was chained inside a cave) is a part of me I had been unaware of; I must confront him instead of fleeing him. I was led down to the bowels, back in time, for the purpose of knowing this and that I could not do it alone but needed both you, Claire, to take me back, way back in time, and my spiritual guide to keep my connection to heaven. Now that I know I am not alone, that I have not one but two guides, I will be able to go back to that place and get a better look at those prehistoric monsters lumbering around inside of me.

I learned a lot from Bruce's explanation of his descent. I also learned to be more open to Bruce's masculine way of descent. I realized that women may have an easier time with their monsters and oozy antediluvian creatures than men. This may be because we do not have to separate completely from the archaic mother realm nor cut the bonds that link mother to daughter in the Mother Line. Thus, women are often much closer to this matriarchal mother world and its decidedly nonrational, fluid, even bloody, and chaotic primeval fecundity. A man, such as Bruce, may need his connection to heaven to safely make the descent while keeping his link to order. It is like the San Francisco analyst

Joseph Wheelwright used to say: "Yes, I go there, but I always keep one foot wrapped tightly about my chair." These are necessary and important threads to keep one grounded in reality. Men often project their fear of the irrational out onto women. Freudian cultural historian Peter Gay (1986) follows this psychologically:

> The fear of women has taken many forms in history. It has been repressed, disguised, sublimated, or advertised, but in one way or another it seems as old as civilization itself . . . It is born of man's early total dependence on his mother, and his longing, frustrated love for her, his defenseless lassitude after intercourse, and the frightening and portentous implications of the female genitals. . . . The Medusa and all the dangers she stands for are a very old story. (pp. 200–201)

As Bruce struggled with his inner Medusas and dragons and "very old stories," he started to perceive another side of the situation. Bruce wrote me a letter while he was making his descent:

> All my life I have suffered from experiencing only a half of life at one time only knowing what I felt from my ego state. Oh, the suffering and hurt I needlessly inflicted on myself. Rather all the joy and ecstasy I missed out on because of my blindness, being lost from the path, disunited and fragmented. This is an emotion like I have never felt before: of ecstasy and pain together: the ecstasy of union, the pain of separation. Feeling one without the other is to be incomplete; like an outer experience of life, maya, an illusion. Not the reality of the inner experience of unity and wholeness: real suffering and joy. Love, the fundamental quality of my archetype anima, I have distorted into lust. At this moment, I love everyone: none can escape, not even my adversaries. I see that my work is to feel these emotions coming through me and to make love to them internally allowing that love to flow through me.

Many months into this difficult internalizing work, Bruce dreamed: There is a new and very small young boy at school. He comes over and sits on Bruce's lap and wants to tell Bruce all about himself.

In a dream shortly after, Bruce sees his mother too busy to notice an unattended similar little boy. His negative judging "minister" part of himself is up on a balcony glaring and spying at the boy, but an old Russian woman gives the boy both rubles and U.S. dollars. Bruce takes the little boy away from the neglectful mother and the "judge" and they go up and outside. The little boy now has a small white puppy with him. Bruce sweeps the boy up in his arms and hugs him. The boy wants to go to New York (where I was then practicing). Bruce tells him yes but we have to take care of the puppy first.

With some integration of the shadow, this young boy—a more natural and feeling aspect of himself—can appear and reveal himself to Bruce. They relate well with each other. The Old Woman, in the guise of a foreigner, the Russian woman, gives the new masculine feeling aspect both conscious and unconscious energy. The dog is animal nature but now in a domesticated, young form that can be cared for and tended. Bruce's feeling that he can do some of the work himself—tend his own young boy and young animal nature himself—takes on significance because of Bruce's growing dependence on my holding and containing him in analysis. By the way, his sometimes slightly self-righteous, minister-like persona had completely fallen away.

At this time, a lot of our work was not on reintegrating and revaluing the masculine and the feminine but on a regression to basic pre-Oedipal infancy issues. These often needed careful attention and cherishing so that his armored self could relax and disarm. He began to experience enough safety to risk growing a more tensile, feeling skin to replace the armor. Bruce felt secure enough now to surrender and feel his dependence, his sense of abandonment, and his crucial need for steady attachment and mirroring.

It was a stormy time for both of us because Bruce now raged at me for all the minor and sometimes big failures I made in holding him. It was not so much the outer detail: something as small, to me that is, as asking him not to mail me things I had to sign for (as it disturbed other patients), but for him, the inner feeling was of my complete rejection and abandonment of him. It re-created his torment as a child whose place was taken again and again by another new baby. To recall his first dream, Bruce had to take turns and I turned into his mother who had no longer had time for him or his needs. However, in place of his mother, I could hear the loneliness, outrage, and pain this had caused. Bruce's aggression and hostility seemed at times crazy to him, as did his almost paranoid need to unlink from me at the same time he clung to me. Countertransferentially, I felt a baby inquisitor was searching for errors in my care of him, and I often felt I was turned into his neglectful and somewhat seductive mother. At the same time, he had an uncanny knack at finding all my very real faults and failings. What a way for an infant self to gain autonomy and trust! I did both cherish and respect him, but I sometimes had to hand over his care to the Archetypal Old Woman standing behind my chair, while I bit my tongue to not lash back at Bruce for his attacks.

At the time of this necessary regression and reintegration, we were over 2 years into the analysis. Bruce dreamed that parts of the inside of his house were a mess and were now under repair. The house would not become livable until he made a journey to Africa (another descent) and came safely back again. The little girl named Joy reappeared as an African girl, now age 6 or 7, but she still couldn't live with him, she told him, because of his possibly somewhat sexualized attitude toward her. She said she didn't think her mother would approve.

In Bruce's case, we were doing the necessary early infantile construction and repair work on the parts of his emotional house that need renovation. This helped him gain a new attitude and balance. It also made him see the way in which his projections messed up his inner living quarters. However, the psyche advised Bruce that he needed to go to Africa first and regain a more natural and primeval part of himself and a less wounded attitude toward the feminine before the little African girl can return. The matriarchal substrate is now no longer represented by antediluvian creatures and descending to the depths but by geographically distant unknowns like traveling to Africa or being helped by someone from Russia.

A few months later, toward the close of this period of regression and consolidation, Bruce dreamed that the African girl did indeed come to live with him and his wife for they now have two little girls, "One is a delightful new little Black girl about 7. She has a big gap in her front teeth; is dressed in white, and has a big smile. She makes us all so happy." Bruce recognizes her as Joy.

As this was happening in Bruce's dream world and in his unconscious, his traditional ego position made a last fight. Bruce raged at me again and almost brought his analysis to an end. He decided to terminate because as he wrote:

> I experienced rage, anger, and bitterness against you, Claire, and women in general for draining [sucking out of me] my power, reducing me to a wimp! I lashed out, calling you every blasphemous name under the sun. These feelings are connected with the dream where I broke my best friend's rose-colored glasses I was wearing. I destroyed my rose-colored view of the feminine" [the other, Virgin Mary side of his and his socioculture's habit of sexualizing and demeaning women].

Bruce went on to accuse me of trying to castrate him and of engaging in a regressive rather than evolutionary process with him. In Active Imagination, I was turned from the Aphrodite-like anima figure into Red Riding Hood and then into the ancient Grandmother, who became bestial as she took her true wolf form. Thus, from the gentle holding, nurturing mother, we now had to deal with the other side of the Old Woman in her wrathful form and as the carrier of the Terrible Mother Archetype.

My good relationship with aspects of the powerful and Dark Feminine that have been turned so monstrous helped me here. This is because I could see Bruce's projection as rising out of fear of the Old Woman's power. It was a power with which I was starting to become familiar, and I was learning when to veil my face against its intensity. Thus, I didn't have to be seized by her, identify with her, or act out her wolfishness. I knew the great strength of the archetype and realized that those who served her with respect seldom needed to feel her wrath.

I had not interpreted Bruce's work on early infancy issues to him in a Kleinian way because I felt the images and feelings he was producing and the dreams he reported showed he was finding his own way. In retrospect, some mapping of the terrain may have eased the journey for both of us. The archetypal potency of the many-sided Great Mother and the suffering of the human infant often filled the room with their energy. I had no wish to defend myself but tried to contain him and his rage as he met the Terrible Mother or the Kleinian bad breast (me) head on. My analytic and human stance here was to hold, contain, and cherish Bruce in a way that humanized the archetypal energy as best I could. I knew it was not about me and also knew about wrestling with my own archetypal rage in places deep inside me that had never been humanized. Our work together humanized by our bearing witness in a cherishing way. We bore witness, as best we could, to the suffering Bruce endured as one of the atrocities experienced, yet too often sealed up, inside us all. I trusted his dreams to show him a way out of his suffering, but I also feel some classical interpretation here may have helped him. And except for the fact that he was a working man who had to travel into the city to see me, we needed more sessions than once a week and the once or twice a week phone sessions in between. They, and therefore I, failed to hold him securely enough at this difficult time.

There followed several dreams where it was suggested and then ordered that he "slow down." He decided not to terminate, but he also started to see a male analyst in his own town (this only lasted for a few sessions). The reasons Bruce gave were that the therapist was male, would give him a masculine perspective, and it would be easier to see him both geographically and emotionally. Suddenly, and at the same time, Bruce wanted, or insisted we needed, a personal relationship. I took all of this as a possible attempt to forcefully enter into a relationship with the feminine. Bruce's psyche came to the rescue again as he dreamed he, as a young boy, was pointing his erection threateningly at some woman he identified with me.

His summation of the sense he made out of all this upheaval I quote:

> The not available woman may well be a projection of my desire for my mother's love transferred in the dream onto Claire, and the erection pointed at her an aggressive nonsexual act—a reaction to her unavailability which triggers the process of: abandonment, feelings of rejection, anger.

He faulted me for sexualizing the dream. I had, indeed, interpreted it as sexualized anger and stressed its hostile aspects. I had focused on his hostility to the analysis and his wish to destroy it through sexualizing our relationship; I also wanted him to look at his anger at the woman (women) whom he felt had too much power over his young self. Bruce quoted the analyst E. C. Whitmont back to me that "an analyst may misinterpret the dream symbols" as sexual when in fact they may simply reflect the dreamer's desire to gain unavailable (rejected) love. I think Bruce may have been surprised when I considered this and said that I may have not sufficiently valued his longing for connection and relationship. That may well have been an error on my part, but he should also ponder the threatening aspect. I did not quote Jung to him but felt, all too well, the truth of Jung's (1937) statement, "The case is not in the least a story of triumph; it is more like a saga of blunders, hesitations, doubts, groping in the dark, and false cues which in the end took a favorable turn" (p. 337).

I am so grateful to Bruce at this point for both pondering, and then taking back the projection, because I felt like I was losing it. I was losing my connection both to him and to the Old Woman. I felt a deep bond with him and also moved by his dedication to his analytic work, but all the woman and Claire bashing that was going on and the urge to make me into a sexual object raised my hackle. I felt the rage of an outlawed, despised, and sexualized being. I began to feel possessed by the negative side of the Old Woman and wanted to project my fury onto Bruce, and then I wasn't at all sure whether it was my rage or his. I had to spend precious time now working hard in my own supervision and training analysis on digesting and integrating both my own anger at the patriarchy (with Bruce as its symbol!) and correcting my own heretofore too rose-colored view of the Mother Archetype and the feminine in general. Just because the Old Woman has been so demonized was no excuse for my trying to turn her into an all-good object. She is much too powerful for that and deserved far more respect.

The alchemical mix of Bruce's and my mutual work resulted in his linking of the threatening erection to an early memory of a bathtub scene where his mother laughed at his erect little body and he felt enraged. He wrote:

> Now ponder the possibility of this pattern projected sexually on women in my life and Claire in the transference. I deceive myself; I use them, and abuse them—never expecting to receive what I really want—thinking that what I want is sex. And when they (e.g., Claire) offer the cherishment I unconsciously seek, I reject it—angrily—feeling rejected because I think I am not getting what I think I want—sex—but what is behind that is a desire for love and attention—relatedness?—non-abandonment and not sex.

Bruce slowly became aware of his mother's unwitting assault on his sense of masculine self and of his almost Adlerian "will to power" as a consequence. Bruce mourned his precarious and easily shamed sense of masculinity. He mourned his defense of himself and the way he protected himself by threatening the women in his life with his masculine power. As he wrestled to integrate all this, he had another house dream:

> I had been working in a huge house off and on for a long time. A large family was living there and remodeling it. I went every morning to supervise. This morning, from the corner of my eye, I noticed the owner's wife wearing a tight orange sweater. She was very attractive. Instantly I turned away. Then I decided to turn and look directly at her face and greet her with a friendly "good morning." She smiled. I returned her smile simply and freely and also smiled at my shadow as he wasn't acting out. Then I was in a vast unused area upstairs I hadn't known was there.

In the dream, Bruce gained a new and less loaded attitude toward women and could greet one simply in a friendly, nonsexualized way. What a relief! The dream also reflects his growth and his access to new energy: the huge new area he hadn't known was there.

We continued to weather storms together that rose from both of our wounded masculine and feminine natures. Bruce's came from his personal upbringing and also from a culture that devalued masculine feeling as it devalued the Old Woman and sexualized her daughter. Bruce's work on the Terrible Mother part of the Mother Archetype, which started by his seeing, and sometimes being overwhelmed by, her negative side, strangely paralleled my work on adjusting my perhaps too positive and glowing feeling toward the Great Mother. It was a deeply corrective experience for both of us. Bruce and I constellated an antidote each for the other. I think we both learned and grew a lot from our struggles, as well as from the deep feeling of connectedness between us. There were increasingly minor storms and discords as he took back more and more projections and also accepted more and more of himself. I wish I could have told him of my own struggle with the Terrible Mother and my passionate exploration of the Old Woman's many other sides, but it is one of those things that bear fruit just as well, if not better, in silence.

Bruce had to return to the foundational basics of his character and experience. He accomplished this through dissolving his outward attitude in the world and his inner defenses (while I painfully integrated more aspects of myself). We had to return to his primordial essence to help him free his energy, trust his own feeling nature, and let him learn how to merge, flow, and release. The alchemical retort at times grew murky and so black that neither of us could see our way. Here Jung's words about therapy proved of inestimable value. As he wrote in "The Psychology of the Transference" (1946):

> *Ars requirit totum hominem* [This art requires the whole person], we read in an old treatise. This is in the highest degree true of psychotherapeutic work. A genuine participation, going right beyond professional routine, is absolutely imperative, unless of course the doctor prefers to jeopardize the whole proceeding by evading his own problems which are becoming more and more insistent. The doctor must go to the limits of his subjective possibilities, otherwise the patient will be unable to follow suit. Arbitrary limits are no use, only real ones. It must be a genuine process of purification where "all superfluities are consumed in the fire" and the basic facts emerge. Is there anything more fundamental than the realization, "This is what I am?" It reveals a unity which nevertheless is—or was—a diversity. No longer the earlier ego with its make-believes and false contrivances, but another "objective" ego, which for this reason is better called the "self." (p. 199)

We had a period of steady deep work that started to focus on his contemplation of his own anima, now far more human than the Aphrodite figure. In Active Imagination, Bruce asked her how she felt to be so naive and inexperienced instead of more evolved. He asked her how she got hurt/wounded and what he could do to help her. He related that she told him she felt walled in; that she is afraid to come out because every time she does, he snaps at her and doesn't let her speak or won't listen to her. She told him she couldn't take much more of it. "I love you," she said, "but I want to be a woman in my own right. I want to play with you, but you frighten me." Bruce then remembered all the times he hadn't paid attention to her or treated her, and the women in his life, harshly or dismissively. He continued:

> I am so sorry for the way I have treated her—including the idea she is naive and inexperienced when, in fact, it is I who am naive. I pleaded for the opportunity to prove my love and understanding and promised to do my best to please her—to allow her to be free to be herself. She said she has always tried, but that I should be alert and learn to play. If I'm not and won't, then I'm more than likely to continue meeting up with her in her witch form.

There were periods of questioning and doubt, and Bruce's old habits reasserted themselves. But the tone became much different, and he used images of his inner anima guide and inner negative witch to help him steer his own way. The Terrible Mother still occasionally appeared to him in dreams, but now he had a way of seeing behind her to what had triggered her rage. After one instance of this, he dreamed of an equal—a friendly woman graduate student. In the dream, Bruce is in church with her, sweeping up a mess on the floor in front of the altar. He feels a little embarrassed because there is a mess but can accept the fact that he probably caused it, he can clean it up, and it is just a regrettable part of life.

The Old Woman as Terrible Mother slowly started to reveal a helpful guiding side. For instance, after a series of more wholesome anima figures in dreams, Bruce found himself, in outer life, in a dubious and troubling situation where he knew he needed a new attitude but wanted to fall back into his old one. The dream that night was just of a voice announcing: "Try the Hag! The experience may help you withdraw your projections." So with the help of the Hag and consulting with me (both the hag's representative and the

Old Woman's Daughter aspects of the Old Woman), Bruce made his way through a delicate and quite perilous situation that kept him in good relationship with his younger inner, and external, anima figures. It was not without cost, experimentation, and sacrifice.

As if to help him, Bruce then dreamed that he, his wife, and little Joy were 12 feet up on a cliff above a lake. He is spading dirt down into the lake both to feed something and to make the drop less steep. He goes on:

> Two strange part duck-like, part human animals came out of the water and up to me. The first had a feminine face—like an old Japanese woman. It was a beautiful face—full of caring and feeling—compassion, with a long far away look as though she had found what she had been searching for but couldn't quite accept it. I was very moved/touched by the feeling of being bonded with her. [He notes that, as a type, he sees her as the Wise Old Woman, what Claire recently called the Crone.] I call my wife to come look at her. She says "Wait till you see the other: a little old man with a wise Jewish face."

So both he and his internal and external feminine are reunited with old and wise aspects of themselves. The duck is related to both Isis and to Penelope in ancient tales. Even further back, she represents that part of the Great Mother Goddess that knows how to dive deep to feed upon the wisdom of the depths. She is commonly representative of "feminine energies . . . and the emotional state of humans . . . Ducks can remind us to drink of the waters of life as well as nurture our own emotional natures" (Andrews, 1996, pp. 134–135). So Bruce's strange part-human, part-animal duck could be seen to represent, what he first projected onto me, his ability to safely descend for the wisdom he needs, to be at home both in the conscious world, the air, and the unconscious, the water. His chthonic self is imaged by a creature primarily representing his long-neglected feeling state.

Bruce summed up the months of turmoil by writing in his journal:

> My life is shattered. There is no semblance of me of myself from the past. My vision of who I am, what I might become, is both exciting and scary. I long for it and run from it. I want so much to consummate new relations—seeking ultimate relatedness—total freedom—to be and become. My marriage restricts this; forbids it. Yet I cannot dissolve it. Duty and responsibility is meaningless without commitment—if to no other at least to God—the God within myself.

Bruce then listed the things he appreciates about his wife and concluded by bringing his analytic work into it:

> Better divorce myself from Claire than from my wife. That's it!! Little Brucey is in a pickle wanting to separate from his mother but at the same time is frightened with the idea of going it alone, becoming his own free man, and all my fears I still project onto Claire.

He continued, with this accomplished:

> I look inside and see Brucey wearing a huge smile; Joy's square white teeth are also exposed. He is happy; she is happy. He wants to make it; she wants to make it. I hope we all do. We are all going to try like hell.

This feels very much to me like a weaving together and integration of the disparate parts of Bruce's self. It also reunites the masculine with the feminine that reunites the family of my dream.

We continued our work together deepening it and still having moments of misunderstanding and anger as well as an increasingly deeper connection until I left New York for California in the early 1990s. Our work had been done, and Bruce's inner family had grown, as had all their abilities to care for each other. As Jung (1946) wrote and I quoted earlier: "It reveals a unity which nevertheless is—or was—a diversity. No longer the earlier ego with its make-believes and false contrivances, but another 'objective' ego, which for this reason is better called the 'self'" (p. 199).

Bruce's final dream uses car symbolism as did my dream of the weaving together of the masculine and feminine, youth and old age. Bruce has a truck (to me, a very masculine image) instead of the cars:

> I am like a truck driver whose work brings him to particular places. My work is not driving the truck. Yet I do. And the particular places I go to are not concrete geographic places but places where I end up depending on the work I have to do while not driving the truck. As I drive I realize I can see for hundreds of miles on the horizon in all directions—360 degrees. I am free; free to move in any direction I choose. It does not matter.

It does not matter because Bruce is free to be the man he is.

In this chapter, I have attempted to demonstrate the weaving together of Bruce's disparate parts that came about through his acceptance and development of his inner feminine and his genuine engagement with both his analyst and his material. Both of us were willing to have a genuine engagement with our own material and with each other. In the process, at one time or another, each of our larger selves (the true Self) came to the rescue as one or more parts of each of our unconscious threatened to scatter and split off into their own disruptive complexes. I hope I have also demonstrated the deep cherishment, what Ellen Siegelman (2002) has referred to as analytic love, I felt and feel for Bruce as well as Bruce's learning to cherish the Old Woman in both himself and in me.

REFERENCES

Andrews, T. (1996). *Animal speak*. St. Paul, MI: Llewellyn.

Gay, P. (1986). *The bourgeois experience: Victoria to Freud*. New York: Oxford University Press.

Jung, C. G. (1929). "Problems of modern psychotherapy," in *Collected works* (Vol. 16). Princeton, NJ: Princeton University Press.

Jung, C. G. (1937). "The realities of practical psychotherapy," in *Collected works* (Vol. 16). Princeton, NJ: Princeton University Press.

Jung, C. G. (1946). "The psychology of the transference," in *Collected works* (Vol. 16.). Princeton, NJ: Princeton University Press.

Siegelman, E. (2002). "The analyst's love: An exploration." *Journal of Jungian Theory and Practice, 3, 1,* 19–33.

Editors' Introduction

Carl Rogers was one of the giants in counseling and psychotherapy as well as in personality theory. He was a sensitive therapist, a master teacher, and for those who knew him, a good friend. He was also a superb researcher and a gifted writer, as the following case will illustrate.

"Mrs. Oak" is a classic case study that documents a client's personal growth during a series of therapy sessions with Dr. Rogers. The experience of unconditional positive regard in the therapeutic relationship allowed Mrs. Oak to increasingly come to like herself and to realize that the core of her personality was positive and healthy. Rogers uses the case as a way to illustrate many of his beliefs about psychotherapy and personality.

Many students are beguiled by the apparent simplicity of person-centered therapy (e.g., reflection), and they become convinced that this is an easy approach to helping people change. As this case clearly demonstrates, considerable skill is required to effectively practice person-centered therapy, and one can spend a lifetime perfecting these techniques.

Unfortunately, this version of "The Case of Mrs. Oak" is the shorter of two, but space limitations precluded the longer and more detailed selection, which can be found in Rogers's and Dymond's book Psychotherapy and Personality Change.

4 | THE CASE OF MRS. OAK

Carl R. Rogers

One aspect of the process of therapy which is evident in all cases might be termed the awareness of experience, or even "the experiencing of experience." I have here labeled it as the experiencing of the self, though this also falls short of being an accurate term. In the security of the relationship with a client-centered therapist, in the absence of any actual or implied threat to self, the client can let himself examine various aspects of his experience as they actually feel to him, as they are apprehended through his sensory and visceral equipment, without distorting them to fit the existing concept of self. Many of these prove to be in extreme contradiction to the concept of self, and could not ordinarily be experienced in their fullness, but in this safe relationship they can be permitted to seep through into awareness without distortion. Thus they often follow the schematic pattern, "I am thus and so, but I experience this feeling which is very inconsistent with what I am"; "I love my parents, but I experience some surprising bitterness toward them at times"; "I am really no good, but sometimes I seem to feel that I'm better than everyone else." Thus at first the expression is that "I am a self which is different from a part of my experience." Later this changes to the tentative pattern, "Perhaps I am several quite different selves, or perhaps my self contains more contradictions than I had dreamed." Still later the pattern changes to some such pattern as this: "I was sure that I could not be my experience—it was too contradictory—but now I am beginning to believe that I can be *all* of my experience."

Perhaps something of the nature of this aspect of therapy may be conveyed from two excerpts from the case of Mrs. Oak. Mrs. Oak was a housewife in her late thirties, who was having difficulties in marital and family relationships when she came in for therapy. Unlike many clients, she had a keen and spontaneous interest in the processes which she felt going on within herself, and her recorded interviews contain much material, from her own frame of reference, as to her perception of what is occurring. She thus tends to put into words what seems to be implicit, but unverbalized, in many clients.

From an early portion of the fifth interview comes material which describes the awareness of experience which we have been discussing.

Client: It all comes pretty vague. But you know I keep, keep having the thought occur to me that this whole process for me is kind of like examining pieces of a jigsaw puzzle. It seems to me I, I'm in the process now of examining the individual pieces which really don't have too much meaning. Probably handling them, now even beginning to think of a pattern. That keeps coming to me. And it's interesting to me because I, I really don't like jigsaw puzzles. They've always irritated me. But that's my feeling. And I mean I pick up little pieces (She gestures throughout this conversation to illustrate her statements.) with absolutely no meaning except I mean the, the feeling that you get from simply handling them without seeing them as a pattern, but just from the touch, I probably feel, well it is going to fit someplace here.

Therapist: And that at the moment that, that's the process, just getting the feel and the shape and the configuration of the different pieces with a little bit of background feeling of, yeah they'll probably fit somewhere, but most of the attention's focused right on, "What does this feel like? And what's its texture?"

C: That's right. There's almost something physical in it. A, a—

T: You can't quite describe it without using your hands. A real, almost a sensuous sense in—

C: That's right. Again it's, it's a feeling of being very objective, and yet I've never been quite so close to myself.

T: Almost at one and the same time standing off and looking at yourself and yet somehow being closer to yourself that way than—

C: Mm-hmm. And yet for the first time in months I am not thinking about my problems. I'm not, actually. I'm not working on them.

T: I get the impression you don't sit down to work on "my problems." It isn't that feeling at all.

C: That's right. That's right. I suppose what I, I mean actually is that I'm not sitting down to put this puzzle together as, as something, I've got to see the picture. It, it may be that, it may be that I am actually enjoying this feeling process. Or I'm certainly learning something.

T: At least there's a sense of the immediate goal of getting that feel as being the thing, not that you're doing this in order to see a picture, but that it's a, a satisfaction of really getting acquainted with each piece. Is that—

C: That's it. That's it. And it still becomes that sort of sensuousness, that touching. It's quite interesting. Sometimes not entirely pleasant, I'm sure, but—

T: A rather different sort of experience.

C: Yes. Quite.

This excerpt indicates very clearly the letting of material come into awareness, without any attempt to own it as part of the self, or to relate it to other material held in consciousness. It is, to put it as accurately as possible, an awareness of a wide range of experiences, with, at the moment, no thought of their relation to self. Later it may be recognized that what was being experienced may all become a part of self.

The fact that this is a new and unusual form of experience is expressed in a verbally confused but emotionally clear portion of the sixth interview.

C: Uh, I caught myself thinking that during these sessions, uh, I've been sort of singing a song. Now that sounds vague and uh—not actually singing—sort of a song without any music. Probably a kind of poem coming out. And I like the idea, I mean it's just sort of come to me without anything built out of, of anything. And in—following that, it came, it came this other kind of feeling. Well, I found myself sort of asking myself, is that the shape that cases take? Is it possible that I am just verbalizing and, at times kind of become intoxicated with my own verbalizations? And then uh, following this, came, well, am I just taking up your time? And then a doubt, a doubt. Then something else occurred to me. Uh, from whence it came, I don't know, no actual logical kind of sequence to the thinking. The thought struck me: We're doing bits, uh, we're not overwhelmed or doubtful, or show concern or, or any great interest when, when blind people learn to read with their fingers, Braille. I don't know—it may be just sort of, it's all mixed up. It may be that's something that I'm experiencing now.

T: Let's see if I can get some of that, that sequence of feelings. First, sort of as though you're, and I gather that first one is a fairly positive feeling, as though maybe you're kind of creating a poem here—a song without music somehow but something that might be quite creative. And then the, the feeling of a lot of skepticism about that. "Maybe I'm just saying words, just being carried off by words that I, that I speak, and maybe it's all a lot of baloney, really." And then a feeling that perhaps you're almost learning a new type of experiencing which would be just as radically new as for a blind person to try to make sense out of what he feels with his fingertips.

C: Mm-hmm. Mm-hmm. (*Pause*) . . . And I sometimes think to myself, well, maybe we could go into this particular incident or that particular incident. And then somehow when I come here, there is, that doesn't hold true, it's, it seems false. And then there just seems to be this flow of words which somehow aren't forced and then occasionally this doubt creeps in. Well, it sort of takes the form of a, maybe you're just making music . . . Perhaps that's why I'm doubtful today of, of this whole thing, because it's something that's not forced. And really I'm feeling that what I should do is, is sort of systematize the thing. Oughta work harder and—

T: Sort of a deep questioning as to what am I doing with a self that isn't, isn't pushing to get things *done, solved?* (*Pause*)

C: And yet the fact that I, I really like this other kind of thing, this, I don't know, call it a poignant feeling, I mean—I felt things that I never felt before. I *like* that, too. Maybe that's the way to do it. I just don't know today.

Here is the shift which seems almost invariably to occur in therapy which has any depth. It may be represented schematically as the client's feeling that "I came here to solve problems, and now I find myself just experiencing myself." And as with this client this shift is usually accompanied by the intellectual formulation that it is wrong, and by an emotional appreciation of the fact that it "feels good."

We may conclude this section saying that one of the fundamental directions taken by the process of therapy is the free experiencing of the actual sensory and visceral reactions of the organism without too much of an attempt to relate these experiences to the self. This is usually accompanied by the conviction that this material does not belong to, and cannot be organized into, the self. The end point of this process is that the client discovers that he can be his experience, with all of its variety and surface contradiction; that he can formulate himself out of his experience, instead of trying to impose a formulation of self upon his experience, denying to awareness those elements which do not fit.

THE FULL EXPERIENCE
OF AN AFFECTIONAL RELATIONSHIP

One of the elements in therapy of which we have more recently become aware is the extent to which therapy is a learning, on the part of the client, to accept fully and freely and without fear the positive feelings of another. This is not a phenomenon which clearly occurs in every case. It seems particularly true of our longer cases, but does not occur uniformly in these. Yet it is such a deep experience that we have begun to question whether it is not a highly significant direction in the therapeutic process, perhaps occurring at an unverbalized level to some degree in all successful cases. Before discussing this phenomenon, let us give it some body by citing the experience of Mrs. Oak. The experience struck her rather suddenly, between the twenty-ninth and thirtieth interview, and she spends most of the latter interview discussing it. She opens the thirtieth hour in this way.

C: Well, I made a very remarkable discovery. I know it's—(*laughs*) I found out that you actually *care* how this thing goes. (*Both laugh.*) It gave me the feeling, it's sort of well—"maybe I'll let you get in the act," sort of thing. It's—again you see, on an examination sheet, I would have had the correct answer, I mean—but it suddenly dawned on me that in the client-counselor kind of thing, you *actually care* what happens to this thing. And it was a revelation, a—not that. That doesn't describe it. It was a—well, the closest I can come to it is a kind of relaxation, a—not a letting down, but a—(pause) more of a straightening out without tension if that means anything. I don't know.

T: Sounds as though it isn't as though this was a new idea, but it was a new experience of really *feeling* that I did care and if I get the rest of that, sort of a willingness on your part to let me care.

C: Yes.

This letting the counselor and his warm interest into her life was undoubtedly one of the deepest features of therapy in this case. In an interview following the conclusion of therapy she spontaneously mentions this experience as being the outstanding one. What does it mean?

The phenomenon is most certainly not one of transference and countertransference. Some experienced psychologists who had undergone psychoanalysis had the opportunity of observing the development of the relationship in another case than the one cited. They were the first to object to the use of the terms transference and countertransference to describe the phenomenon. The gist of their remarks was that this is something which is mutual and appropriate, whereas transference or countertransference are phenomena which are characteristically one-way and inappropriate to the realities of the situation.

Certainly one reason why this phenomenon is occurring more frequently in our experience is that as therapists we have become less afraid of our positive (or negative) feelings toward the client. As therapy goes on the therapist's feeling of acceptance and respect for the client tends to change to something approaching awe as he sees the valiant and deep struggle of the person to be himself. There is, I think, within the therapist, a profound experience of the underlying commonality—should we say brotherhood—of man. As a result he feels toward the client a warm, positive, affectional reaction. This poses a problem for the client who often, as in this case, finds it difficult to accept the positive feeling of another. Yet, once accepted, the inevitable reaction on the part of the client is to relax, to let the warmth of liking by another person reduce the tension and fear involved in facing life.

But we are getting ahead of our client. Let us examine some of the other aspects of this experience as it occurred to her. In earlier interviews she had talked of the fact that she did *not* love humanity, and that in some vague and stubborn way she felt she was right, even though others would regard her as wrong. She mentions this again as she discusses the way this experience has clarified her attitudes toward others.

C: The next thing that occurred to me that I found myself thinking and still thinking, is somehow—and I'm not clear why—the same kind of a caring that I get when I say "I don't love humanity." Which has always sort of—I mean I was always convinced of it. So I mean, it doesn't—I knew that it was a good thing, see. And I think I clarified it within myself—what it has to do with this situation, I don't know. But I found out, no, I don't love, but I do *care* terribly.

T: Mm-hmm. Mm-hmm. I see . . .

C: It might be expressed better in saying I care terribly what happens. But the caring is a—takes form—its structure is in understanding and not wanting to be taken in, or to contribute to those things which I feel are false and—It seems to me that in—

in loving, there's a kind of *final* factor. If you do that, you've sort of done enough. It's a—

T: That's *it,* sort of.

C: Yeah. It seems to me this other thing, this caring, which isn't a good term—I mean, probably we need something else to describe this kind of thing. To say it's an impersonal thing doesn't mean anything because it isn't impersonal. I mean I feel it's very much a part of a whole. But it's something that somehow doesn't stop . . . It seems to me you could have this feeling of loving humanity, loving people, and at the same time—go on contributing to the factors that make people neurotic, make them ill— where, what I feel is a resistance to those things.

T: You care enough to want to understand and to want to avoid contributing to anything that would make for more neuroticism, or more of that aspect in human life.

C: Yes. And it's—(*pause*). Yes, it's something along those lines. . . . Well, again, I have to go back to how I feel about this other thing. It's—I'm not really called upon to give of myself in a—sort of on the auction block. There's nothing final . . . It sometimes bothered me when I—I would have to say to myself, "I don't love humanity," and yet, I always knew that there was something positive. That I was probably right. And—I may be all off the beam now, but it seems to me that, that is somehow tied up in the—this feeling that I—I have now, into how the therapeutic value can carry through. Now, I couldn't tie it up, I couldn't tie it in, but it's as close as I can come to explaining to myself, my—well, shall I say the learning process, the follow-through on my realization that—yes, you *do care* in a given situation. It's just that simple. And I hadn't been aware of it before. I might have closed this door and walked out, and in discussing therapy, said, yes, the counselor must feel thus and so, but, I mean, I hadn't had the dynamic experience.

In this portion, though she is struggling to describe her own feeling, it would seem that what she is saying would be characteristic of the therapist's attitude toward the client as well. His attitude, at its best, is devoid of the *quid pro quo* aspect of most of the experiences we call love. It is the simple outgoing human feeling of one individual for another, a feeling, it seems to me, which is even more basic than sexual or parental feeling. It is a caring enough about the person that you do not wish to interfere with his development, nor to use him for any self-aggrandizing goals of your own. Your satisfaction comes in having set him free to grow in his own fashion.

Our client goes on to discuss how hard it has been for her in the past to accept any help or positive feeling from others, and how this attitude is changing.

C: I have a feeling . . . that you have to do it pretty much yourself, but that somehow you ought to be able to do that with other people. (*She mentions that there have been "countless" times when she might have accepted personal warmth and kindliness from others.*) I get the feeling that I just was afraid I would be devastated. (*She returns to talking about the counseling itself and her feeling toward it.*) I mean there's been this tearing through the thing myself. Almost to—I mean, I felt it—I mean I tried to verbalize it on occasion—a kind of—at times almost not wanting you to restate, not wanting you to reflect, the thing is *mine.* Course all right, I can say it's resistance. But that doesn't mean a damn thing to me now . . . The—I think in—in relationship to this particular thing, I mean, the—probably at times, the strongest feeling was, it's mine, it's *mine.* I've got to cut it down myself. See?

T: It's an experience that's awfully hard to put down accurately into words, and yet I get a sense of difference here in this relationship, that form the feeling that "this is mine," "I've got to do it," "I am doing it," and so on, to a somewhat different feeling that—"I could let you in."

C: Yeah. Now. I mean, that's—that it's—well, it's sort of, shall we say, volume two. It's—it's a—well, sort of, well, I'm still in the thing alone, but I'm not—see—I'm—

T: Mm-hmm. Yes, that paradox sort of sums it up, doesn't it?

C: Yeah.

T: In all of this, there is a feeling, it's still—every aspect of my experience is mine and that's kind of inevitable and necessary and so on. And yet that isn't the whole picture either. Somehow it can be shared or another's interest can come in and in some ways it is new.

C: Yeah. And it's—it's as though, that's how it should be. I mean, that's how it—has to be. There's a—there's a feeling, "and this is good." I mean, it expresses, it clarifies it for me. There's a feeling—in this caring, as though—you were sort of standing back—standing off, and if I want to sort of cut through to the thing, it's a—a slashing of—oh, tall weeds, that I can do it, and you can—I mean you're not going to be disturbed by having to walk through it, too. I don't know. And it doesn't make sense. I mean—

T: Except there's a very real sense of rightness about this feeling that you have, hm?

C: Mm-hmm.

May it not be that this excerpt portrays the heart of the process of socialization? To discover that it is not devastating to accept the positive feeling from another, that it does not necessarily end in hurt, that it actually "feels good" to have another person with you in your struggles to meet life—this may be one of the most profound learnings encountered by the individual, whether in therapy or not.

Something of the newness, the nonverbal level of this experience is described by Mrs. Oak in the closing moments of this thirtieth interview.

C: I'm experiencing a new type, a—probably the only worthwhile kind of learning, a—I know I've—I've often said what I know doesn't help me here. What I meant is, my acquired knowledge doesn't help me. But it seems to me that the learning process here has been—so dynamic, I mean, so much a part of the—of everything, I mean, of me, that if I just get that out of it, it's something, which, I mean—I'm wondering if I'll ever be able to straighten out into a sort of acquired knowledge what I have experienced here.

T: In other words, the kind of learning that has gone on here has been something of quite a different sort and quite a different depth; very vital, very real. And quite worthwhile to you in and of itself, but the question you're asking is: Will I ever have a clear intellectual picture of what has gone on at this somehow deeper kind of learning level?

C: Mm-hmm. Something like that.

Those who would apply to therapy the so-called laws of learning derived from the memorization of nonsense syllables would do well to study this excerpt with care. Learning as it takes place in therapy is a total, organismic, frequently nonverbal type of thing which may or may not follow the same principles as the intellectual learning of trivial material which has little relevance to the self. This, however, is a digression.

Let us conclude this section by rephrasing its essence. It appears possible that one of the characteristics of deep or significant therapy is that the client discovers that it is not devastating to admit fully into his own experience the positive feeling which another, the therapist, holds toward him. Perhaps one of the reasons why this is so difficult is that essentially it involves the feeling that "I am worthy of being liked." This we shall consider in the following section. For the present it may be pointed out that this aspect of therapy is a free and full experiencing of an affectional relationship which may be put in generalized terms as follows: "I can permit someone to care about me, and can fully accept that caring within myself. This permits me to recognize that I care, and care deeply, for and about others."

THE LIKING OF ONE'S SELF

In various writings and researches that have been published regarding client-centered therapy, there has been a stress upon the acceptance of self as one of the directions and outcomes of therapy. We have established the fact that in successful psychotherapy negative attitudes toward the self decrease and positive attitudes increase. We have measured the gradual increase in self-acceptance and have studied the correlated increase in acceptance of others. But as I examine these statements and compare them with our more recent cases, I feel they fall short of the truth. The client not only accepts himself—a phrase which may carry the connotation of a grudging and reluctant acceptance of the inevitable—he actually comes to *like* himself. This is not a bragging or self-assertive liking; it is rather a quiet pleasure in being one's self.

Mrs. Oak illustrates this trend rather nicely in her thirty-third interview. Is it significant that this follows by ten days the interview where she could for the first time admit to herself that the therapist cared? Whatever our speculations on this point, this fragment indicates very well the quiet joy in being one's self, together with the apologetic attitude which, in our culture, one feels is necessary to take toward such an experience. In the last few minutes of the interview, knowing her time is nearly up she says:

C: One thing worries me—and I'll hurry because I can always go back to it—a feeling that occasionally I can't turn out. Feeling of being quite pleased with myself. Again the Q technique.[1] I walked out of here one time, and impulsively I threw my first card, "I am an attractive personality"; looked at it sort of aghast but left it there, I mean, because honestly, I mean, that is exactly how it felt—a—well, that bothered me and I catch that now. Every once in a while a sort of pleased feeling, nothing superior, but just—I don't know, sort of pleased. A neatly turned way. And it bothered me. And yet—I wonder— I rarely remember things I say here, I mean I wondered why it was that I was convinced, and something about what I've felt about being hurt that I suspected in—my feelings when I would hear someone say to a child, "Don't cry." I mean, I always felt, but it isn't right; I mean, if he's hurt, let him cry. Well, then, now this pleased feeling that I have. I've recently come to feel, it's—there's something almost the same there. It's—We don't object when *children* feel pleased with themselves. It's—I mean, there really isn't anything vain. It's—maybe that's how people *should* feel.

T: You've been inclined almost to look askance at yourself for this feeling, and yet as you think about it more, maybe it comes close to the two sides of the picture, that if a child wants to cry, why shouldn't he cry? And if he wants to feel pleased with himself, doesn't he have a perfect right to feel pleased with himself? And that sort of ties in with this, what I would see as an appreciation of yourself that you've experienced every now and again.

C: Yes. Yes.

T: "I'm really a pretty rich and interesting person."

C: Something like that. And then I say to myself, "Our society pushes us around and we've lost it." And I keep going back to my feelings about children. Well, maybe

[1]This portion needs explanation. As part of a research study by another staff member this client had been asked several times during therapy to sort a large group of cards, each containing a self-descriptive phrase, in such a way as to portray her own self. At one end of the sorting she was to place the card or cards most like herself, and at the other end, those most unlike herself. Thus when she says that she put as the first card, "I am an attractive personality," it means that she regarded this as the item most characteristic of herself.

they're richer than we are. Maybe we—it's something we've lost in the process of growing up.

T: Could be that they have a wisdom about that that we've lost.

C: That's right. My time's up.

Here she arrives, as do so many other clients, at the tentative, slightly apologetic realization that she has come to like, enjoy, appreciate herself. One gets the feeling of a spontaneous relaxed enjoyment, a primitive *joie de vivre,* perhaps analogous to the lamb frisking about the meadow or the porpoise gracefully leaping in and out of the waves. Mrs. Oak feels that it is something native to the organism, to the infant, something we have lost in the warping process of development.

Earlier in this case one sees something of a forerunner of this feeling, an incident which perhaps makes more clear its fundamental nature. In the ninth interview Mrs. Oak in a somewhat embarrassed fashion reveals something she has always kept to herself. That she brought it forth at some cost is indicated by the fact that it was preceded by a very long pause, of several minutes duration. Then she spoke.

C: You know this is kind of goofy, but I've never told anyone this (*nervous laugh*) and it'll probably do me good. For years, oh, probably from early youth, from seventeen probably on, I, I have had what I have come to call to myself, told myself were "flashes of sanity." I've never told anyone this (*another embarrassed laugh*), wherein, in, really I feel sane. And, and pretty much aware of life. And always with a terrific kind of concern and sadness of how far away, how far astray that we have actually gone. It's just a feeling once in a while of finding myself a whole kind of person in a terribly chaotic kind of world.

T: It's been fleeting and it's been infrequent, but there have been times when it seems the whole you is functioning and feeling in the world, a very chaotic world to be sure—

C: That's right. And I mean, and knowing actually how far astray we, we've gone from, from being whole healthy people. And of course, one doesn't talk in those terms.

T: A feeling that it wouldn't be *safe* to talk about the singing you[2]—

C: Where does that person live?

T: Almost as if there was no place for such a person to, to exist.

C: Of course, you know, that, that makes me—now wait a minute—that probably explains why I'm primarily concerned with feelings here. That's probably it.

T: Because that whole you does exist with all your feelings. Is that it, you're more aware of feelings?

C: That's right. It's not, it doesn't reject feelings and—that's *it*.

T: That whole you somehow lives feelings instead of somehow pushing them to one side.

C: That's right. (*Pause*) I suppose from the practical point of view it could be said that what I ought to be doing is solving some problems, day-to-day problems. And yet, I, I—what I'm trying to do is solve, solve something else that's a great, that is a great deal more important than little day-to-day problems. Maybe that sums up the whole thing.

T: I wonder if this will distort your meaning, that from a hard-headed point of view you ought to be spending time thinking through specific problems. But you wonder if perhaps maybe you aren't on a quest for this whole you and perhaps that's more important than a solution to the day-to-day problems.

C: I think that's it. That's probably what I mean.

_____

[2]The therapist's reference is to her statement in a previous interview that in therapy she was singing a song.

If we may legitimately put together these two experiences, and if we are justified in regarding them as typical, then we may say that both in therapy and in some fleeting experiences throughout her previous life, she has experienced a healthy, satisfying, enjoyable appreciation of herself as a whole and functioning creature; and that this experience occurs when she does not reject her feelings but lives them.

Here, it seems to me, is an important and often overlooked truth about the therapeutic process. It works in the direction of permitting the person to experience fully, and in awareness, all of his reactions including his feelings and emotions. As this occurs, the individual feels a positive liking for himself, a genuine appreciation of himself as a total functioning unit, which is one of the important end points of therapy.

THE DISCOVERY THAT THE CORE OF PERSONALITY IS POSITIVE

One of the most revolutionary concepts to grow out of our clinical experience is the growing recognition that the innermost core of man's nature, the deepest layers of his personality, the base of his "animal nature," is positive in nature—is basically socialized, forward moving, rational, and realistic.

This point of view is so foreign to our present culture that I do not expect it to be accepted, and it is indeed so revolutionary in its implications that it should not be accepted without thoroughgoing inquiry. But even if it should stand these tests, it will be difficult to accept. Religion, especially the Protestant Christian tradition, has permeated our culture with the concept that man is basically sinful, and only by something approaching a miracle can his sinful nature be negated. In psychology, Freud and his followers have presented convincing arguments that the id, man's basic and unconscious nature, is primarily made up of instincts which would, if permitted expression, result in incest, murder, and other crimes. The whole problem of therapy, as seen by this group, is how to hold these untamed forces in check in a wholesome and constructive manner, rather than in the costly fashion of the neurotic. But the fact that at heart man is irrational, unsocialized, destructive of others and self—this is a concept accepted almost without question. To be sure there are occasional voices of protest. But these solitary voices are little heard. On the whole the viewpoint of the professional worker as well as the layman is that man as he is, in his basic nature, had best be kept under control or under cover or both.

As I look back over my years of clinical experience and research, it seems to me that I have been very slow to recognize the falseness of this popular and professional concept. The reason, I believe, lies in the fact that in therapy there are continually being uncovered hostile and antisocial feelings, so that it is easy to assume that this indicates the deeper and therefore the basic nature of man. Only slowly has it become evident that these untamed and unsocial feelings are neither the deepest nor the strongest, and that the inner core of man's personality is the organism itself, which is essentially both self-preserving and social.

To give more specific meaning to this argument, let me turn again to the case of Mrs. Oak. Since the point is an important one, I shall quote at some length from the recorded case to illustrate the type of experience on which I have based the foregoing statements. Perhaps the excerpts can illustrate the opening up of layer after layer of personality until we come to the deepest elements.

It is in the eighth interview that Mrs. Oak rolls back the first layer of defense, and discovers a bitterness and desire for revenge underneath.

C: You know over in this area of, of sexual disturbance, I have a feeling that I'm beginning to discover that it's pretty bad, pretty bad. I'm finding out that, that I'm bitter, really. Damn bitter. I—and I'm not turning it back in, into myself . . . I think what I probably feel is a certain element of "I've been cheated." (*Her voice is very tight and her throat chokes up.*) And I've covered up very nicely, to the point of consciously not caring. But I'm, I'm sort of amazed to find that in this practice of, what shall I call it, a kind of sublimation that right under it—again words—there's a, a kind of passive force that's, it's pas—it's very passive, but at the same time it's just kind of *murderous.*

T: So there's the feeling, "I've really been cheated. I've covered that up and seem not to care and yet underneath that there's a kind of a, a latent but very much present *bitterness* that is very, very strong."

C: It's very strong. I—that I know. It's terribly powerful.

T: Almost a dominating kind of force.

C: Of which I am rarely conscious. Almost never . . . Well, the only way I can describe it, it's a kind of murderous thing, but without violence . . . It's more like a feeling of wanting to get even . . . And of course, I won't pay back, but I'd like to. I really would like to.

Up to this point the usual explanation seems to fit perfectly. Mrs. Oak has been able to look beneath the socially controlled surface of her behavior, and find underneath a murderous feeling of hatred and a desire to get even. This is as far as she goes in exploring this particular feeling until considerably later in therapy. She picks up the theme in the thirty-first interview. She has had a hard time getting under way, feels emotionally blocked, and cannot get at the feeling which is welling up in her.

C: I have the feeling it isn't guilt. (*Pause. She weeps.*) Of course I mean, I can't verbalize it yet. (*Then with a rush of emotion*) It's just being terribly hurt!

T: Mm-hmm. It isn't guilt except in the sense of being very much wounded somehow.

C: (*Weeping*) It's—you know, often I've been guilty of it myself but in later years when I've heard parents say to their children, "stop crying," I've had a feeling, a hurt as though, well, why should they tell them to stop crying? They feel sorry for themselves, and who can feel more adequately sorry for himself than the child? Well, that is sort of what—I mean, as though I mean, I thought that they should let him cry. And—feel sorry for him too, maybe. In a rather objective kind of way. Well, that's—that's something of the kind of thing I've been experiencing. I mean, now—just right now. And in—in—

T: That catches a little more the flavor of the feeling that it's almost as if you're really weeping for yourself.

C: Yeah. And again you see there's conflict. Our culture is such that—I mean, one doesn't indulge in self-pity. But this isn't—I mean, I feel it doesn't quite have that connotation. It may have.

T: Sort of think that there is a cultural objection to feeling sorry about yourself. And yet you feel the feeling you're experiencing isn't quite what the culture objected to either.

C: And then of course, I've come to—to see and to feel that over this—see, I've covered it up. (*Weeps.*) But I've covered it up with so much bitterness, which in turn I had to cover up. (*Weeping*) *That's* what I want to get rid of! I almost don't *care* if I hurt.

T: (*Softly, and with an empathic tenderness toward the hurt she is experiencing*) You feel that here at the basis of it as you experience it is a feeling of real tears for yourself. But that you can't show, mustn't show, so that's been covered by bitterness that you don't like, that you'd like to be rid of. You almost feel you'd rather absorb the hurt than to—than to feel the bitterness. (*Pause*) And what you seem to be saying quite strongly is, I do *hurt,* and I've tried to cover it up.

C: I didn't know it.

T: Mm-hmm. Like a new discovery really.

C: (*Speaking at the same time*) I never really did know. But it's—you know, it's almost a physical thing. It's—it's sort of as though I were looking within myself at all kinds of—nerve endings and bits of things that have been sort of mashed. (*Weeping*)

T: As though some of the most delicate aspects of you physically almost have been crushed or hurt.

C: Yes. And you know, I do get the feeling, "Oh, you poor thing." (*Pause*)

T: Just can't help but feel very deeply sorry for the person that is you.

C: I don't think I feel sorry for the whole person; it's a certain aspect of the thing.

T: Sorry to see that hurt.

C: Yeah.

T: Mm-hmm. Mm-hmm.

C: And then of course there's this damn bitterness that I want to get rid of. It's—it gets me into trouble. It's because it's a tricky thing. It tricks me. (*Pause*)

T: Feel as though that bitterness is something you'd like to be rid of because it doesn't do right by you.

C: (*Weeps. Long pause*) I don't know. It seems to me that I'm right in feeling, what in the world good would it do to term this thing guilt. To chase down things that would give me an interesting case history, shall we say. What *good* would it do? It seems to me that the—that the key, the real thing is in this feeling that I have.

T: You could track down some tag or other and could make quite a pursuit of that, but you feel as though the core of the whole thing is the kind of experience that you're just having right here.

C: That's right. I mean if—I don't know what'll happen to the feeling. Maybe nothing. I don't know, but it seems to me that whatever understanding I'm to have is a part of this feeling of hurt, of—it doesn't matter much what it's called. (*Pause*) Then I—one can't go around with a hurt so openly exposed. I mean this seems to me that somehow the next process has to be a kind of healing.

T: Seems as though you couldn't possibly expose yourself if part of yourself is so hurt, so you wonder if somehow the hurt mustn't be healed first. (*Pause*)

C: And yet, you know, it's—it's a funny thing (*pause*). It sounds like a statement of complete confusion or the old saw that the neurotic doesn't want to give up his symptoms. But that isn't true. I mean, that isn't true here, but it's—I can just hope that this will impart what I feel. I somehow don't mind being hurt. I mean, it's just occurred to me that I don't mind terribly. It's a—I mind more the—the feeling of bitterness which is, I know, the cause of this frustration, I mean the—I somehow mind that more.

T: Would this get it? That, though you don't like the hurt, yet you feel you can accept that. That's bearable. Somehow it's the things that have covered up that hurt, like the bitterness, that you just—at this moment, can't stand.

C: Yeah. That's just about it. It's sort of as though, well, the first, I mean, as though, it's—well, it's something I can cope with. Now, the feeling of, well, I can still have a hell of a lot of fun, see. But that this other, I mean, this frustration—I mean, it comes out in so many ways, I'm beginning to realize, you see. I mean, just this sort of, this kind of thing.

T: And a hurt you can accept. It's a part of life within a lot of other parts of life, too. You can have lots of fun. But to have all of your life diffused by frustration and bitterness, that you don't like, you don't want, and are now more aware of—

C: Yeah. And there's somehow no dodging it now. You see, I'm much more aware of it. (*Pause*) I don't know. Right now, I don't know just what the next step is. I really don't know. (*Pause*) Fortunately, this is a kind of development, so that it—doesn't carry over too acutely into—I mean, I—what I'm trying to say, I think, is that I'm still functioning. I'm still enjoying myself and—

T: Just sort of want me to know that in lots of ways you carry on just as you always have.

C: That's it. (*Pause*) Oh, I think I've got to stop and go.

In this lengthy excerpt we get a clear picture of the fact that underlying the bitterness and hatred and the desire to get back at the world which has cheated her, is a much less antisocial feeling, a deep experience of having been hurt. And it is equally clear that at this deeper level she has no desire to put her murderous feelings into action. She dislikes them and would like to be rid of them.

The next excerpt comes from the thirty-fourth interview. It is very incoherent material, as verbalizations often are when the individual is trying to express something deeply emotional. Here she is endeavoring to reach far down into herself. She states that it will be difficult to formulate.

C: I don't know whether I'll be able to talk about it yet or not. Might give it a try. Something—I mean, it's a feeling—that—sort of an urge to really get out. I know it isn't going to make sense. I think that maybe if I can get it out and get it a little, well, in a little more matter of fact way, that it'll be something that's more useful to me. And I don't know how to—I mean, it seems as though I want to say, I want to talk about my *self.* And that is of course as I see, what I've been doing for all these hours. But, no, this—it's my *self.* I've quite recently become aware of rejecting certain statements, because to me they sounded—not quite what I meant, I mean, a little bit too idealized. And I mean, I can remember always saying it's more selfish than that, more selfish than that. Until I—it sort of occurs to me, it dawns, yeah, that's exactly what I mean, but the selfishness I mean, has an entirely different connotation. I've been using a word "selfish." Then I have this feeling of—I—that I've never expressed it before of selfish—which means nothing. A—I'm still going to talk about it. A kind of pulsation. And it's something aware all the time. And still it's there. And I'd like to be able to utilize it, too—as a kind of descending into this thing. You know, it's as though—I don't know, damn! I'd sort of acquired someplace, and picked up a kind of acquaintance with the structure. Almost as though I knew it brick for brick kind of thing. It's something that's an awareness. I mean, that—of a feeling of not being fooled, of not being drawn into the thing, and a critical sense of knowingness. But in a way—the reason, it's hidden and—can't be a part of everyday life. And there's something of—at times I feel almost a little bit terrible in the thing, but again terrible not as terrible. And why? I think I know. And it's—it also explains a lot to me. It's—it's something that is *totally* without hate. I mean, just *totally.* Not with love, but *totally without hate.* But it's—it's an exciting thing, too . . . I guess maybe I am the kind of person that likes to, I mean, probably even torment myself, or to chase things down, to try to find the whole. And I've told myself, now look, this is a pretty strong kind of feeling which you have. It isn't constant. But you feel it sometimes, and as you let yourself feel it, you feel it yourself. You know, there are words for that kind of thing that one could find in abnormal psychology. Might almost be like the feeling that is occasionally, is attributed to things that you read about. I mean, there are some elements there—I mean, this pulsation, this excitement, this knowing. And I've said—I tracked down one thing, I mean, I was very, very brave, what shall we say— a sublimated sex drive. And I thought, well, *there* I've got it. I've really solved the thing. And that there is nothing more to it than that. And for awhile, I mean, I was quite pleased with myself. That was it. And then I had to admit, no, that wasn't it. 'Cause that's something that had been with me long before I became so terribly frustrated sexually. I mean, that wasn't—and, but in the thing, then I began to see a little, within this very core is an acceptance of sexual relationship, I mean, the only kind that I would think would be possible. It was in this thing. It's not something that's been—I mean, sex hasn't been sublimated or substituted there. No. Within this, within what I know there—I mean, it's a different kind of sexual feeling to be sure. I mean, it's one that is stripped of all the things that have happened to sex, if you know what I mean. There's no chase, no pursuit, no battle, no—well, no kind of hate, which I think, seems to me, has crept into such things. And yet, I mean, this feeling has been, oh, a little bit disturbing.

T: I'd like to see if I can capture a little of what that means to you. It is as you've gotten very deeply acquainted with yourself on kind of a brick-by-brick experiencing basis, and in that sense have become more *self*-ish, and the notion of really,—in the discovering of what is the core of you as separate from all the other aspects, you come across the realization, which is a very deep and pretty thrilling realization, that the core of that self is not only without hate, but is really something more resembling a saint, something really very pure, is the word I would use. And that you can try to depreciate that. You can say, maybe it's a sublimation, maybe it's an abnormal manifestation, screwball and so on. But inside of yourself, you knew that it isn't. This contains the feelings which could contain rich sexual expression, but it sounds bigger than, and really deeper than that. And yet fully able to include all that could be a part of sex expression.

C: It's probably something like that . . . It's kind of—I mean, it's a kind of descent. It's a going down where you might almost think it should be going up, but no, it's—I'm sure of it; it's kind of going down.

T: This is a going down and immersing yourself in your self almost.

C: Yeah. And I—I can't just throw it aside. I mean, it just seems, oh, it just *is*. I mean, it seems an awfully important thing that I just had to say.

T: I'd like to pick up one of those things too, to see if I understand it. That it sounds as though this sort of idea you're expressing is something you must be going up to capture, something that *isn't* quite. Actually though, the feeling is, this is a going down to capture something that's more deeply there.

C: It is. It really—there's something to that which is—I mean, this—I have a way, and of course sometime we're going to have to go into that, of rejecting almost violently, that which is righteous, rejection of the ideal, the—as—and that expressed it; I mean, that's sort of what I mean. One is a going up into I don't know. I mean, I just have a feeling, I can't follow. I mean, it's pretty thin stuff if you ever start knocking it down. This one went—I wondered why—I mean, has this awfully definite feeling of descending.

T: That this isn't a going up into the thin ideal. This is a going down into the astonishingly solid reality, that—

C: Yeah.

T: —is really more surprising than—

C: Yeah. I mean, a something that you don't knock down. That's there—I don't know—seems to me after you've abstracted the whole thing. That lasts . . .

Since this is presented in such confused fashion, it might be worthwhile to draw from it the consecutive themes which she has expressed.

I'm going to talk about myself as *self*-ish, but with a new connotation to the word. I've acquired an acquaintance with the structure of myself, know myself deeply. As I descend into myself, I discover something exciting, a core that is totally without hate. It can't be a part of everyday life—it may even be abnormal. I thought first it was just a sublimated sex drive. But no, this is more inclusive, deeper than sex. One would expect this to be the kind of thing one would discover by going up into the thin realm of ideals. But actually, I found it by going deep within myself. It seems to be something that is the essence, that lasts.

Is this a mystic experience she is describing? It would seem that the counselor felt so, from the flavor of his responses. Can we attach any significance to such a Gertrude

Stein kind of expression? The writer would simply point out that many clients have come to a somewhat similar conclusion about themselves, though not always expressed in such an emotional way. Even Mrs. Oak, in the following interview, the thirty-fifth, gives a clearer and more concise statement of her feeling, in a more down-to-earth way. She also explains why it was a difficult experience to face.

C: I think I'm awfully glad I found myself or brought myself or wanted to talk about self. I mean, it's a very personal, private kind of thing that you just don't talk about. I mean, I can understand my feeling of, oh, probably slight apprehension now. It's—well, sort of as though I was just rejecting, I mean, all of the things that western civilization stands for, you see. And wondering whether I was right, I mean, whether it was quite the right path, and still of course, feeling how right the thing was, you see. And so there's bound to be a conflict. And then this, and I mean, now I'm feeling, well, of course that's how I feel. I mean there's a—this thing that I term a kind of a lack of hate, I mean, is very real. It carried over into the things I do, I believe in . . . I think it's all right. It's sort of maybe my saying to myself, well, you've been bashing me all over the head, I mean, sort of from the beginning, with superstitions and taboos and misinterpreted doctrines and laws and your science, your refrigerators, your atomic bombs. But I'm just not buying; you see, I'm just, you just haven't quite succeeded. I think what I'm saying is that, well, I mean, just not conforming, and it's—well, it's just that way.

T: Your feeling at the present time is that you have been very much aware of all the cultural pressures—not always very much aware, but "there have been so many of those in my life—and now I'm going down more deeply into myself to find out what I really feel" and it seems very much at the present time as though that somehow separates you a long ways from your culture, and that's a little frightening, but feels basically good. Is that—

C: Yeah. Well, I have the feeling now that it's okay, really . . . Then there's something else—a feeling that's starting to grow; well, to be almost formed, as I say. This kind of conclusion, that I'm going to stop looking for something terribly wrong. Now I don't know why. But I mean, just—it's this kind of thing. I'm sort of saying to myself now, well, in view of what I know, what I've found—I'm pretty sure I've ruled out fear, and I'm positive I'm not afraid of shock—I mean, I sort of would have welcomed it. But—in view of the places I've been, what I learned there, then also kind of, well, taking into consideration what I don't know, sort of, maybe this is one of the things that I'll have to date, and say, well, now, I've just—I just can't find it. See? And now without any—without, I should say, any sense of apology or covering up, just sort of simple statement that I can't find what at this time, appears to be bad.

T: Does this catch it? That as you've gone more and more deeply into yourself, and as you think about the kind of things that you've discovered and learned and so on, the conviction grows very, very strong that no matter how far you go, the things that you're going to find are not dire and awful. They have a very different character.

C: Yes, something like that.

Here, even as she recognized that her feeling goes against the grain of her culture, she feels bound to say that the core of herself is not bad, nor terribly wrong, but something positive. Underneath the layer of controlled surface behavior, underneath the bitterness, underneath the hurt, is a self that is positive, and that is without hate. This I believe is the lesson which our clients have been facing us with for a long time, and which we have been slow to learn.

If hatelessness seems like a rather neutral or negative concept, perhaps we should let Mrs. Oak explain its meaning. In her thirty-ninth interview, as she feels her therapy drawing to a close, she returns to this topic.

C: I wonder if I ought to clarify—it's clear to me, and perhaps that's all that matters really, here—my strong feeling about a hate-free kind of approach. Now that we have brought it up on a rational kind of plane, I know—it sounds negative. And yet in my thinking, my—not really my thinking but my feeling, it—and my thinking, yes, my thinking, too—it's a far more positive thing than this—than a love—and it seems to me a far easier kind of a—it's less confining. But it—I realize that it must sort of sound and almost seem like a complete rejection of so many things, of so many creeds and maybe it is. I don't know. But it just to me seems more positive.

T: You can see how it might sound more negative to someone but as far as the meaning that it has for you is concerned, it doesn't seem as binding, as possessive I take it, as love. It seems as though it actually is more—more expandable, more usable, than—

C: Yeah.

T: —any of these narrower terms.

C: Really does to me. It's easier. Well, anyway, it's easier for me to feel that way. And I don't know. It seems to me to really be a way of—of not—of finding yourself in a place where you aren't forced to make rewards and you aren't forced to punish. It is—it means so much. It just seems to me to make for a kind of freedom.

T: Mm-hmm. Mm-hmm. Where one is rid of the need of either rewarding or punishing, then it just seems to you there is so much more freedom for all concerned.

C: That's right. (*Pause*) I'm prepared for some breakdowns along the way.

T: You don't expect it will be smooth sailing.

C: No.

This section is the story—greatly abbreviated—of one client's discovery that the deeper she dug within herself, the less she had to fear; that instead of finding something terribly wrong within herself, she gradually uncovered a core of self which wanted neither to reward nor punish others, a self without hate, a self which was deeply socialized. Do we dare to generalize from this type of experience that if we cut through deeply enough to our organismic nature, that we find that man is a positive and social animal? This is the suggestion from our clinical experience.

BEING ONE'S ORGANISM, ONE'S EXPERIENCE

The thread which runs through much of the foregoing material of this chapter is that psychotherapy (at least client-centered therapy) is a process whereby man becomes his organism—without self-deception, without distortion. What does this mean?

We are talking here about something at an experiential level—a phenomenon which is not easily put into words, and which, if apprehended only at the verbal level, is by that very fact, already distorted. Perhaps if we use several sorts of descriptive formulation, it may ring some bell, however faint, in the reader's experience, and cause him to feel "Oh, now I know, from my own experience, something of what you are talking about."

Therapy seems to mean a getting back to basic sensory and visceral experience. Prior to therapy the person is prone to ask himself, often unwittingly, "What do others think I should do in this situation?" "What would my parents or my culture want me to do?" "What do I think *ought* to be done?" He is thus continually acting in terms of the form which should be imposed upon his behavior. This does not necessarily mean that he always acts in *accord* with the opinions of others. He may indeed endeavor to act so as to contradict the expectations of others. He is nevertheless acting *in terms* of the expectations (often introjected expectations) of others. During the process of therapy the individual comes to ask himself, in regard to ever-widening areas of his life-space, "How do I experience this?" "What does it mean to me?" "If I behave in a certain way how do I symbolize the meaning which it *will* have for me?" He comes to act on a basis of what may be termed realism—a realistic balancing of the satisfactions and dissatisfactions which any action will bring to himself.

Perhaps it will assist those who, like myself, tend to think in concrete and clinical terms, if I put some of these ideas into schematized formulations of the process through which various clients go. For one client this may mean: "I have thought I must feel only love for my parents, but I find that I experience both love and bitter resentment. Perhaps I can be that person who freely experiences both love and resentment." For another client the learning may be: "I have thought I was only bad and worthless. Now I experience myself at times as one of much worth; at other times as one of little worth or usefulness. Perhaps I can be a person who experiences varying degrees of worth." For another: "I have held the conception that no one could really love me for myself. Now I experience the affectional warmth of another for me. Perhaps I can be a person who is lovable by others—perhaps I am such a person." For still another: "I have been brought up to feel that I must not appreciate myself—but I do. I can cry for myself, but I can enjoy myself, too. Perhaps I am a richly varied person whom I can enjoy and for whom I can feel sorry." Or, to take the last example from Mrs. Oak, "I have thought that in some deep way I was bad, that the most basic elements in me must be dire and awful. I don't experience that badness, but rather a positive desire to live and let live. Perhaps I can be that person who is, at heart, positive."

What is it that makes possible anything but the first sentence of each of these formulations? It is the addition of awareness. In therapy the person adds to ordinary experience the full and undistorted awareness of his experiencing—of his sensory and visceral reactions. He ceases, or at least decreases, the distortions of experience in awareness. He can be aware of what he is actually experiencing, not simply what he can permit himself to experience after a thorough screening through a conceptual filter. In this sense the person becomes for the first time the full potential of the human organism, with the enriching element of awareness freely added to the basic aspect of sensory and visceral reaction. The person comes to *be* what he *is,* as clients so frequently say in therapy. What this seems to mean is that the individual comes to *be*—in awareness—what he is—in experience. He is, in other words, a complete and fully functioning human organism.

Already I can sense the reactions of some of my readers. "Do you mean that as a result of therapy, man becomes nothing but a human *organism,* a human *animal?* Who will control him? Who will socialize him? Will he then throw over all inhibitions? Have you merely released the beast, the id, in man?" To which the most adequate reply seems to be, "In therapy the individual has actually *become* a human organism, with all the richness which that implies. He is realistically able to control himself, and he is incorrigibly socialized in his desires. There is no beast in man. There is only man in man, and this we have been able to release."

So the basic discovery of psychotherapy seems to me, if our observations have any validity, that we do not need to be afraid of being "merely" *homo sapiens.* It is the discovery that if we can add to the sensory and visceral experiencing which is characteristic of the whole animal kingdom, the gift of a free and undistorted awareness of which only the human animal seems fully capable, we have an organism which is beautifully and constructively realistic. We have then an organism which is as aware of the demands of the culture as it is of its own physiological demands for food or sex—which is just as aware of its desire for friendly relationships as it is of its desire to aggrandize itself—which is just as aware of its delicate and sensitive tenderness toward others, as it is of its hostilities toward others. When man's unique capacity of awareness is thus functioning freely and fully, we find that we have, not an animal whom we must fear, not a beast who must be controlled, but an organism able to achieve, through the remarkable integrative capacity of its central nervous system, a balanced, realistic, self-enhancing, other-enhancing behavior as a resultant of all these elements of awareness. To put it another way, when man is less than fully man—when he denies to awareness various aspects of his experience—then indeed we have all too often reason to fear him and his behavior, as the present world situation testifies. But when he is most fully man, when he is his complete organism, when awareness of experience, that peculiarly human attribute, is most fully operating, then he is to be trusted, then his behavior is constructive. It is not always conventional. It will not always be conforming. It will be individualized. But it will also be socialized.

A CONCLUDING COMMENT

I have stated the preceding section as strongly as I am able because it represents a deep conviction growing out of many years of experience. I am quite aware, however, of the difference between conviction and truth. I do not ask anyone to agree with my experience, but only to consider whether the formulation given here agrees with his own experience.

Nor do I apologize for the speculative character of this paper. There is a time for speculation, and a time for the sifting of evidence. It is to be hoped that gradually some of the speculations and opinions and clinical hunches of this paper may be put to operational and definitive test.

Editors' Introduction

Albert Ellis was trained as a psychoanalyst but found he was not getting the results he wanted so, in characteristic style, he created his own system, known as rational emotive behavior therapy (REBT). REBT is the precursor of many of today's cognitive and cognitive-behavioral therapies.

Ellis's style is inimitable, as anyone knows who has heard him speak or who has had the good fortune to observe him in a therapy session. He is direct, forceful, confident, and convinced of the correctness of his views.

In the case that follows we have an opportunity to observe Ellis working with a young woman whose thinking is clearly irrational and who presents the type of problem with which REBT therapists seem to excel. We also see Ellis making mistakes in therapy, acknowledging them, and critiquing his own work.

The reader will find it interesting to contrast Ellis's style with Rogers's treatment of Mrs. Oak in the preceding case study. Ellis is known as a master clinician, and Rogers had the same reputation. However, as this case clearly demonstrates, their therapy styles are dramatically different.

How much do you know about the imbroglio involving Albert Ellis and the Albert Ellis Institute? Do you have a position on the decisions that were made on both sides?

How do you think your own personality will influence your decision about which therapeutic approach to adopt? Which therapist would you rather have treating you—Rogers or Ellis? Do you believe some clients are a better fit for person-centered therapy, while others are a better fit for REBT? If so, why?

5 | A TWENTY-THREE-YEAR-OLD WOMAN GUILTY ABOUT NOT FOLLOWING HER PARENTS' RULES[1]

Albert Ellis

Martha, a twenty-three-year-old woman, came for help because she claimed she was self-punishing, compulsive, afraid of males, had no goals in life, and was guilty about her relationship with her parents.

SEGMENTS FROM THE FIRST SESSION

C-1:   Well, for about a year and a half since I graduated from college, I've had the feeling that something was the matter with me. I seem to have a tendency toward punishing myself. I'm accident-prone. I'm forever banging myself or falling down stairs, or something like that. And my relationship with my father is causing me a great deal of trouble. I've never been able to figure out where is the responsibility and what my relationship with my parents should be.

T-2:   Do you live with them?

C-3:   No, I don't. I moved out in March.

T-4:   What does your father do?

C-5:   He is a newspaper editor.

T-6:   And your mother is a housewife?

C-7:   Yes.

T-8:   Any other children?

C-9:   Yes, I have two younger brothers. One is twenty; the other is sixteen. I'm twenty-three. The sixteen-year-old has polio, and the other one has an enlarged heart. We never had much money, but we always had the feeling that love and security in life are what count. And the first thing that disturbed me was, when I was about sixteen years old, my father began to drink seriously. To me he had been the infallible person. Anything he said was right. And since I moved out and before I

From Ellis, A. (1974). *Growth through Reason* (pp. 223–286). Hollywood: Wilshire Books. Reprinted by permission of the author.

[1] In this early case of REBT, I stress the cognitive and philosophic techniques commonly used in this therapy. From the beginning, however, REBT has been highly behavioral, especially in its use of in vivo desensitization or exposure with clients like Martha, who are afraid to risk failure and rejection. REBT makes use of operant conditioning, stimulus control, relapse prevention, and many other behavioral methods. It is also very forceful, emotive, and experiential, and uses many affective methods such as shame-attacking exercises, rational emotive imagery, forceful coping statements, and vigorous disputing of clients' irrational beliefs.

   Details on these methods are given in my books *The Practice of Rational Emotive Behavior Therapy* (New York: Springer); *A Guide to Rational Living* (Hollywood, CA: Wilshire Books); *Rational Emotive Behavior Therapy: A Therapist's Guide* (San Luis Obispo, CA: Impact Publishers); *How to Control Your Anxiety Before It Controls You* (Secaucus, NJ: Carol Publishing Group); and in other REBT publications.

moved out, I've wondered where my responsibility to my family lies. Because if they would ask me to do something, if I didn't do it, I would feel guilty about it.

T-10:   What sort of things did they ask you to do?

C-11:   Well, they felt that it just wasn't right for an unmarried girl to move out. Also, I find it easier to lie than to tell the truth, if the truth is unpleasant. I'm basically afraid of men and afraid to find a good relationship with a man that would lead to marriage. My parents have never approved of anyone I have gone out with. In thinking about it, I wonder whether I, subconsciously maybe, went out of my way to find somebody they wouldn't approve of.

T-12:   Do you go with anyone now?

C-13:   Yes, two people.

T-14:   And are you serious about either one?

C-15:   I really don't know. One is sort of serious about me, but he thinks there's something the matter with me that I have to straighten out. I have also at various times been rather promiscuous, and I don't want to be that way.

T-16:   Have you enjoyed sex?

C-17:   Not particularly. I think—in trying to analyze myself and find out why I was promiscuous, I think I was afraid not to be.

T-18:   Afraid they wouldn't like you?

C-19:   Yes. This one fellow that I've been going with—in fact, both of them said I don't have a good opinion of myself.

T-20:   What do you work at?

C-21:   I'm a copywriter for an advertising agency. I don't know if this means anything, but when I was in college, I never could make up my mind what to major in. I had four or five majors. I was very impulsive about the choice of college.

T-22:   What did you finally pick?

C-23:   I went to the University of Illinois.

T-24:   What did you finally major in?

C-25:   I majored in—it was a double major: advertising and English.

T-26:   Did you do all right in college?

C-27:   Yes, I was a Phi Beta Kappa. I graduated with honors.

T-28:   You had no difficulty—even though you had trouble in making up your mind— you had no difficulty with the work itself?

C-29:   No, I worked very hard. My family always emphasized that I couldn't do well in school, so I had to work hard. I always studied hard. Whenever I set my mind to do anything, I really worked at it. And I was always unsure of myself with people. Consequently, I've almost always gone out with more than one person at the same time, maybe because of a fear of rejection by one. Also, something that bothers me more than anything is that I think that I have the ability to write fiction. But I don't seem to be able to discipline myself. Instead of spending my time wisely, as far as writing is concerned, I'll let it go, let it go, and then go out several nights a week— which I know doesn't help me. When I ask myself why I do it, I don't know.

T-30:   Are you afraid the writing wouldn't be good enough?

C-31:   I have that basic fear.

T-32:   That's right: it is a *basic* fear.

C-33:   Although I have pretty well convinced myself that I have talent, I'm just afraid to apply myself. My mother always encouraged me to write, and she always encouraged me to keep on looking for something better in everything I do. From the time I started to go out with boys, when I was about thirteen or fourteen, she never wanted me to get interested in one boy. There was always something better somewhere else. "Go out and look for it." And if somebody didn't please me in all respects, "Go out and look for somebody else." I think that this has influenced the feeling that I've always had that when I might be interested in one person, I'm always looking for someone else.

T-34:   Yes, I'm sure it probably has.

C-35:   But I don't know what I'm looking for.

T-36:   You seem to be looking for perfection. You're looking for security, certainty.

Generally, in doing psychotherapy, I first obtain a moderate degree of background information to identify a symptom that I can concretely use to show her what her basic philosophy or value system is and how she can change it. I thus asked her, in T-30, "Are you afraid the writing wouldn't be good enough?" because I assume, on the basis of rational emotive behavior theory, that there are only a few reasons why she is not writing, and that this is probably one of them. Once she admits she has a fear of failure in writing, I emphasize that this is probably her general or basic fear—so that she will begin to see that her fear of failure is all-pervasive and may explain some other dysfunctional behavior she has mentioned. In T-36, I flatly tell her that I think she's looking for perfection and certainty. I hope she will be somewhat startled by this statement. I intend eventually to show her that her writing fears (and other symptoms) largely stem from her perfectionism. As it happens, she does not appear ready yet to take up my hypothesis; so I bide my time, knowing that I will sooner or later get back to forcing her to look at some of the concepts behind her disturbed behavior.

C-37:   The basic problem is that I'm worried about my family. I'm worried about money. And I never seem to be able to relax.

T-38:   Why are you worried about your family? Let's go into that, first of all. What's to be concerned about? They have certain demands which you don't want to adhere to.

C-39:   I was brought up to think that I mustn't be selfish.

T-40:   Oh, we'll have to knock that out of your head!

C-41:   I think that that is one of my basic problems.

T-42:   That's right. You were brought up to be Florence Nightingale.

C-43:   Yes, I was brought up in a family of sort of would-be Florence Nightingales, now that I analyze the whole pattern of my family history. . . . My father became really alcoholic sometime when I was away in college. My mother developed a breast cancer last year, and she had one breast removed. Nobody is healthy.

T-44:   How is your father doing now?

C-45:   Well, he's doing much better. He's been going to AA meetings, and the doctor he has been seeing has been giving him pills to keep him going. He spends quite a bit of money every week on pills. And if he misses a day of pills, he's absolutely unbearable. My mother feels that I shouldn't have left home—that my place is with them. There are nagging doubts about what I should—

T-46:   Why are there doubts? Why *should* you?

C-47:   I think it's a feeling I was brought up with that you always have to give of yourself. If you think of yourself, you're wrong.

T-48:   That's a *belief*. Why do you have to keep believing that—at your age? You believed a lot of superstitions when you were younger. Why do you have to retain them? Your parents indoctrinated you with this nonsense, because that's *their* belief. But why do you still have to believe that one should not be self-interested; that one should be self-sacrificial? Who needs that philosophy? All it's gotten you, so far, is guilt. And that's all it ever *will* get you!

C-49:   And now I try to break away. For instance, they'll call up and say, "Why don't you come Sunday?" And if I say, "No, I'm busy," rather than saying, "No, I'll come when it's convenient," they get terribly hurt, and my stomach gets all upset.

T-50:   Because you tell yourself, "There I go again. I'm a louse for not devoting myself to them!" As long as you tell yourself that crap, then your stomach or some other part of you will start jumping! But it's your *philosophy,* your *belief,* your sentence to *yourself*—"*I'm* no god-damned good! How could I do that lousy, stinking thing?" *That's* what's causing your stomach to jump. Now, that is a false sentence. Why are you no goddamned good because you prefer you to them? For that's what it amounts to. *Who* said you're no good—Jesus Christ? Moses? Who said so? The answer is: your parents said so. And you believe it because they said so. But who the hell are they?

C-51:   That's right. I was brought up to believe that everything your parents say is right. And I haven't been able to stop believing this.

T-52:   You haven't *done* it. You're *able* to, but you haven't. And *you're* now saying, every time you talk to them, the same crap to yourself. And you've got to see you're saying this drivel! Every time a human being gets upset—except when she's in physical pain—she has always told herself some bullshit the second before she gets upset. Normally, the bullshit takes the form, "This is terrible!"— in your case, "It's terrible that I don't want to go out there to see them!" Or people tell themselves, "*I shouldn't* be doing this!"—in your case, "*I shouldn't* be selfish!" Now, those terms—"This is *terrible!*" and "*I shouldn't* be doing this!"— are assumptions, premises. You cannot sustain them scientifically. You *believe* they're true, without any evidence, mainly because your parents indoctrinated you to believe that they're true. . . . Not only believe it, but *keep* indoctrinating yourself with it. That's the real perniciousness of it. That's the reason it persists—not because they taught it to you. It would just naturally die after a while. But you keep saying it to yourself. It's these simple declarative sentences that you tell yourself every time you make a telephone call to your parents. And unless we can get you to see that you are saying them, and contradict and challenge them, you'll go on saying them forever. Then you will keep getting pernicious results: headaches, self-punishment, lying, and whatever else you get. These results are the logical consequences of an irrational cause, a false premise. And it's this premise that has to be questioned.

As soon as Martha, in C-45, says that she has nagging doubts whenever she thinks of herself first, I try to show her that this idea is only an opinion, that it cannot be empirically justified, and that it will lead to poor results. I am herewith being classically rational emotive: not only explicating but attacking Martha's self-defeating premises and values, and trying to actively teach her how to attack her basic mistaken views.

C-59:   I get so mad at myself for being so illogical.

T-60:   There you go again! You are not only saying that you *are* illogical, but that you *shouldn't* be. Why *shouldn't* you be? It's a pain in the ass to be illogical; it's a nuisance. But who says it's *wicked* for you to be wrong? *That's your parents'* philosophy.

C-61:   Yes, and also there's the matter of religion. I was brought up to be a strict, hard-shelled Baptist. And I can't quite take it any more. This has been going on for— (*Pause*) Well, the first seeds of doubt were sown when I was in high school. Nobody answered my questions. And I kept asking the minister, and he didn't answer my questions. And when I went to college, I started reading. I tried very hard, the first two years in college. I went to church all the time. If I had a question, I'd ask the minister. But pretty soon I couldn't get any answers. And now I really don't believe in the Baptist Church.

T-62:   All right, But are you *guilty* about not believing?

C-63:   Not only am I guilty, but the worst part about it is that I can't tell my parents that I don't believe.

T-64:   But why do you have to? What's the necessity? Because they're probably not going to accept it.

C-65:   Well, they didn't accept it. I was going to get married to a Jewish fellow as soon as I graduated from college. And, of course, the problem of religion came up then. And I didn't stand up for what I believed. I don't know; rather than have scenes, I took the coward's way out. And when I spend Saturdays and Sundays with them now—which is rare—I go to church with them. And this is what I mean by lying, rather than telling the truth.

T-66:   I see. You're probably going to extremes there—going to church. Why do you have to go to church?

C-67:   I always hate to create a scene.

T-68:   You mean you always sell your soul for a mess of porridge?

C-69:   Yes, I do.

T-70:   I don't see why you should. That leaves you with no integrity. Now it's all right to do whatever you want about being quiet, and not telling your parents about your loss of faith—because they're not going to approve and could well upset themselves. There's no use in throwing your irreligiosity in their faces. But to let yourself be forced to go to church and thereby to give up your integrity—that's bullshit. You can even tell them, if necessary, "I don't believe in that any more." And if there's a scene, there's a scene. If they commit suicide, they commit suicide! You can't really hurt them, except physically. You can't hurt anybody else except with a baseball bat! You can do things that they don't like, that they take too seriously, and that they hurt themselves with. But you can't really hurt them with words and ideas. That's nonsense. They taught you to believe that nonsense: "You're hurting us, dear, if you don't go along with what we think you ought to do!" That's drivel of the worst sort! They're hurting themselves by fascistically demanding that you do a certain thing, and then making themselves upset when you don't do it. You're not doing the hurting—they are. If they get hurt because you tell them you're no longer a Baptist, that's their doing. They're hurting themselves; you're not hurting them. They'll say, "How can you do this to us?" But is that *true?* Are you doing anything to them or are *they* doing it to themselves?

C-71:   No, I'm not.

T-72:   But you *believe* that you're hurting them. It's crap! . . .

T-104: . . . What you had better do is relatively simple—but it's not easy to do. And that is—you've already done parts of what needs to be done. You have changed some of your fundamental philosophies—particularly regarding religion—which is a big change for a human being to make. But you haven't changed enough of your philosophy; you still believe some basic dogmas. Most people—whether Jew, Catholic, or Protestant—believe certain dogmas. The main dogmas are that we should devote ourselves to others before ourselves; that we must be loved, accepted, and adored by others, especially by members of our own family; and that we must do well, we must achieve greatly, succeed, do right. And you firmly believe these major ideas. You'd better get rid of them!

C-105: How do I do that?

T-106: By seeing, first of all, that every single time you get upset . . . you told yourself some superstitious creed—some bullshit. That, for example, you're no good because you aren't successful at something; or that you're a louse because you are unpopular, or are selfish, or are not as great as you should be. Then, when you see that you have told yourself this kind of nonsense, you have to ask yourself the question, "*Why* should I have to be successful? *Why* should I always have to be accepted and approved? *Why* should I be utterly loved and adored? Who said so? Jesus Christ? Who the hell was he?" There is no evidence that these things *should* be so; and you are just parroting, on faith, this nonsense, this crap that most people in your society believe. And it's not only your parents who taught it to you. It's also all those stories you read, the fairy tales you heard, the TV shows you saw. They all include this hogwash!

C-107: I know. But every time you try to overcome this, you're faced with it somewhere else again. And I realize—I've come to realize—you know, the thing that made me try to straighten myself out was that I know I've got to learn to have confidence in my own judgment.

T-108: While you've really got confidence in this other crap!

C-109: Yes, I'm very unconfident.

T-110: You have to be—because you believe this stuff.

I continue actively teaching and depropagandizing Martha. Not only do I deal with the irrational philosophies that she brings up, but I prophylactically mention and attack others as well. I keep trying to expose to her a few basic groundless ideas—such as the ideas that she must be loved and must perform well—and to show her that her symptoms, such as her self-sacrificing and her lack of self-confidence, are the natural results of these silly ideas. . . .

C-127: . . . I also want to find out—I suppose it's all basically the same thing—why I have been promiscuous, why I lie—

T-128: For love. I get the impression you think you're such a worm that the only way to get worth, value, is to be loved, approved, accepted. And perhaps you're promiscuous to gain love, because it's an easy way: you can gain acceptance easily that way. You may lie because you're ashamed. You possibly feel that they wouldn't accept you if you told the truth. These are very common results; anybody who desperately needs to be loved—as you think you do with your crummy philosophy—will be promiscuous, will lie, will do other things which are silly, rather than do the things she really wants to do and rather than gain her own self-approval.

C-129: That's what I don't have; I don't have any.

T-130: You never tried to get it! You've been working your butt off to get other people's approval. Your parents' first, but other people's second. That's why the promiscuity; that's why the lying. And you're doing no work whatever at getting your own self-acceptance, because the only way you get self-respect is by not giving that much of a damn what other people think. There is no other way to get it; that's what self-acceptance really means: to thine *own* self be true!

In my response, T-130, I epitomize one of the main differences between REBT and most other "dynamic" systems of psychological treatment. Whereas a psychoanalytically-oriented therapist would probably have tried to show Martha that her promiscuity and lying stemmed from her early childhood experiences, I believe nothing of the sort. I assume that her childhood lying, for example, was mainly caused by her own innate tendencies toward crooked thinking—which in turn led her to react inefficiently to the propaganda her parents may have imposed on her. What is important, therefore, is her own reactivity and not her parents' actions. I also believe, on theoretical grounds, that the reason for Martha's present promiscuity and lying is probably her current need to be inordinately loved; and she freely seems to admit (as she also previously did in C-19) that my educated guess about this is true.

If I were proved to be wrong in this guess, I would not be perturbed but would look for another hypothesis—for example, her promiscuity might be a form of self-punishment, because she thought she was unworthy on some other count. As a rational emotive behavior therapist, I am willing to take a chance on being wrong with my first hypothesis because, if I am right, I usually save my client a good deal of time. Moreover, by taking a wrong tack, I may well help myself and the client get to the right tack. If, however, I try the psychoanalytic, history-taking path, to arrive at the "real" reasons for my client's behavior, (a) I may never find what these "real" reasons are (for they may not exist, or years of probing may never turn them up); (b) I may still come up with the wrong reasons; and (c) I may sidetrack the client so seriously that she may never discover what her basic disturbance-creating philosophy is and therefore never do anything about changing it. For a variety of reasons, then, I took a very direct approach with Martha.

C-131: You have to develop a sort of hard shell towards other people?

T-132: Well, it isn't really a callous shell. It's really that you have to develop your own goals and your own confidence so much that you do not allow the views and desires of others to impinge that much on you. Actually, you'll learn to be kinder and nicer to other people if you do this. We're not trying to get you to be against others, to be hostile or resentful. The less vulnerable you get to what others think of you, actually the more sensitive, kindly, and loving you can often be. Because you haven't been really loving, but largely maintaining a facade with your parents. Underneath, you've been resentful, unloving.

C-133: I can be loving, though.

T-134: That's right. But you'd better be true to yourself first; and through being true to yourself then you'll be able to care more for other people. Not all people, and maybe not your parents. There's no law that says you have to love your parents. They may just not be your cup of tea. In fact, it looks like in some ways they aren't. Tough! It would be nice if they were: it would be lovely if you could love them and have good relationships. But that may never really be. You may well have to withdraw emotionally from them, to some extent—not from everybody, but probably from them somewhat—in order to be true to yourself. Because it seems to me they act like leeches, fascists, emotional blackmailers.

C-135: Yes, that's the term: emotional blackmailers. This I know; this has been evidenced all through my life. Emotional blackmail!

At every point, I try to show Martha that she does not have to feel guilty with withdrawing emotionally from her parents, nor for doing what she wants to do or thinking what she wants to think. I do not try to get her to condemn her parents or to be hostile to them. Quite the contrary! But I do consistently show her that they have their own problems in logical thinking and that she'd better resist their emotional blackmailing. As it turns out, she seems to have always known this; but my actively bringing it to her attention will presumably help her to act, now, on what she knows and feels. I am thereby helping her, through frank and therapist-directed discussion, to get in touch with her real feelings and to follow them in practice.

T-136: Right. And you've been accepting this blackmail. You had to accept it as a child— you couldn't help it, you were dependent. But you don't *still* have to accept it. You now can see that they're blackmailing; and now you can calmly resist it, without being resentful of them. Then their blackmail won't take effect. They'll probably foam at the mouth, have fits, and everything. Tough!—so they'll foam. Well, there's no question that you can change. We haven't got any more time now. But the main problem—as I said awhile ago—is your philosophy, which is an internalizing, really, of their philosophy. And if there ever was evidence of how an abject philosophy affects you, there it is: they're thoroughly miserable. And you'll be just as miserable if you continue this way. If you want to learn to *change* your philosophy, this is what I do in therapy: beat people's crazy ideas over the head until they stop defeating themselves. That's all you're doing: defeating yourself!

I keep utilizing material from Martha's own life to consistently show her what is going on in her head, philosophically, and what she'd better do about changing her thinking. This first interview with Martha indicates how REBT, right from the start, encourages the therapist to talk much more about the client's value system than about her symptoms and how it uses the information she gives to highlight her own disturbance-creating ideas and to attack them. I think that this session also shows that although I do not hesitate to contradict Martha's assumptions at several points, I am essentially supportive in that I keep showing her (a) that I am on her side, (b) that I think I can help her, (c) that I am fairly sure what the real sources of her disturbances are, and (d) that if she works at seeing these sources and at doing something to undermine them, the chances are excellent that she will become much less upsettable. My "attack," therefore, is one that would ordinarily be called "ego-bolstering." Or, in REBT terminology, it is one that is designed to help Martha fully accept rather than severely condemn herself.

To this end, I consistently have what Carl Rogers calls "unconditional positive regard" for Martha, for I accept her in spite of her difficulties and inanities, and believe that she is capable of overcoming her crooked thinking by living and working primarily for herself. I also show that I am on Martha's side, not because I personally find her attractive, bright, or competent, but because I feel that every human has the right to choose to live primarily for himself or herself.

SEGMENTS FROM THE SECOND SESSION

This session takes place five days after the first session. Martha has already made some progress, has calmed down considerably, and is now in a better condition to work on some of her basic problems.

T-1:   How are things?

C-2:   Things are okay. I went to visit my parents on Monday night. And every time I was tempted to fall prey to their emotional blackmail, I remembered what you said, and I was able to fight it.

T-3:   Fine!

C-4:   My mother is having a rough time yet, because of having her breast removed. She hardly says anything. She's really in a fog. She gets confused, and she uses the confusion to give her a hold on the family. She was putting on a martyr act the other night; and usually I would have given in to her, but I said, "Quit being a martyr! Go to bed." She just looked at me as though I was a strange creature!

T-5:   And you didn't get upset by it?

C-6:   No, I didn't get upset by it. I had the feeling that I was doing the right thing. And that was, I think, the major accomplishment in the past few days.

T-7:   Yes; well that was quite a good accomplishment.

C-8:   Now if there are any bigger crises that will come, I don't know how I'll face them; but it looks like I can.

T-9:   Yes; and if you keep facing these smaller crises as they arise—and they tend to be continual—there's no reason why you shouldn't be able to face the bigger ones as well. Why not?

C-10:   I guess it's a case of getting into a good habit.

T-11:   Yes, that's right: getting ready to believe that no matter what your parents do, no matter how hurt they get, that's not your basic problem. You're not deliberately doing them in; you're just standing up for yourself.

As often occurs in REBT, although this is only the second session, Martha is already beginning to implement some of the major ideas that were discussed during the first session and is beginning to change herself. I deliberately support her new notion that she can handle herself with her parents, and I keep reiterating that she does not have to react to their views and behavior by getting upset. I thereby am approving her new patterns and rewarding or reinforcing her. But I am also repetitively teaching—taking every opportunity to reassert that she can think for herself and does not have to react negatively because her parents or others view her unfavorably. . . .

C-40: In school, if I didn't do well in one particular thing, or even on a particular test—and little crises that came up—if I didn't do as well as I had wanted to do . . .

T-41: You beat yourself over the head?

C-42: Yes.

T-43: But why? What's the point? Are you supposed to be perfect? Why shouldn't human beings make mistakes, be imperfect?

C-44: Maybe you always expect yourself to be perfect.

T-45: Yes. But is that *sane?*

C-46: No.

T-47: Why do it? Why not give up that unrealistic expectation?

C-48: But then I can't accept myself.

T-49: But you're saying, "It's shameful to make mistakes." Why is it shameful? Why can't you go to somebody else when you make a mistake and say, "Yes, I made a mistake"? Why is that so awful?

C-50: I don't know.

T-51: There *is* no good reason. You're just *saying* it's so. Recently I wrote an article for a professional publication, and they accepted it, and they got another psychologist to write a critique of it. He wrote his critique—a fairly savage one—and he pointed out some things with which I disagree, so I said so in my reply. But he pointed out some things which he was right about; where I had overstated my case and made a mistake. So, I merely said about this in my rejoinder, "He's right; I made a mistake here." Now, what's the horror? Why shouldn't I make a mistake? Who am I—Jesus Christ? Who are you—the Virgin Mary? Then, why shouldn't you be a fallible human being like the rest of us and make mistakes?

C-52: It might all go back to, as you said, the need for approval. If I don't make mistakes, then people will look up to me. If I do it all perfectly—

T-53: That is an erroneous belief; that if you never make mistakes everybody will love you and that it is necessary that they do. That's a big part of it. But is it true? Suppose you never did make mistakes—would people love you? Maybe they would hate your guts because you were so perfect, wouldn't they?

C-54: And yet, not all the time. There are times—this is rare, I grant you—but sometimes I'll take a stand on something that other people don't like. But this is rare!

T-55: Yes, but what about the times when you know you're wrong? Let's take those times—that's what we're talking about. You know you're wrong, you made a mistake, there's no question about it. Why are you a louse at *those* times? Why is it shameful to admit your mistake? Why can't you accept yourself as a fallible human being—which we all are?

C-56: (*Pause*) Maybe I have the idea that if I keep telling myself how perfect I am, I won't realize how imperfect I am.

T-57: Yes, but why shouldn't one accept the fact that one is imperfect? That's the real question. What's shameful about being imperfect? Why must one be an angel—which you're trying to be?

C-58: Probably there's no good reason.

T-59: No. Then why don't you look at *that?* There's no good reason. It's a definitional thing, saying "To be good, to be perfect, to be a worthwhile human being, I must be perfect. If I have flaws, I'm no damned good." And you can't substantiate that proposition. It's a senseless proposition; but you believe it. The reason you believe it is your society believes it. This is the basic creed of your silly society.

Certainly, your parents believe it. If they knew one-sixtieth of your errors and mistakes—especially your sex errors!—they'd be horrified, wouldn't they?

C-60: Yes.

T-61: You have the same silly horror! Because *they* think you ought to be a sexless angel, you think you ought to be.

C-62: (*Silence*)

T-63: You've accepted their idiotic judgments—the same judgments that have driven your father to drink and made your mother utterly miserable. They both have been miserable all your life. That's what perfectionism leads to. A beautiful object lesson there! Anybody who is perfectionistic tends to become disturbed, unhappy—ultimately often crazy. The gospel of perfection!

C-64: That's what I have to work on. Because I don't want to get like they are.

T-65: No, but you are partly like they are already—we had better change that. It isn't a matter of getting—you've already got! Let's face it. You don't do the same kind of behavior as they do, but you hate yourself when you don't. You make the mistakes; they don't make them. But then you say, "I'm no good! How could I have done this? This is terrible! I'm not Florence Nightingale. I go to bed with guys. I do bad things. I make blunders. How awful!" That's the same philosophy that they have, isn't it? And it's an impossible philosophy, because we'd really literally have to be angels to live up to it. There *are* no angels! Not even your parents!

I make a mistake when I tell Martha that she believes she is worthless largely because her parents and her society teach her to believe this. I fail to note that practically all humans seem to be born with a tendency to believe this sort of drivel; that they must be pretty perfect and are no good if they are not; and that therefore their parents and their society are easily able to convince them that this is "true."

Clinically, however, I felt when I talked to Martha that she was already prejudiced against her parents' views and that she might therefore see the perniciousness of her own ideas if I emphasized how similar they were to those of her parents. As a rational emotive behavior therapist, I am a frank propagandist, since I deliberately use appeals that I think will work with a given client. But I only propagandize in accordance with what appears to be the empirical reality that some people do define themselves as worthless slobs. I do not propagandize only to win Martha's approval, but to dramatically (emotively) bring to her attention the realities of life.

Rational emotive behavior therapists are sometimes accused of foisting on their clients their own prejudiced views of the world. Actually, they base their views on the facts of human existence and the usual nature of people. And they teach individuals with disturbances to look at these facts and to realistically accept and work with them. They may teach through dramatic or emotive methods in order to put a point over more effectively, taking into consideration that clients generally hold their wrong-headed views in a highly emotionalized, not easily uprootable manner.

C-66: (*Pause*) I guess that's this great fear of failure. That might have been what was keeping me from concentrating on writing, which I really want to do. I'm afraid that I might make a mistake, you know.

T-67: Yes, that's the other grim tragedy. Two things happen if you have a terrible, grim fear of failure. One is, as you just said, you get anxious, unhappy, ashamed. Two, you don't live; you don't do the things you want to do. Because if you did them, you might make a mistake, an error, be a poor writer—and wouldn't that be awful, according to your definition? So you just don't do things. That's your parents again. How could they be happy, when they haven't done anything? And you have been following the same general pattern. You haven't taken it to their extremes as yet, but it's the same bullshit, no matter how you slice it. And in your case you're afraid to write; because if you wrote, you'd commit yourself. And if you committed yourself, how horrible *that* would be!

C-68:   I've done a lot of thinking since the last time I saw you. And I've gone at the type-writer with a fresh burst of enthusiasm. I'm really anxious to get to my writing—I want to get home from work so I can write. Nothing big has happened, but I feel as though if I concentrate on it and keep feeling this way, all I have to do is to keep working at it.

T-69:   And one of two things will happen. Either you'll become a good writer, with enough work and practice; or you'll prove that you're not—which would be a good thing, too. It would be far better to prove you're not a good writer by work-ing at it than not to write. Because if you don't write, you may go on for the rest of your life hating yourself; while if you really work solidly day after day, and you just haven't got it in this area, that's tough. So you won't be a writer—you'll be something else. It would be better to learn by that experience.

C-70:   That's right. Because—I don't know—I felt so different, sitting at the typewriter and working at it, that it got to be enjoyable.

T-71:   It will!

C-72:   But it was painful before.

T-73:   It was painful because you were *making* it painful by saying, "My God! Look what would happen if I failed! How awful!" Well, anything would become painful if you kept saying that.

C-74:   Another thing that bothers me, I guess—it's the whole pattern of behavior; the way everything has been in my life. It's a sort of—"Go ahead and do it now, and then something will come along and take care of it." Like my parents always said, "We'll go ahead and do this, even though we don't have the money for it, and it'll come from somewhere."

T-75:   Right: "In God we trust!" . . .

C-84:   . . .And when I tell myself, "Don't be silly; you can't do it, so don't," I'm tempted to go ahead and do it anyway.

T-85:   Yes, because you're telling yourself stronger and louder: "It'll take care of itself. Fate will intervene in my behalf. The Lord will provide!"

C-86:   And I get mad at myself for doing it—

T-87:   That's illegitimate! Why not say, "Let's stop the crap!" instead of getting mad at yourself? How will getting mad at yourself help?

C-88:   It doesn't. It just causes more tension.

T-89:   That's exactly right. It doesn't do any good whatsoever. Let's cut out all the self-blame. That's doesn't mean cut out all criticism. Say, "Yes, I am doing this wrongly, so how do I not do it wrongly?"—instead of: "I am doing it wrongly; what a louse I am! I'm no good; I deserve to be punished!"

I persist at showing Martha that she can take chances, do things badly, and still not condemn herself. At every possible turn, I get back to her underlying philosophies con-cerning (a) failing and defining herself as a worthless individual and (b) unrealistically relying on the world or fate to take care of difficult situations. She consistently describes her feelings, but I bring her back to the ideas behind them. Then she seems to accept my interpretations and to seriously consider working against her disturbance-creating ideas. My persistence and determination may importantly induce her to tentatively accept my explanations and to use them herself.

C-90:   When I am particularly worried about anything, I have very strange dreams. I have dreams that I can't describe, but I have them several times a week.

T-91:   There's nothing unusual about that. They're probably anxiety dreams. All the dreams say—if you told me what they are, I could show you right away—the same kind of things you're saying to yourself during the day. They're doing it in a vague and more abstract way. But that's all they are, just repetitious of the crap you're telling yourself during the day. In dreams, our brain is not as efficient as it is when we're awake; and therefore it uses symbols, vague representations, indirectness, and so on. But the dreams tell us the same crap we think during the day.

C-92:   I had a dream last week that disturbed me. I dreamed that I ran off somewhere with my boss, and his wife found us in bed; and I was so upset over that—I really was. Because I never consciously thought of my boss in a sexual way.

T-93:   That doesn't mean that that's what the dream represented, that you thought of your boss in a sexual way. There's a more obvious explanation of the dream. All the dream is really saying is: You did the wrong thing and got found out.

C-94:   I never thought of that.

T-95:   That's all it was saying, probably. And what's one of the wrongest things you can do in our society? Have intercourse with your boss and have his wife find out! That's all. It probably has little to do with sex at all; and you're probably not going around unconsciously lusting after your boss.

C-96:   No, I don't think I am.

T-97:   No. But it would be the wrong move, if you did have sex with him; it might, of course, jeopardize your job. So that's all you're saying in your dream: if I do the wrong thing, I'm no goddamned good; I may lose my job; I may get terribly penalized; and so on. That's what you say all day, isn't it? Why should you not translate it into dreams at night? It's the same crap!

In REBT, dreams are not overemphasized and are often used only to a small extent; for, as I say to Martha, they are hardly the royal road to the unconscious (as Freud believed), but seem to be rather distorted and muddled representations of the same kind of thinking and feeling that the individual tends to do during his waking life. Since they are experienced in symbolic, vague, and ambiguous ways, and since they can easily be misinterpreted (according to whatever biases the individual therapist happens to hold), the REBT practitioner would rather stick with the client's conscious thoughts, feelings, and behaviors and with the unconscious (or unaware) thoughts and feelings that can be deduced from them. Dreams are rather redundant material, and can consume a great deal of therapeutic time if they are taken too seriously. Moreover, long-winded dream analysis can easily (and dramatically!) distract the client from what he'd better do most of all: look at his philosophies of life and work hard at changing them.

The beauty of the REBT approach is that no matter what the client seems to be upset about, the therapist can quickly demonstrate that there is no good reason for her upsetness. Thus, if Martha's dream represents (a) her lusting after her boss, (b) her being out of control, or (c) any other kind of mistake, REBT theory holds that she cannot be a rotter and that she therefore need not be terribly anxious, guilty, angry, or depressed. She creates her disturbed feelings, not from the dream events, nor from her foolish motives that may be revealed in these events, nor from the happenings in her real life, nor from anything *except* her own attitudes about these events, motives, or happenings. And I, as her therapist, am concerned much more with her attitudes than with things transpiring in her waking or sleeping life. So if REBT is consistently followed, *any* emotional problem may be tracked down to its philosophic sources (or the ways in which the individual blames herself, others, or the world); and these philosophies may then be challenged, attacked, changed, and uprooted.

C-192:   I guess the main thing is to keep in mind that a lot of the thoughts I have—whenever I get a thought like that, I'd better challenge it.

T-193:   That's right, to see that it is invalid. First you start with the feeling—the upset. Then you know, on theoretical grounds, that you have an invalid thought, because you don't get negative feelings without first having some silly thought. Then you look for the thought—which is pretty obvious most of the time. You're invariably blaming yourself or saying that something is horrible when it isn't. Then you say, "Why is this horrible? Why would it be dreadful if such-and-such a thing happened?" Challenge it; question it; counter it. That's the process. And if you go through that process, your thoughts can't persist. Because they're your irrational thoughts now. They're no longer your parents' ideas. You have internalized them.

C-194: (*Long pause*) I guess it has to be done.

T-195: Yes. And you will get immense benefit from doing it—as you've already been deriving this week. It felt good when you acted that way, didn't it?

C-196: Since I have been back at the typewriter again, I've been thinking differently. I can see myself falling back, as I used to be able to do, into a clear pattern of thought. I mean, I'm not just thinking in symbols and metaphors, but am able to describe things incisively, or at least have descriptive impressions of things.

T-197: Yes. That's because you're letting yourself go—you're not pouncing on yourself so much.

C-198: Yes, you're right. Not that I've done very much in this last week, but I do feel like I'm loosening up more.

T-199: That's very good progress in one week's time! All you have to do is keep that up—and go a little further.

C-200: And another thing I've done: I haven't called up my father because I felt I had to. And he hasn't called me—so that means something.

T-201: Fine! When would you like to make the next appointment?

Martha's apparent progress represents a common occurrence in REBT. After one or two active-directive sessions, clients frequently report that something they thought they were never able to do before is now in their repertoire. This does not mean that they are truly "cured" of their emotional disturbances. But it often does seem to mean that they are well on the way to resolving at least one or two major aspects of these disturbances.

Even if clients such as Martha are quickly helped, this hardly means that all or most individuals who try REBT encounters are similarly relieved; many of them, of course, are not. I assume, however, that a certain large minority of people can almost immediately profit by the REBT approach; and I assume that a given individual with whom I am talking may be one of this minority. If my assumption proves to be correct, fine! If it does not, I am prepared, if necessary, to doggedly continue with the approach for as many sessions as are desirable—until the client finally begins to see that she is causing her own upsets, that she can observe the specific meanings and beliefs by which she causes them, that she can vigorously and consistently dispute and challenge these beliefs, and that she can thereby become considerably less disturbed.

THIRD SESSION

The third session with Martha was uneventful. Because she was afflicted with some expensive physical ailments and had financial difficulties, she decided to discontinue therapy for a time.

SEGMENTS FROM THE FOURTH SESSION

The fourth session with Martha took place nine months after the third session. She had expected to come back to therapy sooner than she actually did, but she was able to get along nicely and didn't feel impelled to return until she had a specific problem to discuss. She now comes with this problem—her relations with men.

T-1:   How are things with you?

C-2:   Pretty well, I would say. I've been hearing good things about you from some of the people I sent to see you. From Matt, in particular. He thinks that you've helped him immensely.

T-3:   I'm glad that he thinks so.

C-4:   And I see that you're making yourself comfortable, as usual. That's the way I found you last time: shoes off, feet up.

T-5:   Yes; that's the way I usually am.

C-6:   I came to you back in January because I needed some help in writing; and also I didn't know how to handle my parents.

T-7:   Yes.

C-8:   Well, I think I solved those two problems fairly well. I get along very well with my parents now. Not because I'm giving in to them at all. I've sort of established myself as a human being, apart from them completely. And I also found some other work. I was working, as I told you, for an advertising agency. But it didn't have any interest for me at the time. I was terribly bored, and I felt I could write on my own. But I was afraid. Then I got an idea for a novel, and a publisher has taken an option on it, and I've been working on it ever since. It will be published in the spring by the same publisher who has been having such success recently with several young novelists.

T-9:   I see. That's fine!

C-10:   So that's all working out very well. But there's something that is bothering me, that I thought you could help me with. I've been thinking of getting married. I've been thinking of marriage in general, first of all. But before that—maybe I'm not quite sure that I really know how to love anybody. Not that I consider that there's a formula. But I've always, in a way, been somewhat afraid of men. The other thing is that there is someone in particular who would like to marry me. And—maybe I'd better tell you how this all happened.

T-11:   Sure.

C-12:   In trying to analyze it—in trying to figure it out—I guess it all started to go back to my father. My father was a nice guy, but he has been alcoholic since I was twelve; and he has been getting worse since I last saw you. But I was absolutely adoring of my father when I was a little girl. And then I realized he was a human being, and he fell off his pedestal. Now I don't know how much can be attributed to that, but I don't think I ever trusted a man. I guess I was afraid that if I devoted myself to that person completely, sooner or later he would walk out on me. And this has always terrified me, no matter what kind of associations I've had. I always have to keep one step ahead of them.

T-13:   All right; it *would* terrify you if you keep saying to yourself, "They'll find out how worthless I am and leave me!"

C-14:   I guess you're right.

T-15:   And if you get rid of that fear—and as you said yourself, a couple of minutes ago, it is a fear—then you can be pretty sure that you'll love someone. I don't know *whom* you'll love—this person you're talking about, who wants to marry you, or anybody else—but I'm sure you have the *capacity* to love if you're not absorbed in, "Oh, my God! What a louse I am! When is he going to find it out?" See? . . .

C-40:   Another thing that I seem to do: every time I get interested in someone, I find myself looking at other men.

T-41:   Yes, that's possible. But it's also possible that if you think of one man in terms of marrying him and you still get interested in other men, you may not be so sure as yet, in terms of your experience, that it should be the first one. And therefore you'd like to try others. So some of what you feel may be normal, and some of it may be your fear of getting involved. The basic problem still is getting you to be unfearful—to realize yourself that you don't have to be afraid of anything . . .

C-42:   Well, I would like to overcome this. I don't want to be afraid of them—that they might leave me.

T-43:   The basic thing they can do, as you said before, is reject you. Now, let's suppose that they do. Let's suppose that you went with this guy, and you really let yourself go with him, and he finally did reject you, for whatever his reasons might be. What could you conclude should this happen?

C-44:   I could always suppose that he was the one who had shortcomings, rather than me.

T-45:   But let's suppose he doesn't have serious shortcomings, and he rejects you. Let's suppose he's perfect and then he spurns you. Now what does that prove?

C-46:   I don't know.

T-47:   All it proves is that he doesn't like you for some deficiencies. It proves, assuming that he's objective about your deficiencies, that you have certain defects. But does having these defects prove that you're worthless? Or that you're thoroughly inadequate, that you're no good?

C-48:   It doesn't.

T-49:   That's exactly right! And yet that's what you automatically think every single time: that it means something bad about you. That's what your parents believe: that if you are deficient and somebody finds it out, that proves that you're worthless, as a total human. Isn't that their philosophy?

C-50:   I guess so.

T-51:   They've told you that in so many words, so many times—as you told me they did awhile ago. When they found out something about you that they didn't like—such as your not running to their beck and call—you were not just a daughter who didn't like them that much (which is all that was evident); no, you were a louse—no good! They called you every name under the sun. They tried to make you guilty, you told me. Over the phone, they'd call you several times—and so on. Isn't that right? They assume that when someone is deficient in their eyes, that person is a slob. That's their philosophy: that unless you're an angel, you are no good.

C-52:   I guess I just carried it with me. I let myself carry it with me.

T-53:   That's right. You've let yourself carry it with you—which is normal enough. Most people do. But look at the results! If it had good results, if it really made you happy, we might say, "Go carry it!" But the result is the normal result—or the abnormal result, in your case. You can't give to a man because you're always worrying, "How worthless I am! And how soon will he see it? And before he sees it, maybe I'd better do something to get rid of him." Which is your logical conclusion from an irrational premise, the premise being that if people do find your deficiencies and therefore reject you, you're totally no good. Actually, there are *two* premises here. One, that they'll find your deficiencies and therefore will reject you—which is quite an assumption! Two, that if they do reject you, you're no damned good. These are two completely irrational premises. They're not supported by any evidence.

I try to show Martha that it is not her boyfriend but her own attitudes about herself that are upsetting her, and that no matter how defective she is, and no matter how badly her boyfriend (or anyone else) rejects her, she can still fully accept herself and try to better her relationships. Although I am therefore ruthless about insisting that she acknowledge her deficiencies, I am (in a typical REBT manner) highly supportive about the possibility of her unconditionally accepting herself. In REBT, the therapist generally does not give warm, personal affection (since there is the always existing danger that the client will, in getting it, wrongly think he is "good" *because* the therapist or group cares for him).

Instead, the rational emotive behavior therapist (and group) tries to give unconditional acceptance, that is, complete tolerance and lack of condemnation of the client no matter what his or her faults are. I think an incisive reading of these sessions with Martha will show that I am rarely loving or warm to her but that I frequently show full acceptance of her.

C-56:   How do I go about convincing myself that this is wrong?

T-57:   The first thing you'd better do before you convince yourself that this is wrong is to convince yourself—that is, fully admit to yourself—that you very strongly have this belief. You can't very well tackle a belief and change it unless you fully admit that you have it. After seeing this, the second thing is to see the degree—which is enormous and intense—to which you have it. You can at first do this by inference—by observing your behavior and asking yourself what ideas lie behind it. For your behavior itself is not necessarily fearful. It may take the form of your *feeling* in a state of panic, or it may be defensive.

C-58:   Well, my behavior is mostly defensive.

T-59:   All right. Then we have to start with your defensive behavior. Look at it, question it, challenge it, and see—by inference, at first—that it could only be this way if you *were* fearful. For why would you be defensive if you were not, underneath, also afraid of something? If we can get you to see how many times a day you're unduly restricted, defensive—and therefore fearing—until you see the real frequency and intensity of your fears, then at least we get you to see what the cancer really is. You can't really understand the cancer without seeing the depths of it. Okay, we have the first step, then, which is to make you see fully what the depths of your cancerous ideation are. Then, as you begin to see this, the second step is to get you to calmly assess it. The first cancer is your defense and your fear behind it. The second cancer is—and this is the reason why so many people *are* defensive—if you admit to yourself, "My God! What a terribly fearful person I am!" you will then tend to blame yourself for that. In other words, you say on level number one, "My heavens, I'm a wrongdoing person, am therefore terribly worthless, and I'd better not let anyone know this." So you become defensive because your real philosophy is: "What a worthless slob I am because I'm imperfect; I have deficiencies; I have faults." So the first level is to make yourself fearful because of your feelings of worthlessness—the philosophy that human beings who are deficient are no damned good. Then, as a derivative of that first level, you come to the second level: "Because I'm deficient, because I'm fearful, because I'm neurotic, I'm a louse and am worthless for *that* reason. So I'd better deny that I'm really that fearful *(a)* because people will find out about it and hate me and *(b)* because I'll use my fear to prove to myself what a louse I am."

   So first we have to get you to admit the fact that you're fearful, defensive, and so on—that you are a perfectionist who tends to bring on feelings of worthlessness. Then we have to get you to see that by admitting your fear and defensiveness you're not a louse for having these traits; and to get you to see that simply because you have a *feeling* you're worthless doesn't mean that you really *are*. So we have to get you to *(a)* admit that you feel like a skunk; *(b)* objectively perceive—and not blamefully perceive—that you believe you're one; and *(c)* (which is really just an extension of b) start tackling your concept of being a skunk. . . .

C-72:   But actually, your parents bring you up that way. Because you are naughty, you stand in a corner; you don't get your supper; you get spanked; or someone says to you, "That wasn't very nice; that wasn't very good!"

T-73:   That's right. They don't only spank you—that wouldn't be so bad, because then they would just penalize you—but they also say, "You're no good!" And the attitude they take in doing the spanking is an angry attitude; and the whole implication of the anger is that you're worthless. People do this in order to train you when you're a child; and it's a very effective method of training. But look at the enormous harm it does! Incidentally, one of the main reasons we would want you to undo your self-blaming tendencies is that if you do get married and have children, you will tend to do the same kind of thing to them that was done to you—unless you see very clearly what was done to you and what you're doing now to continue it.

C-74: And also, I'm absolutely terrified of being somebody's mother.

T-75: Yes, that's right. Just look how incompetent you might be, and how you might screw it up! And wouldn't *that* be awful!

C-76: You know, I've been asking myself that a hundred thousand times.

T-77: All right; but those are the times we have to clip. Let's just take that sentence, "Suppose I was somebody's mother and brought my child up badly." That's what you're saying. How are you *ending* the sentence?

C-78: Wouldn't that be awful! Wouldn't I be terrible!

T-79: That's right. Now is that a logical conclusion to make from the observed facts? Let's suppose the facts were true—that you did bring up a child badly. Let's suppose that. Would it still follow that you'd be a worthless slob?

C-80: No, it wouldn't. Because I'd be defining—that's what it is—I'd be defining *worthless* in terms of whatever it is I lack, whatever it is that I do badly in.

T-81: That's right. The equation you'd be making is: my deficiency equals my worthlessness. That's exactly the equation—and it's a definition. Now is it a *true* definition?

C-82: No.

T-83: It's a true or an accurate definition if you *make* it true—if you *insist* that it's true.

C-84: But it's not necessarily a correct one.

T-85: That's right. And what happens when you make that definition?

C-86: Then you feel worthless, because you define yourself as worthless.

T-87: Yes, pragmatically, you defeat yourself. If it were a definition that led to good results, that might be fine. But *does* it lead to that?

C-88: No. Because you tend to look at everything negatively, rather than—I hate to say positively, because it sounds like "positive thinking," and that's not it.

T-89: Yes, let's say it makes you look at things negatively rather than looking at them without prejudice.

C-90: Yes, without prejudice.

From responses T-77 to T-89, I resort to a questioning dialogue, instead of my previous use of straight lecturing and explaining. I keep asking Martha various questions about what she's telling herself, what results she is thereby getting, and whether the things she is saying to herself and the definitions she is setting up about her behavior are really accurate. She shows, by her answers, that she is following what I have previously explained and that she can probably use this material in her future living. . . .

T-95: . . . a child will lots of times define himself as a blackguard on his own. Because if he fails and does so lots of times—as he inevitably will—even if Mommy didn't call him a slob, he would probably tend to think he is worthless. It's sort of a normal, natural conclusion for a young child, who can't think straight because of his youth, to say, "Because I failed at A, B, C, and D, I'm bound to fail at X, Y, and Z; and therefore I'm thoroughly incompetent at everything." That's what we call overgeneralization; and human beings, especially young children, tend to overgeneralize. Now, unfortunately, we also help them to do this, in our society— in fact, in most societies. But they might well do it without social help, though probably to a lesser degree. Anyway, it behooves us to help them to think in a less overgeneralized manner. We'd better take the child who tends to overgeneralize and calmly show him, a thousand times if necessary, "Look, dear, because you did A, B, C, and D mistakenly, that doesn't mean—"

C-96:   "—that you're going to do X, Y, and Z wrongly."

T-97:   That's right! "And even if you do A, B, C, and D badly, and also do X, Y, and Z wrongly, that doesn't mean that you're a louse. It means, objectively, that you have deficiencies. So you're not Leonardo da Vinci. Tough!" But we don't teach them anything of the kind.

C-98:   No. "You have to excel in everything. If you don't, that's bad!"

T-99:   "That's terrible!" We don't even say it's bad. Because it is, of course, objectively bad; it's inconvenient; it's a nuisance when you fail; and you will get certain poor results if you keep failing. But it doesn't say anything about you personally, as a *human being,* except that you're the kind of a creature who often fails. It doesn't say that you're a worm—unless you define it so.

C-100: Well, I think I'll know what to look for.

T-101: Yes. It will take a little practice. It won't take very long, I'm sure, in your case, because you see the outlines, and I think you're very able to do this kind of thinking, which is highly important. Many people deliberately shy away from doing it, so they never see it. They're hopeless because, in a sense, they don't *want* to see it; they want the world to change, or others to change, rather than wanting to change themselves. But you want to see it, and you have seen a large hunk of it already, in dealing recently with your parents. Considering the short length of time that I saw you and that you've been working on it, you've done remarkably well. Now there's no reason why you can't see the bigger hunk of it—which applies to you much more than to your relations with your father and mother.

So you go off and look for these things we've been talking about. As I said, make a list, if you're not going to remember the things that come up during the week that you bother yourself about. Make a list of the major times when you feel upset, or when you believe you acted defensively instead of feeling overtly upset. Look for these things; come in, and we'll talk about them. I'll check what you find, just as I'd check your lessons if I were teaching you how to play the piano. You'll then be able to see your own blockings more clearly. There's no reason why not.

I continue to be encouraging to show Martha that she has been able to make good progress so far and that she should be able to continue to do so. But I stress that she well may not be able to do this entirely on her own at the present time and that therefore it would be best if she kept coming in to see me, to check her own impressions of what is bothering her and to make sure that she works concertedly against her internalized philosophies that lead her astray.

C-102: Because I know I need this right now. I mean I can feel the need for it. Logically, I know that my hang-up with relating to males is a big stumbling block; and this is something I have to overcome.

T-103: Yes. What I would advise you to do is to see me every week or so for therapy, or every other week or so; and also, if possible, join one of my therapy groups for awhile, where you'll see and relate to others who have similar problems to yours. You may get some insight into some of the things you're doing by watching them and showing them how to solve some of their difficulties. That's another helpful way, because we're often just too close to ourselves. But if we see the same kind of behavior in someone else, we say, "Ah, I do that, too!"

C-104: When do the groups meet? . . .

The client came for one more individual session and several group sessions of therapy, and then felt that she was doing very well and that she could manage things on her own. She returned, over the years, for other sessions from time to time, mainly to discuss the problems of her parents, her husband, her children, or other close associates. She continues to get along remarkably well. She is still in touch with me at intervals, largely to refer her friends and relatives for therapy sessions. She has reality (rather than emotional) problems with her parents; she is happily married and has two lively and seemingly little-disturbed children; she gets along well with her husband, in spite of his personal hang-ups; and she keeps writing successful books and taking great satisfaction in her work. She is hardly free from all disturbances, since she still has a tendency to become overwrought about people treating her unfairly. But she seems almost fully to accept herself, and most of her original problems are solved or managed. She still marvels at, and keeps telling her new acquaintances about, the relatively few sessions of REBT that helped her to look at, understand, and change her basic anxiety-creating and hostility-inciting philosophy of life.

Editors' Introduction

This case illustrates an important behavioral technique, covert sensitization, applied to a serious clinical problem, pedophilia. There is widespread pessimism among clinicians regarding the treatment of pedophilia, and this makes the success of this case all the more remarkable.

We selected the case because it illustrates how behavior therapists have embraced the use of cognitions as therapeutic tools. In addition, the case was written by Dr. David Barlow, arguably the most important figure in contemporary behavior therapy. Dr. Barlow has been an outspoken and eloquent advocate for the use of empirically supported treatments (ESTs).

Careful reading of this case will dispel the myth that behavior therapists are indifferent to relationship variables and the false belief that behavioral methods are applied in a lockstep manner without consideration for personality factors and family dynamics. We quickly see that Dr. Barlow is a sensitive therapist who tailors his treatment to the unique needs of his patient, and the case provides a glimpse of the genuine concern this therapist has for this very troubled patient.

It will be useful for students to think about how practitioners of the other therapeutic approaches represented in Case Studies in Psychotherapy *would have conceptualized the etiology and maintenance of this particular problem, and to speculate about how treatment—and outcome—might have differed. How would you have approached the case? Can a therapist's revulsion about a behavior like pedophilia influence his or her ability to help a client? How can a therapist put aside strong personal feelings in the interest of his or her clients?*

6 | COVERT SENSITIZATION FOR PARAPHILIA

David H. Barlow

CASE BACKGROUND

At the time of presentation, Reverend X was a 51-year-old married minister from the Midwest. He had three grown children, two females and a male, the youngest of whom was his 19-year-old daughter. He was tall and quite serious and although cooperative, did not volunteer a great deal of information at the initial interview. He came to my office after referral by a prominent psychiatrist in another state for assessment and possible treatment of heterosexual pedophilic behavior.

Reverend X reported that he had been touching and caressing girls between the ages of 10 and 16 for more than 20 years. He estimated at this time that there were probably more than 50 girls with whom he had had some interaction. Most typically this interaction was restricted to hugging or caressing their breasts. On occasion, he would also touch their genitals. He did not expose himself to girls nor did he ask them to touch him in any way. Generally, he reported achieving a partial erection during this type of contact but never ejaculated during one of these encounters. He did not report this to be primarily an erotic experience but rather continued to suggest that the emphasis was on an exchange of affection. In fact, during the initial interview he reported feeling little remorse about his activities for this reason, although he was deeply concerned over the effect of being "found out" on his family and his career.

Some 12 years before he presented for treatment, his activities were discovered for the first time and he was forced to leave his church in another state in the Midwest, but the matter was kept relatively quiet and he was able to take up a new position in a different state, a position he retained until just prior to treatment. Although he sought treatment and agreed to refrain from any physical interaction with young girls in his new church, he was soon as active as ever. This behavior continued on until several months before presenting for treatment.

According to Reverend X, in most of the cases the young girls responded positively to his advances and did not seem offended or frightened. In several instances this type of activity would continue with the girl for several months and it was with these girls that genital touching occurred.

During these years, although responsible administratively and spiritually for the entire parish, he took particular interest in activities involving young adolescent girls, such as the local Girl Scout troop. In addition to this activity, Reverend X, who was particularly attracted to the small breasts characteristic of young adolescent girls, would masturbate once or twice a week to pictures of girls with these features, which he found in

From *Covert Conditioning Casebook,* First Edition, by J. R. Cautela, A. J. Kearney, L. Ascher, A. Kearney, M. Kleinman, and 17 others. © 1993. Reprinted with permission of Wadsworth, a division of Thomson Learning.

what he referred to as "nudist magazines." In fact, he subscribed to a rather extensive series of pedophilic pornographic magazines, which, much to the embarrassment of himself and his family, continued to arrive at his old rectory for months after his discovery only to be received by the new occupants.

Several months before presenting for treatment he was confronted by the parents of an 11-year-old Girl Scout who were hearing "strange stories" about physical touching from their daughter and wanted to discuss them. His behavior was presented as a misunderstanding and the incident died down until the parents of another young girl with similar experiences mentioned them to the parents of the first girl. The story spread like wildfire and quickly led to outrage and dismissal from the parish by the bishop and suspension as a minister with strong recommendations to seek treatment.

Reverend X grew up a rather inhibited teenager with few lasting social contacts with girls. When he married at age 26, he engaged in sexual intercourse for the first time. He had begun dating at approximately age 22 and on only one occasion before marriage had he engaged in even light petting. Masturbatory fantasies in high school were centered on developing breasts.

After discovery 12 years ago at his previous parish, he was the client in a number of long-term psychotherapeutic relationships. He reported that none of these had had the slightest effect whatsoever on his sexual arousal patterns. At least one of his previous therapists had taken the approach that there must be something wrong within his marital relationship. This only angered him and was disconfirmed by his wife, who reported a normal and satisfying sexual and marital relationship.

Despite the incident, his relationship with his family remained excellent and his wife was extremely supportive, determined to stick by him through "thick and thin." His children were also quite supportive but seemed to largely dismiss the incidents or deny that they were anything but exaggerations and innuendos. He had never approached any of his children sexually.

ASSESSMENT AND BEHAVIOR ANALYSIS

The most striking aspect of the presentation of Reverend X alluded to previously and also mentioned by his referring psychiatrist was the absence of any remorse. Reverend X himself also commented on his relative absence of remorse and seemed puzzled by it since he had at least an intellectual appreciation of the seriousness of his acts. It became clear that before attempting formal intervention with covert sensitization it would be necessary to deal with his motivation to change, which would be likely to affect his compliance with covert sensitization procedures. Thus it became necessary to strip away some of the rationalizations that were interfering with his motivation for treatment.

The primary rationalization commonly found in pedophiles is the notion that they are somehow providing love and affection to children that is beneficial to them and that this affection may be restricted or absent from other sources. Indeed, this rationalization was clearly present in Reverend X, who considered his behavior to be primarily affectionate despite the occasional genital contact and masturbatory activity to "nudist magazines." The client was instructed to make a list of various specific rationalizations. He began working on these rationalizations at home. He was also asked to contemplate how his contacts were received by the girls and whether or not he was oblivious to any negative cues. It became apparent that he had established a strong "boundary" between "proper and improper" pedophilic behavior. For example, intercourse with a child or coercion was as repugnant to him as it would be to the average person. But fondling breasts and genitals was affectionate. Evidence for rationalization was present in the following reports or observations: (1) he reported that most children were very responsive to his advances; (2) his description of many of his episodes was objectified by his use of third person speech; (3) he was very indignant over the angry manner with which most of his congregation responded to him after discovery, thinking they were somehow ungrateful for all of his years of service to the parish (this included his bishop, whom he accused of not providing appropriate support); and (4) he had established boundaries between "good and bad" pedophilic behavior, as mentioned earlier.

In an attempt to break down some of these barriers, two scenarios were presented to him for consideration. First, he was asked how he would react if he discovered that one of his daughters had been fondled or molested by a strange adult male. Initially he digressed into problems of hypothetical questions but then replied that he had never considered that possibility and had probably blocked it out. In fact, in the remainder of the session he refused to consider the topic despite subsequent attempts to introduce it. In regard to the reaction of his parishioners, he was asked what his reaction would be if it was discovered that his bishop had been raping women in the back alleys of the city for several years on Saturday night. He was able to admit that his behavior was at least as repugnant as the hypothetical behavior of his bishop and that it would seem quite shocking indeed.

Thinking about these issues in and between the first several sessions sensitized Reverend X to several facets of his problem, and he was able to recognize, at least at a rational level, the horror that his behavior evoked in others and by inference, the repugnant nature of the behavior itself. Nevertheless, he was now requested in sessions to imagine that his daughter was being molested and to picture it as vividly as possible. He was instructed to feel it emotionally and then report his reactions. Second, he was asked to imagine a similar situation in which he was engaging in genital contact with his most recent victim with all of the parishioners watching.

During this time he was also given materials to read on the consequences of sexual abuse of children. In fact, he reported that he had been familiar with some of these materials before but had read them in a more abstract intellectual manner. During the next several weeks he reported that his masturbatory fantasies began to incorporate images of nameless, faceless people watching him and that his fantasies became a bit fuzzy, much like static on a television set.

By approximately the fourth session the patient clearly began to experience some of the horror and aversiveness of his behavior and actually demonstrated some negative affect and a few tears. This was a marked change from previous sessions characterized by little or no affect of any kind while discussing his behavior. Masturbation of any kind stopped. At this point steps preliminary to implementing covert sensitization were begun.

Detailed descriptions of his behavior and preliminary explorations of the most aversive consequences he could imagine allowed a behavior analysis prior to implementing formal covert sensitization. Self-monitoring revealed infrequent pedophilic fantasies at this time. The decreased frequency of his fantasies most likely related to the punishing effect of his recent discovery. Nevertheless, his pattern of pedophilic behavior was fairly consistent. Typically he would playfully approach a young girl who happened to be alone in a room at the church recreation center or perhaps in his car if he were driving her somewhere. He would then put his arms on her or around her and gradually move his hands to the breast area or, on occasion, the genital area. He would be very careful to ascertain if the girl would be likely to be responsive beforehand and if she remained responsive during the encounter. If there was any sign of resisting or lack of responsiveness he would quickly desist or revert to a wrestling or playing type of activity that did not involve breast or genital contact. On rare occasions the same behavior might occur during the summer while swimming in a nearby lake.

In addition to these rather restricted behavioral patterns, the client would experience a number of urges upon seeing young girls in various locations. These urges would range from a full-blown sexual thought sequence while watching a young girl to what he would call a "glimpse." During a glimpse he would not be aware of any frank sexual thoughts but would notice himself glancing at a young girl who was not directly in his line of sight and therefore represented someone who probably would not attract his attention if she were not the appropriate age and sex.

Since no behavior was occurring at this time and since fantasies (sexual thoughts in the absence of young girls) were also absent, self-monitoring was restricted to "urges" such as those described above. This "urge" once again was defined as a sexual thought, image, or impulse upon seeing a young adolescent girl. The client recorded all sexual urges on a self-monitoring record that he carried with him at all times. The record was divided into daily segments in which the patient could total the number of occurrences of full-blown urges or "glimpses" each day. The patient was instructed to record these urges or glimpses as soon as possible after their occurrence. Physiological assessment of sexual arousal patterns was also conducted using penile strain gauge measures. This assessment revealed continued marked responsiveness to pedophilic stimuli.

One further assessment procedure necessary before beginning covert sensitization is a determination of the worst possible consequences of the behavior in the patient's own mind. Reverend X reported, consistent with his reaction during the first several sessions of treatment, that being observed engaging in this behavior provoked a particularly strong negative emotional reaction in him. He also displayed some sensitivity to images of nausea and vomiting, which comprise a common set of aversive scenes in covert sensitization. In cases where nausea and vomiting are not particularly aversive, scenes of blood and injury or scenes of snakes or spiders crawling on one's skin can be very effective. With this information the patient was ready to begin covert sensitization trials.

TREATMENT PROGRAM

Prior to my initiating covert sensitization, I presented Reverend X with the following therapeutic rationale:

> We will now initiate a procedure with the purpose of directly reducing remaining arousal to young girls using a technique called covert sensitization. This procedure involves having you imagine sexual scenes with young girls similar to those interactions you have actually experienced or masturbate to, and to pair an aversive image with that scene. This procedure has been successfully employed with individuals with similar problems in the past and we have every reason to believe that it will be very helpful in your case.
>
> The purpose of covert sensitization is to neutralize what has become a very automatic uncontrollable sexual arousal to young girls. This will be accomplished by repeatedly imagining a very unpleasant scene in association with your typically sexually arousing scenes. It is very important that you imagine, as vividly as possible, all of the scenes that I present. In addition, this procedure is very useful because you will be learning a skill that you can apply to situations where in the past you would have become aroused. That is, if you find yourself becoming aroused by young girls you can utilize your aversive images in a self-control fashion and very quickly eliminate the arousal. Since this is basically a skill that you are learning, it is also very important that you do a fair amount of homework between sessions.
>
> Initially, I will be presenting vivid descriptions of sexually arousing scenes based on everything we have talked about thus far. I want you to make yourself comfortable, close your eyes, and imagine the scene as if you are actually there. It is very

important that you "live" the scene. You should feel, hear, and sense every part of the image. You should not see yourself in the scene but should actually be there. We will also develop some aversive scenes along the lines we have already discussed to be associated with the arousing scenes.

As noted, Reverend X had identified being caught in the act and observed by his family and close friends as perhaps the most aversive naturally occurring event he could think of. In addition, some preliminary exploration revealed a sensitivity to nausea and vomiting. Therefore, these two aversive scenes were used throughout covert sensitization trials.

> Sit back in the chair and get as relaxed as possible. Close your eyes and concentrate on what I'm saying. Imagine yourself in the recreation room of the church. Notice the furniture . . . the walls . . . and the feelings of being in the room. Standing to one side is Joan, a 13-year-old girl. As she comes toward you, you notice the color of her hair . . . the clothes she is wearing . . . and the way she is walking. She comes over and sits by you. She is being flirtatious and very cute. You touch her playfully and begin to get aroused. She is asking you questions about sex education and you begin to touch her. You can feel your hands on her smooth skin . . . on her dress . . . and on her breasts under her shirt.

> As you become more and more aroused, you begin taking off her clothes. You can feel your fingers on her dress as you slip it off. You begin touching arms . . . her back and her breasts . . . Now your hands are on her thighs and her buttocks. As you get more excited, you put your hand between her legs. She begins rubbing your penis. You're noticing how good it feels. You are stroking her thighs and genitals and getting very aroused.

> You hear a scream! As you turn around you see your two daughters and your wife. They see you there—naked and molesting that little girl. They begin to cry. They are sobbing hysterically. Your wife falls to her knees and holds her head in her hands. She is saying "I hate you, I hate you!" You start to go over to hold her, but she is afraid of you and runs away. You start to panic and lose control. You want to kill yourself and end it all. You can see what you have done to yourself.

The aversive scenes were presented in great detail in order to elicit arousal and to facilitate the imagery process. Initially, they were presented late in the chain of behavior. As treatment progressed, the aversive scenes were introduced earlier in the arousing sequence.

In addition to these scenes where Reverend X was caught by his family, other images involving nausea and vomiting were used. In these images as he would begin genital contact with young girls he would feel himself becoming more and more nauseous . . . feel the vomit working its way up into his throat and begin swallowing hard to attempt to keep it down. At that point he would start gagging uncontrollably until vomit and mucus began spilling out of his mouth and nose all over his clothes and the clothes of the young girl. In this particular case I embellished the scene by having him continue to vomit all over the lap of the young girl until the girl's flesh would actually begin to rot before his eyes and worms and maggots would begin crawling around in it. These embellishments are not effective with everyone but were very effective with Reverend X. During the scenes he would become visibly tense, rise in his chair, and be quite drained by the end of the session. During vomiting scenes patients on occasion will bring in a fresh shirt for fear that they might actually vomit during the sessions. This illustrates once again that there is no limit to the vividness of the scenes, and some dramatic presentations on the part of the therapist, at least initially, can be very helpful if the patient is able to process them in such a way that they are effective.

In the example presented earlier, the patient progressed rather far in the chain of sexual behaviors before the aversive scene was introduced. In general, as treatment progresses, the aversive scenes are introduced earlier in the arousing sequence. In this fashion, aversive scenes are paired with the very early parts of the chain, often the first glimpse, by the end of treatment. It is this early pairing that is rehearsed in a self-control fashion.

In this particular case these scenes were presented in two different formats. In the first format, referred to as "punishment," the sexually arousing scene was presented and resulted in the aversive scenes mentioned earlier. In the second format, described as "escape," the patient would begin the sexually arousing scene, contemplate briefly the aversive consequences, and then turn and flee the situation as quickly as possible, feeling greatly relieved and relaxed as he got farther away from the situation.

For Reverend X a typical session involved presenting five of the scenes, either three punishment and two escape or vice versa. The location of the scenes would be varied to conform to the typical locations that were relevant for this particular patient. The two aversive scenes would also be alternated in a random fashion or sometimes integrated or combined.

When it was clear that the patient could imagine these images vividly and was fully processing the information, he was asked to go through the trial himself in the presence of the therapist. Methods for overcoming difficulties in achieving clear images were discussed and practiced. The self-administered practices within sessions were interspersed with therapist-conducted trials. After several sessions, when it was clear that the patient could self-administer the procedure as effectively as the therapist, homework assignments were prescribed. The patient monitored the intensity of his self-administered sessions on a scale of 0 to 100, where 0 equaled no intensity whatsoever and 100 represented an intensity as vivid as real life. Initially, his practice sessions were rated in the 10% to 50% range. As time went on the practice sessions were more consistently rated in the 50% to 70% range, which was judged to be sufficiently intense to produce the desired effects. Initially sessions were prescribed once a day in which he would be asked to conduct three trials (imagine three scenes). After several weeks this was cut back to two practices a week to maximize the intensity. Scenes were varied slightly by the patient to prevent habituation.

During this time self-monitoring revealed occasional urges and glimpses but still no fantasies or masturbatory activity. In fact, the patient had cut back on masturbatory activity shortly after his apprehension and ceased altogether just before treatment began, as noted earlier. Nevertheless, occasional interviews with his wife, who remained extremely supportive, revealed some increase in sexual activity in their relationship, averaging two to three times per week. This relationship was described by both as improved and entirely satisfactory.

At this time the final phase of covert sensitization was introduced. In this phase the patient used the aversive images in vivo in a self-control fashion whenever an urge or even a glimpse occurred. This information was also noted on self-monitoring forms such that any urge or glimpse would be immediately consequated by an aversive image. While he found this somewhat difficult at first, Reverend X reported increasing facility in carrying out his part of the treatment and noted a gradually decreasing number of urges and glimpses.

RESULTS

Rather early in the course of treatment a reaction to Reverend X's behavior on the part of his community threatened to disrupt progress. Although he had moved out of the rectory and away from the church, some of his family remained in his hometown. On occasion he would return to town from his temporary residence, which was convenient to my office, to assist with some practical matters concerning an upcoming move that he and his wife were planning. He would also see a few old friends. During this period a very ugly reaction to his earlier apprehension occurred in the community. Rumors circulated describing very exaggerated accounts of his behavior as well as the fact that he was living in another state simply to wait out the statute of limitations and avoid criminal charges. It was also rumored that he had stopped seeking treatment and had a cavalier attitude toward his problem. This community reaction, which also affected his family, had a serious impact on therapy. A brief but deep state of depression retarded progress and forced a temporary cessation of covert sensitization sessions while the implications of the community reaction were discussed. In fact, Reverend X was deeply distressed by the incident, not only because of the vicious allegations, but also because it became clear that he still harbored some illusions that the community, which had showed deep support and respect for him during his years of service, would somehow welcome him back with open arms once his treatment was completed. Only when he fully appreciated that this was not going to happen and began to make realistic plans about permanently relocating was he able to continue on with therapy.

Four months after treatment began, pedophilic urges had dropped to zero and remained there. At this time Reverend X and his wife permanently relocated to another state, where he obtained work in a local hardware store. He would continue to commute approximately five hours each way for remaining treatment sessions such that he would have one long session every two weeks. Six months after treatment began, a full assessment revealed an excellent response. Treatment was terminated with plans for the first follow-up session to occur one month later and then at decreasing intervals after that as indicated.

Periodic follow-ups were conducted during the ensuing 18 months. A full evaluation at that time, including penile plethysmography, revealed no return of pedophilic arousal patterns. This pattern of results was supported by lengthy interviews with Reverend X as well as independent and separate interviews with his wife. Both individuals reported a satisfactory adaptation to their new location, where Reverend X had worked steadily and productively for the same employer and had been asked to take on additional supervisory responsibilities. The marital relationship, if anything, had continued to improve during the past year. He had begun to engage in extensive volunteer activity in his community.

DISCUSSION

Covert sensitization has proven very effective for paraphilic patterns of arousal, as noted earlier. Nevertheless, there were several aspects of this case that undoubtedly facilitated treatment. Reverend X received deep and sustaining support from his family not only during the initial crisis but also throughout treatment. This support extended to at least some of his old friends in his community who were aware of his problem and, increasingly, friends that he met in his new community, who, of course, were not aware of his problem. In view of the stigma so often attached to sexual offenders and the outright desertion by even close family and friends that often occurs, this support was undoubtedly very valuable to Reverend X.

In addition, throughout this period he maintained his deeply religious attitude and convictions. He attended service regularly and continued to express a desire to resume the provision of some service to the church, even if not on a full-time basis. Nevertheless, despite several inquiries to the church hierarchy, he received no response to his request and began to give up hope of resuming any vestiges of a career that had been at the very center of his existence and had provided deep meaning to his life for some 25 years.

More than two years following this contact and nearly four years after beginning treatment, another follow-up visit confirmed no return of pedophilic arousal patterns whatsoever. Reverend X continued to do extremely well in his new job and was now second-in-command of a small chain of hardware stores. He continued to be active in his community. The church continued to ignore his occasional letters asking for clarification of his status, and he had given up all hope of any return to even part-time duties. Nevertheless, he still hoped against hope that some day the church that he had served for so long might at least lift the suspension and allow him to occasionally conduct religious services for his immediate family. Beyond that his thoughts centered on his day-to-day life in his new community and the distant plan of retirement with his wife somewhere in the South in another 10 or 15 years.

Editors' Introduction

Aaron Beck, the leading figure in cognitive therapy, is an authority on suicide and depression. In the case that follows, the reader has an opportunity to see how Beck works with a depressed professional woman.

The cognitive approach to therapy is precise, straightforward, and methodological. Beck lays out a sort of road map for therapy in the introduction to the case and then illustrates how the actual therapy sessions link to the therapy plan. Like Ellis, he challenges his patient's irrational beliefs, but he does so in a more probing, Socratic manner consistent with the philosophy of collaborative empiricism that is the foundation of cognitive therapy. This case is especially interesting because the depressed individual being treated is a clinical psychologist.

We believe this case nicely illustrates the sometimes subtle differences between cognitive therapy and two related approaches to therapy: rational emotive behavior therapy and cognitive behavior therapy. Once again, the student is given an opportunity to observe a master therapist at work, listening to the actual language used in the therapy sessions. Dr. Beck has earned the admiration and respect of almost everyone in the world of psychotherapy, and he is the individual most responsible for the tremendous interest in cognitive therapy currently found with almost all practicing psychotherapists.

Almost every therapist and counselor will at some point treat suicidal clients, and most experienced therapists have lost patients to suicide. What feelings do you experience reading about this woman's suicidal ideation? How do you evaluate lethality in patients with suicidal thoughts? Will you feel comfortable working with deeply depressed individuals?

7 | AN INTERVIEW WITH A DEPRESSED AND SUICIDAL PATIENT

Aaron T. Beck

Perhaps the most critical challenge to the adequacy of cognitive therapy is its efficacy in dealing with the acutely suicidal patient. In such cases the therapist often has to shift gears and assume a very active role in attempting to penetrate the barrier of hopelessness and resignation. Since intervention may be decisive in saving the patient's life, the therapist has to attempt to accomplish a number of immediate goals either concurrently or in rapid sequence: establish a working relationship with the patient, assess the severity of the depression and suicidal wish, obtain an overview of the patient's life situation, pinpoint the patient's "reasons" for wanting to commit suicide, determine the patient's capacity for self-objectivity, and ferret out some entry point for stepping into the patient's phenomenological world to introduce elements of reality.

Such a venture, as illustrated in the following interview, is taxing and demands all the qualities of a "good therapist"—genuine warmth, acceptance, and empathetic understanding—as well as the application of the appropriate strategies drawn from the system of cognitive therapy.

The patient was a 40-year-old clinical psychologist who had recently been left by her boyfriend. She had a history of intermittent depressions since the age of 12 years, [and] had received many courses of psychotherapy, antidepressant drugs, electroconvulsive therapy, and hospitalizations. The patient had been seen by the author five times over a period of 7 or 8 months. At the time of this interview, it was obvious that she was depressed and, as indicated by her previous episodes, probably suicidal.

In the first part of the interview, the main thrust was to *ask appropriate questions* in order to make a clinical assessment and also to try to elucidate the major psychological problems. The therapist, first of all, had to make an assessment as to how depressed and how suicidal the patient was. He also had to assess her expectations regarding being helped by the interview (T-1; T-8) in order to determine how much leverage he had. During this period of time, in order to keep the dialogue going, he also had to repeat the patient's statements.

It was apparent from the emergence of suicidal wishes that this was the salient clinical problem and that her hopelessness (T-7) would be the most appropriate point for intervention.

Several points could be made regarding the first part of the interview. The therapist accepted the seriousness of the patient's desire to die but treated it as a topic for further examination, a problem to be discussed. "We can discuss the advantages and disadvantages" (T-11). She responded to this statement with some amusement (a favorable sign). The therapist also tried to test the patient's ability to look at herself and her problems

Excerpt from Aaron T. Beck et al., *Cognitive Therapy of Depression* (pp. 225–243). Published in 1979 by Guilford Publications, Inc. Reprinted by permission of the publisher.

with objectivity. He also attempted to test the rigidity of her irrational ideas and her acceptance of his wish to help her (T-13–T-20).

In the first part of the interview the therapist was not able to make much headway because of the patient's strongly held belief that things could not possibly work out well for her. She had decided that suicide was the only solution, and she resented attempts to "get her to change her mind."

In the next part of the interview, the therapist attempted to isolate the participating factor in her present depression and suicidal ideation, namely, the breakup with her boyfriend. It becomes clear as the therapist tries to explore the significance of the breakup that the meaning to the patient is, "I have nothing" (P-23). The therapist then selects, "*I have nothing*" as a target and attempts to elicit from the patient information contradictory to this conclusion. He probes for a previous period of time when she did *not* believe "I have nothing" and also was not having a relationship with a man. He then proceeds (T-26) to probe for other goals and objects that are important to her; he seeks concrete sources of satisfaction (T-24–T-33). The therapist's attempt to establish that the patient does, indeed, "have something" is parried by the patient's tendency to discount any positive features in her life (P-32).

Finally, the patient does join forces with the therapist, and it is apparent in the latter part of the interview that she is willing to separate herself from her problems and consider ways of solving them. The therapist then moves to a consideration of the basic assumption underlying her hopelessness, namely, "I cannot be happy without a man." By pointing out disconfirming past experiences, he tries to demonstrate the error of this assumption. He also attempts to explain the value of shifting to the assumption, "I can make myself happy." He points out that it is more realistic for her to regard herself as the active agent in seeking out sources of satisfaction than as an inert receptacle dependent for nourishment on the whims of others.

The taped interview, which was edited down from 60 minutes to 35 minutes for practical reasons, is presented verbatim. (The only changes made were to protect the identity of the patient.) The interview is divided into five parts.

PART 1
QUESTIONING TO ELICIT VITAL INFORMATION

1. How depressed is the patient? How suicidal?
2. Attitude about coming to appointment (expectancy about therapy).
3. Emergence of suicidal wishes: immediate critical problem.
4. Attempt to find the best point for therapeutic intervention: hopelessness—negative attitude toward future (P-7).
5. Accept seriousness of patient's desire to die but treat it as a topic for further examination—"Discuss advantages and disadvantages" (T-11).
6. Test ability to look at herself—objectivity; test rigidity of her irrational ideas; test responsiveness to therapist (T-13–T-20).

PART 2
BROADENING PATIENT'S PERSPECTIVE

1. Isolate the precipitating factor—breakup with boyfriend; reduce use of questioning.
2. Determine meaning to patient of the breakup.
3. Immediate psychological problem: "I have nothing."

4. Question the conclusion, "I have nothing."

5. Probe for other objects that are important to her: concrete sources of satisfaction (T-24–T-33).

6. Shore up reality-testing and positive self-concept (T-35–T-37).

PART 3
"ALTERNATIVE THERAPY"

1. Therapist very active in order to engage patient's interest in understanding and dealing with her problem. Induce patient to examine options (T-38). "Eliminate" suicide as an option.

2. Undermine patient's all-or-nothing thinking by getting her to regard herself, her future, and her experiences in quantitative probabilities (T-45).

3. Feedback: important information as to success of interview. Look for (a) affect shift, (b) positive statements about herself, (c) consensus with patient regarding solution of problem (P-47).

PART 4
OBTAINING MORE ACCURATE DATA

1. More therapeutic collaboration: discussion about therapeutic techniques and rationale.

2. Testing her conclusions about "no satisfaction," indirectly disproving her conclusion.

3. Patient's spontaneous statement, "Can I tell you something positive?"

4. Periodic attempts to evoke a mirth response.

PART 5
CLOSURE

Reinforce independence (T-106), self-help, optimism.

Therapist (T-1): Well, how have you been feeling since I talked to you last? . . .
Patient (P-1): Bad.
T-2: You've been feeling bad . . . well, tell me about it?
P-2: It started this weekend . . . I just feel like everything is an effort. There's just completely no point to do anything.
T-3: So, there are two problems; everything is an effort, and you believe there's no point to doing anything.
P-3: It's because there's no point to doing anything that makes everything too hard to do.
T-4: (*Repeating her words to maintain interchange. Also to acknowledge her feelings.*) Because there's no point and everything feels like an effort . . . And when you were coming down here today, were you feeling the same way?
P-4: Well, it doesn't seem as bad when I am working. It's bad on weekends and especially on holidays. I sort of expected that it would happen.
T-5: (*Eliciting expectancy regarding session*) You expected to have a hard time on holidays . . . And when you left your office to come over here, how were you feeling then?

P-5:   Kind of the same way. I feel that I can do everything that I have to do, but I don't *want* to.

T-6:   You don't want to do the things you have to.

P-6:   I don't want to do anything.

T-7:   Right . . . and what kind of feeling did you have? Feel low?

P-7:   (*Hopelessness to be target*) I feel that there's no hope for me. I feel my future . . . that everything is futile, that there's no hope.

T-8:   And what idea did you have about today's interview?

P-8:   I thought that it would probably help as it has always happened in the past . . . that I would feel better—temporarily. But that makes it worse because then I know that I am going to feel bad again.

T-9:   That makes it worse in terms of how you feel?

P-9:   Yes.

T-10:   And the reason is that it builds you up and then you get let down again?

P-10:   (*Immediate problem—suicide risk*) I feel like it's interminable, it will just go this way forever, and I am not getting any better . . . I don't feel any less inclined to kill myself than I ever did in my life . . . In fact, if anything, *I feel like I'm coming closer to it.*

T-11:   Perhaps we should talk about that a little bit because we haven't talked about the advantages and disadvantages of killing yourself.

P-11:   (*Smiles*) You make everything so logical.

T-12:   (*Testing therapeutic alliance*) Is that bad? Remember you once wrote something . . . that reason is your greatest ally. Have you become allergic to reason?

P-12:   But I can't try anymore.

T-13:   Does it take an effort to be reasonable?

P-13:   (*Typical "automatic thoughts"*) I know I am being unreasonable; the thoughts seem so real to me . . . it does take an effort to try to change them.

T-14:   Now, if it came easy to you—to change the thoughts, do you think that they would last as long?

P-14:   No . . . see, I don't say that this wouldn't work with other people. I don't try to say that, but I don't feel that it can work with me.

T-15:   So, do you have any evidence that it did work with you?

P-15:   It works for specific periods of time, and that's like the Real Me comes through.

T-16:   Now, is there anything unusual that happened that might have upset the apple cart?

P-16:   You mean this weekend?

T-17:   Not necessarily this weekend. As you know, you felt you were making good progress in therapy and you decided that you were going to be like the Cowardly Lion Who Found His Heart. What happened after that?

P-17:   (*Agitated, bows head*) It's too hard . . . it would be easier to die.

T-18:   (*Attempts to restore objectivity. Injects perspective by recalling previous mastery experience.*) At the moment, it would be easier to die—as you say. But, let's go back to the history. You're losing sight and losing perspective. Remember when we talked and made a tape of that interview and you liked it. You wrote a letter the next day and you said that you felt you had your Heart and it wasn't any great effort to reach that particular point. Now, you went along reasonably well until you got involved. Correct? Then you got involved with Jim. Is that correct? And then very predictably when your relationship ended, you felt terribly let down. Now, what do you conclude from that?

P-18:   (*Anguish, rejects therapist's venture*) My conclusion is that I am always going to have to be alone because I can't stay in a relationship with a man.

T-19:   All right, that's one possible explanation, What other possible explanations are there?

P-19:   That's the only explanation.

T-20:   Is it possible you just weren't *ready* to get deeply involved and then let down?

P-20A: But, I feel like I'll never be ready. (*Weeps*)

P-20B: I have never given up on him, even when I couldn't see him for a year at a time. He was always in my mind, all the time. So how can I think now that I can just dismiss him.

T-21:   This was never final until now. There was always the hope that . . .

P-21:   There wasn't, and he told me very clearly that he could not get involved with me.

T-22:   Right, but before January, it was very quiescent. You weren't terribly involved with him. It started up in January again. He did show serious interest in you.

P-22:   For the first time in four years.

T-23:   (*Attempts to restore perspective*) All right, so that's when you got involved again. Prior to January, you weren't involved, weren't thinking of him every minute and you weren't in the situation you are in now, and you were happy at times. You wrote that letter to me that you were happy, right? Okay. So that was back in January, you were happy and you did not have Jim. Now comes May, and you're unhappy because you have just broken up with him. Now, why do you still have to be unhappy, say, in July, August, or September?

P-23:   (*Presents specific target belief*) I have nothing.

T-24:   You weren't unhappy in January, were you?

P-24:   At first I was, that's why I called.

T-25:   All right, how about December? December you weren't unhappy. What did you have in December? You had something that made you happy.

P-25:   I was seeing other men. That made me happy.

T-26:   There are other things in your life besides men that you said you liked very much.

P-26:   Yes and I . . .

T-27:   (*Aims at target beliefs. Shows she had and has something.*) Well, there were other things you say were important that are not important right now. Is that correct? What were the things that were important to you back in December, November, and October?

P-27:   Everything was important.

T-28:   Everything was important. And what were those things?

P-28:   It's hard to even think of anything that I cared about.

T-29:   Okay, now how about your job?

P-29:   My job.

T-30:   Your job was important. Did you feel that you were accomplishing something on the job?

P-30:   Most of the time I did.

T-31:   (*Still aiming*) Most of the time, you felt you were accomplishing something on the job. And what about now? Do you feel you are accomplishing on the *job now?*

P-31:   (*Discounts positive*) Not as much as I could.

T-32:   (*Reintroduces positive*) You're not accomplishing as much as you could but even when you are "off," I understand that you do as well [as] or better than many of the other workers. Is that not correct?

P-32:   (*Disqualifies positive statement*) I can't understand why you say that. How do you know that? Because I told you that. How do you know that's true?

T-33:   I'm willing to take your word for it.

P-33:   From somebody who is irrational.

T-34:   (*Presents positive evidence of satisfactions and achievements.*) Well, I think that somebody who is as irrationally down on herself as you, is very unlikely to say something positive *about herself* unless the positive thing is so strong that it is unmistakable to anybody . . . In any event, you do get some satisfaction out of the job right now and you do feel you are doing a reasonably good job, although you are not doing as well as you would like to, but as well as you are capable. You're still doing a reasonably good job. You can see for yourself. Your clients' plans are improving? Are they being helped? Does anyone say they are appreciative of your efforts?

P-34:   Yes.

T-35:   They do tell you? Yet you are saying you are so irrational that I can't believe anything you say. Do you say, "You're just a dumb client . . . no judgment at all," to your clients?

P-35:   I wouldn't say that about somebody.

T-36:   Well, do you think it about yourself?

P-36:   Yes.

T-37:   (*Points out inconsistency. Underscores her capacity for rationality. Fortifies her professional role.*) So, you trust the word of your clients, but you won't trust your own word. You won't think of your clients as being irrational, and yet, you think of you—when you are the client—as being irrational. How can you be rational when you are the therapist and irrational when you are the patient?

P-37A: I set different standards for myself than what I set for anybody else in the world.

P-37B: Suppose I'll never get over it?

T-38:   (*Changes the options—consider nonsuicidal solutions. Sweat it out or fight to solve problem.*) Suppose you'll never get over it? Well, we don't know whether you'll never get over it or not . . . so there're two things you can do. One is, you can take it passively and see, and you might find that you will get over it, since almost everybody gets over grief reactions. Or, you can attack the problem aggressively and actively build up a solid basis for yourself. In other words, you can capitalize on the chance . . .

P-38:   (*Thinks of finding another man.*) I feel desperate. I feel that I have to find somebody right now—right away.

T-39:   All right, now if you found somebody right away, what would happen?

P-39:   The same thing would happen again.

T-40:   (*Omits suicide as one of the options.*) Now, remember when we talked about Jim and you said back in January you decided that you would take that chance and you'd chance being involved, with the possibility that something would come of it positively. Now, you have two choices at this time. You can either stick it out now and try to weather the storm with the idea that you are going to keep fighting it, or you can get involved with somebody else and not have the opportunity for this elegant solution. Now, which way do you want to go?

P-40:   (*Compulsion to get involved with somebody.*) I don't want to, but I feel driven. I don't know why I keep fighting that, but I do. I'm not involved with anybody now and I don't want to be, but I feel a compulsion.

T-41:   That's right, because you're hurting very badly. Isn't that correct? If you weren't hurting you wouldn't feel the compulsion.

P-41:   But I haven't done anything yet.

T-42:   (*Emphasizes ideal option. Also turning disadvantage into advantage.*) Well, you know it's your decision. If you do seek somebody else, nobody is going to fault you on it. But I'm trying to show that there's an opportunity here. There's an unusual opportunity that you may never have again—that is to go it alone . . . to work your way out of the depression.

P-42:   That's what I'll be doing the rest of my life . . . that's what worries me.

T-43:   You really just put yourself in a "no-win" situation. You just acknowledged that if you get involved with another man, probably you would feel better.

P-43:   Temporarily, but then, I'd go through the same thing.

T-44:   I understand that. So now, you have an opportunity to not have to be dependent on another guy, but you have to pay a price. There's pain now for gain later. Now are you willing to pay the price?

P-44:   I'm afraid that if I don't involve myself with somebody right away . . . I know that's dichotomous thinking . . . I think if I don't get immediately involved, that I will never have anybody.

T-45:   That's all-or-nothing thinking.

P-45:   I know.

T-46:   (*Seeking a consensus on nonsuicidal option.*) That's all-or-nothing thinking. Now, if you are going to do it on the basis of all-or-nothing thinking, that's not very sensible. if you are going to do it on the basis of, "The pain is so great that I just don't want to stick it out anymore," all right. Then you take your aspirin temporarily and you'll just have to work it out at a later date. The thing is—do you want to stick it out right now? Now, what's the point of sticking it out now?

P-46:   I don't know.

T-47:   *You* don't really believe this.

P-47:   (*Reaching a consensus.*) Theoretically, I know I could prove to myself that I could, in fact, be happy without a man, so that if I were to have a relationship with a man in the future, I would go into it not feeling desperate, and I would probably eliminate a lot of anxiety and depression that have in the past been connected to this relationship.

T-48:   So, at least you agree, theoretically, on a logical basis this could happen. If you try to stick it out . . . Now, what do you think is the probability that this could happen?

P-48:   For me?

T-49:   For you.

P-49:   For another person I'd say the probability is excellent.

T-50:   For one of your clients?

P-50:   Yeah.

T-51:   For the average depressed person that comes to the Mood Clinic . . . most of whom have been depressed 7 years or more. You would still give them a high probability.

P-51:   Listen, I've been depressed all of my life. I thought of killing myself when I was 14 years old.

T-52:   (*Undermining absolutistic thinking by suggesting probabilities.*) Well, many of the other people that have come here too have felt this way. Some of the people that have come here are quite young and so have not had time to be depressed very long . . . Okay, back to this. Hypothetically, this could happen. This could happen with almost anybody else, this could happen with anybody else. But you don't think it can happen to you. Right . . . It can't happen to you. But what is the possibility . . . (you know, when we talked about the possibility with Jim, we thought it was probably five in a hundred that a good thing could come from it) . . . that you could weather the storm and come out a stronger person and be less dependent on men than you had been before?

P-52:   I'd say that the possibility was minimal.

T-53:   All right, now is it minimal like one in a hundred, one in a million . . . ?

P-53:   Well, maybe a 10% chance.

T-54:   10% chance. So, you have one chance in ten of emerging from this stronger.

P-54:   (*More perspective; disqualifies evidence.*) Do you know why I say that . . . I say that on the basis of having gone through that whole summer without a man and being happy . . . and then getting to the point where I am now. That's not progress.

T-55:   (*Using database.*) I'd say that is evidence. That summer is very powerful evidence.

P-55: (*Discredits data.*) Well, look where I am right now.

T-56: The thing is, you did very well that summer and proved as far as any scientist is concerned that you could function on your own. But you didn't prove it to your own self. You wiped out that experience as soon as you got involved with a man. That experience of independence became a nullity in your mind after that summer.

P-56: (*Mood shift. A good sign.*) Is that what happened?

T-57: Of course. When I talked to you the first time I saw you, you said "I cannot be happy without a man." We went over that for about 35 or 40 minutes until I finally said, "Has there ever been a time when you didn't have a man?" And you said, "My God, that time when I went to graduate school." You know, suddenly a beam of light comes in. You almost sold me on the idea that you couldn't function without a man. But that's *evidence.* I mean, if I told you I couldn't walk across the room, and you were able to demonstrate to me that I could walk across the room, would you buy my notion that I could not walk across the room? You know, there is an objective reality here. I'm not giving you information that isn't valid. There are people . . .

P-57: I would say, how could you negate that if it didn't happen?

T-58: What?

P-58: (*Asks for explanation. A good sign.*) I'd say what's wrong with my mind, having once happened, how can I negate it?

T-59: (*Alliance with patient's rationality.*) Because it's human nature, unfortunately, to negate experiences that are not consistent with the prevailing attitude. And that is what attitude therapy is all about. You have a very strong attitude, and anything that is inconsistent with that attitude stirs up cognitive dissonance. I'm sure you have heard of that, and people don't like to have cognitive dissonance. So, they throw out anything that's not consistent with their prevailing belief.

P-59: (*Consensus gels.*) I understand that.

T-60: (*Optimistic sally.*) You have a prevailing belief. It just happens, fortunately, that that prevailing belief is wrong. Isn't that marvelous? To have a prevailing belief that makes you unhappy, and it happens to be wrong! But it's going to take a lot of effort and demonstration to indicate to you, to convince you that it is wrong. And why is that?

P-60: I don't know.

T-61: (*Since patient is now collaborating, he shifts to didactic strategy. Purpose is to strengthen patient's rationality.*) Do you want to know now why? Because you've always had it. Why? First of all, this belief came on at a very early age. We're not going into your childhood, but obviously, you made a suicide attempt or thought about it when you were young. It's a belief that was in there at a very young age. It was very deeply implanted at a very young age, because you were so vulnerable then. And it's been repeated how many times since then in your own head?

P-61: A million times.

T-62: A million times. So do you expect that five hours of talking with me is going to reverse in itself something that has been going a million times in the past?

P-62: Like I said, and you agreed, my reason was my ally. Doesn't my intelligence enter into it? Why can't I make my intelligence help?

T-63: Yeah, that's the reason intelligence comes into it, but that's exactly what I'm trying to get you to do. To use your intelligence.

P-63: There's nothing wrong with my intelligence. I know that.

T-64: I understand that. Intelligence is fine, but intelligence has to have tools, just as you may have the physical strength to lift up a chair, but if you don't believe at the time that you have the strength to do it, you're not going to try. You're going to say, "It's pointless." On the other hand, to give you a stronger example, you may have the physical strength to lift a heavy boulder, but in order to really lift it, you might have to use a crowbar. So, it's a matter of having the correct tool. It isn't simply a matter of having naked, raw intelligence, it's a matter of using the right tools. A person who has intelligence cannot solve a problem in calculus, can he?

P-64:   If she knows how to. (*Smiles.*)

T-65:   (*Reinforces confidence in maturity.*) All right. Okay. You need to have the formulas, that's what you're coming in here for. If you weren't intelligent, you wouldn't be able to understand the formulas, and you know very well you understand the formulas. Not only that, but you use them on your own clients with much more confidence than you use them on yourself.

P-65:   (*Self-praise, confirms therapist's statement.*) You wouldn't believe me if you heard me tell things to people. You'd think I was a different person. Because I can be so optimistic about other people. I was encouraging a therapist yesterday who was about to give up on a client. I said, "You can't do that." I said, "You haven't tried everything yet," and I wouldn't let her give up.

T-66:   All right, so you didn't even have a chance to use the tools this weekend because you had the structure set in your mind, and then due to some accidental factor you were unable to do it. But you concluded on the weekend that the tools don't work since "I am so incapable that I can't use the tools." It wasn't even a test was it? Now for the next weekend . . .

P-66:   (*Agrees.*) . . . It wasn't a true test . . .

T-67:   No, it wasn't even a fair test of what you could do or what the tools could do. Now for weekends, what you want to do is prepare yourself for the Fourth of July. You prepare for the weekends by having the structure written down, and you have to have some backup plans in case it gets loused up. You know you really do have a number of things in your network that can bring you satisfaction. *What are some of the things you have gotten satisfaction from last week?*

P-67:   I took Margaret to the movies.

T-68:   What did you see?

P-68:   It was a comedy.

T-69:   What?

P-69:   A comedy.

T-70:   That's a good idea. What did you see?

P-70:   (*Smiles*) It was called *Mother, Jugs and Speed.*

T-71:   Yeah, I saw that.

P-71:   Did you see that?

T-72:   Yeah, I saw that on Friday.

P-72:   (*Smiles*) I liked it.

T-73:   It was pretty good. A lot of action in that. So you enjoyed that. Do you think you could still enjoy a good movie?

P-73:   I can. If I get distracted, I'm all right.

T-74:   So what's wrong with that?

P-74:   Because then what happens . . . while I'm distracted the pain is building up and then the impact is greater when it hits me. Like last night I had two friends over for dinner. That was fine. While they're there . . . I'm deliberately planning all these activities to keep myself busy . . . and while they were there I was fine. But when they left . . .

T-75:   That's beautiful.

P-75:   The result was that the impact was greater because all this pain had accumulated . . .

T-76:   We don't know because you didn't run a control, but there is no doubt there is a letdown after you've had satisfactory experience . . . so that what you have to do is set up a mechanism for handling the letdown. See what you did is you downed yourself, you knocked yourself and said, "Well . . . it's worse now than if I hadn't had them at all." Rather than just taking it phenomenologically: "They were here and I felt good when they were here, then I felt let down afterward." So then obviously the thing to pinpoint is what? The letdown afterward. So what time did they leave?

P-76: About 9.

T-77: And what time do you ordinarily go to bed?

P-77: About 10.

T-78: So you just had one hour to plan on.

P-78: To feel bad . . .

T-79: All right, one hour to feel bad. That's one way to look at it. That's not so bad, is it? It's only one hour.

P-79: But then I feel so bad during the hour. That's when I think that I want to die.

T-80: All right, what's so bad about feeling bad? You know what we've done with some of the people? And it's really worked. We've assigned them. We've said, "Now we want to give you one hour a day in which to feel bad." Have I told you about that? "I want you to feel just as bad as you can," and in fact sometimes we even rehearse it in the session. I don't have time today but maybe another time.

P-80: It's time-limited.

T-81: (*Alliance with patient as a fellow therapist.*) Yeah, and we have the people—I'd say, "Why don't you feel as bad as you can—just think of a situation, the most horribly devastating, emotionally depleting situation you can. Why don't you feel as bad as you possibly can?" And they really can do it during a session. They go out and after that they can't feel bad again even though they may even want to. It's as though they've depleted themselves of the thing and they also get a certain degree of objectivity toward it.

P-81: (*Helping out.*) It has to be done in a controlled . . .

T-82: It has to be done in a structured situation.

P-82: It has to be controlled.

T-83: That's true. It has to—that's why I say, "Do it in here, first."

P-83: Yes.

T-84: Then, I can pull them out of it . . .You need to have a safety valve.

P-84: If you do it at home . . . you might . . .

T-85: Right, the therapist has to structure it in a particular way. I'm just saying that one hour of badness a day is not necessarily antitherapeutic. And so it doesn't mean you have to kill yourself because you have one bad hour. What you want to do is to think of this as "my one bad hour for today." That's one way of looking at it. And then you go to sleep at 10 o'clock and it's over. You've had one bad hour out of 12. That's not so terrible. Well, you told yourself during that time something like this. "See, I've had a pretty good day and now I've had this bad hour and it means I'm sick, I'm full of holes, my ego is . . ."

P-85: See I'm thinking, "It never ends."

T-86: For one hour, but yeah, but that's not even true because you thought that you couldn't have any good times in the past, and yet as recently as yesterday you had a good day.

P-86: But what gives it momentum is that thought that it's not going to end.

T-87: Maybe the thought's incorrect. How do you know the thought is incorrect?

P-87: I don't know.

T-88: (*Retrospective hypothesis-testing.*) Well, let's operationalize it. What does it mean, "It's not going to end?" Does that mean that you're never going to feel good again in your whole life? Or does that mean that you're going to have an unremitting, unrelenting, inexorable sadness day in, day out, hour after hour, minute after minute. I understand that is your belief. That's a hypothesis for the moment. Well, let's test the hypothesis retrospectively. Now you have that thought: "This is never going to end." You had that thought when? Yesterday at 9 a.m.

P-88:   Yes.

T-89:   Now that means that if that hypothesis is correct, every minute since you awoke this morning, you should have had unending, unrelenting, unremitting, inevitable, inexorable sadness and unhappiness.

P-89:   (*Refutes hypothesis.*) That's not true.

T-90:   It's incorrect.

P-90:   Well, you see, when I wake up in the morning, even before I'm fully awake the first thing that comes to my mind inevitably is that I don't want to get up. That I have nothing that I want to live for. And that's no way to start the day.

T-91:   That's the way a person who has a depression starts the day. That's the perfectly appropriate way to start the day if you're feeling depressed.

P-91:   Even before you're awake?

T-92:   Of course. When people are asleep they even have bad dreams. You've read the article on dreams. Even their dreams are bad. So how do you expect them to wake up feeling good after they have had a whole night of bad dreams? And what happens in depression as the day goes on? They tend to get better. You know why? Because they get a better feel of reality—reality starts getting into their beliefs.

P-92:   Is that what it is?

T-93:   Of course.

P-93:   I always thought it was because the day was getting over and I could go to sleep again.

T-94:   Go to sleep to have more bad dreams? The reality encroaches and it disproves this negative belief.

P-94:   That's why it's diurnal.

T-95:   Of course, and we have already disproven the negative belief, haven't we? You had that very strong belief last night—strong enough to make you want to commit suicide—that this would be unremitting, unrelenting, inevitable, and inexorable.

P-95:   (*Cheerful*) Can I tell you something very positive I did this morning?

T-96:   (*Kidding*) No, I hate to hear positive things. I'm allergic. Okay. I'll tolerate it. (*Laughs.*)

P-96:   (*Recalls rational self instruction.*) I got that thought before I was even awake, and I said, "Will you stop it, just give yourself a chance and stop telling yourself things like that."

T-97:   So what's wrong with saying that?

P-97:   I know. I thought that was a very positive thing to do. (*Laughs.*)

T-98:   (*Underscores statement.*) That's terrific. Well, say it again so I can remember.

P-98:   I said, "Stop it and give yourself a chance."

T-99:   (*More hopeful prediction. Self-sufficiency.*) When you had your friends over, you found intrinsic meaning there. This was in the context of *no man* . . . Now when the pain of the breakup has washed off completely, do you think you're going to be capable of finding all these goodies, yourself, under your own power, and attaching the true meaning to them?

P-99:   I suppose if the pain is less . . .

T-100:   Well, the pain's less right now.

P-100:   Does it matter?

T-101:   Yeah.

P-101:   But that doesn't mean it won't continue.

T-102:   Well, in the course of time, you know, it's human nature that people get over painful episodes. You've been over painful episodes in the past.

P-102: Suppose I keep on missing him forever.

T-103: What?

P-103: Suppose I keep on missing him forever?

T-104: There's no reason to expect you to miss him forever. That isn't the way people are constructed. People are constructed to forget after a while and then get involved in other things. You had them before.

P-104: You spoke of a man who missed a mother for 25 years.

T-105: (*Emphasizes self-sufficiency.*) Well, I don't know . . . this may have been one little hang-up he had, but, I don't know that case . . . In general, that isn't the way people function. They get over lost love. All right? And one of the ways we can speed the process is by you, yourself, attaching meaning to things that are in your environment that you are capable of responding to . . . You demonstrated that . . .

P-105: Not by trying to replace a lost love right away?

T-106: (*Reinforcing independence.*) Replace it? What you're trying to do is find another instrument to happiness. He's become your mechanism for reaching happiness. That's what's bad about the whole man hang-up. It is that you are interposing some other unreliable entity between you and happiness. And all you have to do is to move this entity out of the way, and there's nothing to prevent you from getting happiness. But you want to keep pulling it back in. I say, leave it out there for a while, and then you'll see. Just in the past week you found that when you didn't have a man, you were able to find happiness without a man. And if you leave the man out of the picture for a long enough period of time, you'll see that you don't need him. Then if you want to bring him in as one of the many things that can bring satisfaction, that's fine, you can do that. But if you see him as the *only* conduit between you and happiness, then you are right back to where you were before.

P-106: Is it an erroneous thing to think that if I get to the point where I really believe that I don't need him, that I won't want him?

T-107: Oh, you're talking about him. I think it will just . . .

P-107: Any man . . . any man?

T-108: (*Undermines regressive dependency.*) . . . Well, you might still want him, like you might like to go to a movie, or read a good book, or have your friends over for dinner. You know, you still have to have relationships with your friends. But if they didn't come over for dinner last night it wouldn't plunge you into a deep despondency. I'm not underestimating the satisfaction that one gets from other people . . . but it's not a necessity . . . It's something that you, yourself, can relate to on a one-to-one basis . . . but one does, as one individual to another. You're relating to a man the way a child does to a parent, or the way a drug addict does to his drugs. He sees the drug as the mechanism for achieving happiness. And you know you can't achieve happiness artificially. And you have been using men in an artificial way. As though they are going to bring you happiness . . . rather than they are simply one of the things external to yourself by which you, yourself, can bring yourself happiness. *You* must bring *you* happiness.

P-108: I can . . . I've been focusing on dependency.

T-109: (*Emphasizing available pleasures.*) Well, you've done it. You've brought yourself happiness by going to the movies, by working with your clients, by having friends over for dinner, by getting up in the morning and doing things with your daughter. You have brought you happiness . . . but you can't depend on somebody else to bring you happiness the way a little girl depends on a parent. It doesn't work. I'm not opposed to it . . . I have no religious objection to it . . . It just doesn't work. Pragmatically, it is a very unwise way to conduct one's life. And in some utopian society after this, children will be trained not to depend on others as the mechanism for happiness. In fact, you can even demonstrate that to your daughter . . . through your own behavior, she can find that out.

P-109: She's a very independent child.

T-110: (*Probing for adverse reaction to interview.*) Well, she's already found that out. Okay, now do you have any questions? Anything that we discussed today? Is there anything that I said today that rubbed you the wrong way?

P-110: You said it would be damaging . . . not damaging . . . but you think it would deprive me of more opportunity to test this out if I were to go to another man.

T-111: Well, it's an unusual opportunity . . .

P-111: It's not so unusual, because I might get involved with somebody else.

T-112: (*Turning disadvantage into advantage.*) Well, yes, but this is like the worst—you said this is the worst—depression you felt for a long time. It's a very *unusual* opportunity to be able to demonstrate how you were able to pull yourself from the very deepest depths of depression onto a very solid independent position. You may not have that opportunity again, really, and it would be such a very sharp contrast. Now, you don't have to do it, but I'm saying it's really a very rich chance, and it does mean possibly a lot of gain. I don't want to make any self-fulfilling hypotheses, but you've got to expect the pain and not get discouraged by it. What are you going to say to yourself . . . if you feel the pain tonight? Suppose you feel pain after you leave the interview today, what are you going to say to yourself?

P-112: "Present pain for future gain."

T-113: Now where are you now on the hopelessness scale?

P-113: Down to 15%.

T-114: It's down to 15% from 95%, but you have to remember that the pain is handled in a structured way, the way I told you about the people who make themselves feel sad during that one period. It has to be structured. If you can structure your pain, this pain is something that's going to build you up in the future, and, indeed, it will. But if you see yourself as just being victimized by these forces you have no control over, . . . you're just helpless in terms of the internal things and external things . . . then you are going to feel terrible . . . And what you have to do is convert yourself from somebody who feels helpless, right? . . . And you are the only person who can do it . . . I can't make you strong and independent . . . I can show you the way, but if you do it, you haven't done it by taking anything from me; you've done it by drawing on resources within yourself.

P-114: How does it follow then that I feel stronger when I have a man? If things are going . . .

T-115: (*Counteracts assumption about getting strength from another person. Empirical test.*) You mean you make yourself feel strong because you yourself think, "Well, I've got this man that's a pillar of strength, and since I have him to lean on, therefore, I feel strong." But, actually, nobody else can give you strength. That's a fallacy that you feel stronger having a man, but you can't trust your feelings. What you're doing is just probably drawing on your own strength. You have the definition in your mind. "I'm stronger if I have a man." But the converse of that is very dangerous . . . which is, "I am weak if I don't have a man . . ." What you have to do, if you want to get over this is to disprove the converse, "I am weak if I don't have a man." Now, are you willing to subject that to the acid test? Then you will know. Okay, well suppose you give me a call tomorrow and let me know how you're going and then we can go over some of the other assignments.

It was apparent by the end of the interview that the acute suicidal crisis had passed. The patient felt substantially better, was more optimistic, and had decided to confront and solve her problems. She subsequently became involved in cognitive therapy on a more regular basis and worked with one of the junior staff in identifying and coping with her intrapersonal and interpersonal problems.

This interview is typical of our crisis intervention strategies but is a departure from the more systematic approach used during the less dramatic phases of the patient's depression. We generally attempt to adhere to the principle of collaborative empiricism in our routine interviews and deviate from standard procedures for a limited period of time only. Once the crisis is over, the therapist returns to a less intrusive and less active role and structures the interview in such a way that the patient assumes a greater responsibility for clarifying and devising possible solutions to problems.

Editors' Introduction

This case study is taken from an important book edited by Kirk Schneider and Rollo May titled The Psychology of Existence. *You will immediately notice the author's frequent and fascinating use of quotations from great literature; Mendelowitz quotes the Bible, José Ortega y Gasset, Chuang-tzu, Lao-tzu, Martin Buber, Søren Kierkegaard, Friedrich Nietzsche, Fritjof Capra, Otto Rank, Milan Kundera, and many others. This is a common characteristic of existential writing, as existential therapists have been influenced as much by philosophers and novelists as by researchers and scientists.*

The case presented involves an unhappy 24-year-old man who appears to meet diagnostic criteria for a diagnosis of obsessive-compulsive personality disorder. Note that the therapist spends as much time talking about the human *condition as he does talking about his* patient's *condition. You see Ron, the patient, increasingly taking responsibility for his life and the decisions he makes; as this occurs, the initial presenting problems resolve. There are still issues that can be addressed in therapy, most especially a less than satisfying marriage, but one senses that Ron is developing the courage necessary to successfully confront these ordinary problems of living.*

Do you agree that change is primarily the responsibility of the client? Are you comfortable with the idea that therapists are simply midwives to a process of growth that is inherent in all people? Do you find the frequent literary allusions absolutely fascinating or a nuisance that slows your reading and interferes with your comprehension of the points the author wants to make? Your answers to these questions should tell you whether or not you would be happy and effective practicing existential psychotherapy.

8 | CASE STUDY OF AN OBSESSIVE-COMPULSIVE PERSONALITY

Ed Mendelowitz

> *His disciples questioned him and said to him, "Do you want us to fast? How shall we pray? Shall we give alms? What diet shall we observe?" Jesus said, "Do not tell lies and do not do what you hate."*
>
> —The Gospel of Thomas
>
> *Life is essentially a drama, because it is a desperate struggle—with things and even with our character—to succeed in being in fact that which we are in design.*
>
> —José Ortega y Gasset (1964)

There is a Hasidic tale told by Rabbi Hanokh and retold by Martin Buber (1948) of a stupid man, one who could not live without lists and rules. Indeed, so difficult was it for this man to think for himself that he almost hesitated to go to sleep at night for fear of the difficulty he would have in finding his clothes upon waking. One evening, it occurred to the man to make yet another list and so—pencil and paper in hand—he duly noted where he lay each article of clothing as he undressed. The next morning, the man was very well pleased to consult this list and find hat, pants, shirt, and so on exactly where he had placed them the night before. "That's all very well," thought the man when he was fully dressed, "but now where am I myself? Where in the world am I?" "He looked and looked, but it was a vain search; he could not find himself. 'And that is how it is with us,' said the rabbi."

I relate this little story as a prelude to the present case study because it occurs to me that we psychologists are also often stupid, preoccupied with lists and charts, theories and techniques, and do not know ourselves any better than the foolish man in the *rebbe's* tale. Ours is a guild of obsessive-compulsives busily jumping our way through countless academic hoops, overcoming innumerable obstacles on our way toward professional respectability and accomplishment such that we scarcely fare any better than our poor Hasid when thrown back on ourselves and left to our own devices. Otto Rank (1945) referred to this process as one of "partialization," the all-too-human attempt to encounter the world in manageable doses. The result is a necessarily reduced and leveled down image of existence and human being.

Rollo May (1967) makes this same point in *Psychology and the Human Dilemma,* where he unwittingly echoes the Hasidic tale with one of his own, this time of the over-confident and ever-industrious psychologist (here we do no laugh so freely!) who is

From *The Psychology of Existence: An Integrative, Clinical Perspective.* (Kirk J. Schneider & Rollo May, 1995, McGraw-Hill College). Reprinted by permission of the authors.

denied eternity because of the crime of *nimis simplicandum*. In short, our accomplished colleague is chastised for a lifetime of oversimplification and an attendant career of professional reduction. "You have spent your life making molehills out of mountains," he is told by an incredulous Saint Peter. "We sent you to earth for seventy-two years to a Dantean circus, and you spent your days and nights at sideshows! *Nimis simplicando!*" (p. 4). The psychologist protests and cravenly submits his many publications and countless awards for consideration but to no avail. "Please! Not your well-practiced chatter," Saint Peter retorts; "Something new is required . . . something new" (p. 6).

Thus humbled, let us proceed to the story at hand.

I first met Ron in the early summer of 1990. He was 24 years old at that time and had received my name from a social worker following his fiancée's unexpected disclosure that she had an abortion at the age of 16. A good obsessive-compulsive, Ron had a strong, indeed rigid, moral code and reacted to this revelation with anger, anxiety, vindictiveness, and feelings of jealousy, indeed once even hitting his fiancée. The day after the news, he was talking to his EAP counselor and from there quickly found his way to my office.

Now, I do not strike a particularly formal or formidable pose for a psychologist and believe that the therapist works ideally through his or her own person rather than through some acquired and often disingenuous pose of professionalism or false show of confidence. (It was Alfred Adler, I believe, who taught that the therapist's most important asset was her or his own self; a simple matter, perhaps, but one which many psychotherapists seem nonetheless not to get.)

I can still remember quite clearly Ron's initial presentation: meticulously dressed in a business suit with attaché case in hand. Ron himself seemed to pick up *intuitively* on the incongruity of the situation by elaborating on how organized he was, even momentarily opening his perfectly arranged attaché case to prove his point. I immediately liked this young man. He had a sense of humor about himself and was not so far gone as to be unable to poke fun at himself. For the obsessive-compulsive character, this is saying something indeed.

During this and subsequent hours, I tried mostly to listen to Ron, asking questions not *compulsively* from some textbook evaluative procedure but rather to let an incipient rapport gradually evolve and allow the client's story to further unfold. In so doing, I learned the following: Ron had been born in rural New England and had moved to an industrialized southern New Hampshire with his family at the end of his first year of school. He had been diagnosed as dyslexic in childhood and had spent his boyhood summers at a special camp for children with learning disabilities. There were other childhood maladies as well (problems with his legs requiring a brace, a lazy eye, etc.), bringing to mind Adler's ideas about "organ inferiority" and "power striving" (Ansbacher & Ansbacher, 1956). Certainly, the client was well aware of his bitter disappointment at not having been able to play varsity sports as an adolescent and even now engaged in any number of compensatory athletic activities.

Ron described his father as "very successful" though difficult to talk to. His mother, he said, was easier to communicate with but had not earned Ron's respect insofar as her world was, as he put it, simply "too small." Ron's mother had been married once previously as a teenager and had two older children from that brief relationship. The client, then, had a half-sister, 29 years of age, whom he described as a recovering alcoholic stuck in a dependent marriage to a similarly recovering spouse. He had also a half-brother, 27 years of age, working on a doctorate somewhere in the Midwest.

Although Ron was not close to his siblings, it was clear that he struggled with turbulent and ambivalent feelings regarding his parents. Thus, his father was a self-made man who was both authoritarian and benefactor. He had not only assisted in Ron's schoolwork but had actually done much of it for his son! While Ron had, no doubt, a "magic helper" (Fromm, 1941) at his disposal and possessed consequently a sense of "specialness"

(Yalom, 1981), he never really got the feeling of accomplishing anything of significance in his own right. Consciously, Ron both admired his father and emulated his high standards. Subconsciously, however, he harbored enormous resentment. His father had become quite successful as an independent salesperson of paper-processing machinery. Ron himself at the time was selling, as we might well have anticipated, stationery products.

Feelings about Ron's mother were similarly unsettled. He could, as we have noted, relate to her more comfortably, for she was warmer and more accessible. He felt, however, that her life was too severely limited and that she was too dependent on her husband. (Ron's mother had herself become pregnant during her teenage years, a situation forcing a marriage from which Ron's father—always the hero—had eventually "rescued" her.) The client could easily see women as "weak," and indeed, his fiancée often frustrated him insofar as he felt that she was lacking "a life of her own."

These, then, are some of the facts of Ron's circumstances to the point when he began working with me. Superficially, it was clear that Ron bore the earmarks of the obsessive-compulsive personality: perfectionism; restlessness; preoccupation with details, rules, and public performance; excessive devotion to work and productivity; inflexibility concerning matters of morality and ethics; restricted capacity for the expression of affection; and so forth. Ordinarily, it seems, the client's diagnosis and history are meant to provide some sort of key to treatment methodology and objectives. The therapist is only too *anxious* to objectify the data into a neatly defined evaluation and corresponding treatment plan. All of this has its relevance, but first let us pause.

I often think about Rollo May's (1981) conception of freedom as the pause between stimulus and response. It is a profound observation. If we rush in impulsively to act without adequate pause, then it seems to me that we are simply instruments in that great chain of cause and effect and are ourselves hardly free to actualize the client's flagging potential in any meaningful way. Is it not appropriate, moreover, to define compulsivity quite simply as *the failure to pause between stimulus and response?* It is important to underscore this point, for we have already noted a professional (to say nothing at all about societal) bias toward compulsivity, and it is clear that nothing of consequence will be accomplished when both therapist and client are similarly misguided. Sages from the East (with their penchant for paradox) have long understood this in a way most Westerners do not:

> If it could be talked about, everybody would have told his brother.
>
> —Chuang-tzu

> Not knowing that one knows is best.
>
> —Lao-tzu, *Tao te Ching*

Polish poet Czeslaw Milosz (1951/1981, p. 29) explains:

> The man of the East cannot take Americans seriously because they have never undergone experiences that teach men how relative their judgments and thinking habits are. Their resultant lack of imagination is appalling.

It is all too easily for left-brained and articulate professionals to theorize and discuss endlessly (often wielding arcane and sophisticated mental apparatuses in so doing) without, nonetheless, truly or deeply understanding. May, we recall, had already chided us concerning the hazards of "well-practiced chatter." "A dog is not recognized as good because it barks well," says Chuang-tzu, "and a man is not reckoned wise because he speaks skillfully." Let us slow down, then, and give these matters more appropriate thought.

Czech novelist Milan Kundera (1986/1988) suggests that the means toward approaching the enigmatic self lies in grasping "the essence of [that self's] existential problem": *to grasp one's "existential code"* (p. 29). Increasingly, I find that this is what I am attempting to get at in my clinical work. It is not simply a matter of affixing this or that diagnosis but rather an approach to understanding, encounter. I say "approach" because I mean to emphasize that the self can never be apprehended with certainty. We may become aware of our themes and those of our clients, but the themes are never static or fixed, never resolved in any absolute way.

What, then, can we say about Ron's existential code? First, Ron struggles significantly with tension between freedom and destiny. He is ambitious, a go-getter, a young man of action. Superficially, one might say, he is his own person. This, however, is hardly the case. He still lives with his parents, and even if he did not, his freedom would nonetheless be severely curtailed. He idealizes a father who, albeit well intended and generous, has undermined self-esteem. He has done this by remaining a kind of "ultimate rescuer" (Yalom, 1980), such that Ron has never genuinely learned to trust in himself. Ron is discontentedly employed in his father's own field and yet adamantly believes that this path, if persevered and navigated successfully, will bring eventual fulfillment. It will not. If one travels the wrong path, one does not find fulfillment—external reward and validation, perhaps, but not fulfillment.

> Are you—the real you—a mere corruption? . . . Why do you not examine your own self, and see that you have arisen?
> —*Treatise on Resurrection* (in Pagels, 1979, p. 12)

> The Baal-Shem said: "Every man should behave according to his 'rung.' If he does not, if he seizes the 'rung' of a fellow man and abandons his own, he will actualize neither the one nor the other."
> —Martin Buber (in Kaufmann, 1961, p. 430)

"I work hard at living, at getting to the next step," states Ron in his initial hour. There is a question, however, concerning the path on which those steps are taken.

Without knowing it more fully, Ron is very angry at this state of affairs. There is consequently a significant history of acting out of aggression: episodic bouts of drinking, periodic frays with authority and the law, even, shortly after the onset of therapy, a vandalized automatic teller machine which failed to operate. One might say that such behavior is a bad sign for an obsessive-compulsive personality. I, however, consider it a good omen, for it indicates a man who is in touch—indeed, violently so—with his daimon. The task will be to harness the daimonic forces in *willing one's own life.*

This tension between freedom and destiny is played out, also, in Ron's relationship with his fiancée and in his attitude toward women in general. His fiancée is herself the daughter of alcoholic parents and, in general, very much a product of anxious family enmeshment. The client is frustrated concerning the limitations of a relationship based, in the end, on reciprocal insecurities, mutual *fear of becoming,* and yet lacks the courage to move beyond it in the pursuit of a more satisfying connection. The women Ron sees as being on his own level are devalued as weak and dependent; they are resented and yet desperately needed to divert attention from his own failure of nerve. Stronger, more confident women, their worlds not so finite or anxiously circumscribed, are seen as highly desirable yet off limits. Ron does not feel deserving of them and rather prefers to deny their existence. They give the lie to Ron's mock show of autonomy. Anxiety, as Kierkegaard (1944, p. 55) had said, is "the dizziness of freedom." Indeed, the tension is played out in other aspects of the client's interpersonal life, such that—although he is rarely aware of it—extant relationships fail to assuage a chronic existential loneliness. He is forever afraid of moving further out into life where he might find circumstances more rewarding.

Finally, yet related to these themes, is Ron's spiritual void, a thoroughly modern dilemma. From the earliest sessions, the client speaks to a "need to find meaning in life," a desire that "life ought to matter." Although brought up in a Protestant home, Ron considers converting to Catholicism in an effort to ease his religious discontent. Certainly, we may view this along the lines of the perennial human struggle between meaning and nothingness, but this, too, correlates with our basic polarity between freedom and destiny. To the extent that one avoids personal responsibility for one's own life, one forfeits a sense of fulfillment at living authentically:

> From becoming an individual no one is excluded, except he who excludes himself by becoming a crowd.
>
> —Søren Kierkegaard (1939, p. 121)

> What does your conscience say?—"You shall become who you are."
>
> —Friedrich Nietzsche (1974, p. 219)

Irrespective of external rewards that may accrue, the client is unable, in his avoidance of himself, to experience a genuine sense of peace with self or world.

These, then, are some of the more pertinent themes that I take to comprise Ron's existential code. Certainly, these themes define to a greater or lesser extent all human beings insofar as they are ontological themes and, more particularly, the compulsive personality in which life has become constricted, cerebral, and leveled down. We are not, however, primarily concerned with apprehending Ron as a member of this or that diagnostic category but rather as a unique individual. This, to my way of thinking, is the distinguishing feature of the existential emphasis in psychotherapy. Theories, techniques, and diagnostic formulae are all important aspects of our work yet always ancillary to the living human being with whom we are present. We seek first "to understand, to uncover, to disclose human existence" (May, 1958b, p. 24). If these conceptions appear only obliquely relevant to the psychotherapist's workaday endeavors, I would suggest that they circumscribe a foundation without which creative work cannot occur.

The existential approach to therapy proceeds with an emphasis on the real relationship between therapist and client. Without a genuine encounter, it is doubtful that the therapeutic process will be anything but superficial. As Frieda Fromm-Reichmann admonishes, the client needs an experience rather than an explanation (cited in May, 1958a, p. 81). This encounter, moreover, can be accomplished only to the extent that the therapist herself or himself has achieved some degree of authenticity. This point is crucial insofar as I think that this quality is a very rare bird these days, the more so among professionals who have spent years upon years in training programs unwittingly learning to define themselves from the outside in, by Kierkegaardian "externals":

> In Christendom he too is a Christian, goes to church every Sunday, hears and understands the parson, yea, they understand one another; he dies; the parson introduces him into eternity for the price of $10—but a self he was not, and a self he did not become . . .
>
> For the immediate man does not recognize his self, he recognizes himself only by his dress . . . he recognizes that he has a self only by externals. There is no more ludicrous confusion, for a self is just infinitely different from externals.
>
> —Søren Kierkegaard (1954, pp. 186–187)

Early in therapy, I tried, as we have noted, to relate genuinely to Ron and listen carefully to his story. Obvious as this may seem, it is a rare enough occurrence for most of us: to be heard without preconceived judgment or theory. In this way, Ron was tacitly encouraged to take the themes that he had himself brought into therapy seriously, to bear responsibility for them above and beyond pro forma expressions of significance. This contrasted sharply with others in Ron's life and past who had typically discouraged authentic confrontation of his anxiety and disease. A thoroughly modern philosophy, really: *kitsch,* we may say, or *the denial of the ontological dimension.*

Ron was not used to this sort of reception and tested it as he would any seemingly authoritarian arrangement. Early in treatment, he missed an appointment, several days following which I received the following courteous and matter-of-fact, if unspectacular, note:

> Dr. Mendelowitz:
>
> I'm sorry that I missed my appointment. I forgot all about it. I've had a lot on my mind. You can bill me for the appointment because it was my fault.
>
> I believe that the treatment is helping but I have a long way to go. Thanks for your help. I think we have a good relationship.
>
> I will call you later this week to reschedule and won't forget about the appointment again.
> Take care,
>
> Ron

When Ron arrived at his next appointment, he apologized once again. I accepted his apology graciously and without fanfare, commenting only that it would be helpful to have advance notice of a missed session. I did not interpret his "forgetfulness" as resistance, which it likely was on a certain level. Resistance, it is understood, has many dimensions and refers at its deepest level to the all-too-human tendency toward self-betrayal, the maneuvering by which one avoids, first and foremost, oneself.

> Perhaps the most tragic thing about the human situation is that a man may try to supplant himself, that is, to falsify his life.
>
> —José Ortega y Gasset (1964, p. 295)

Or as Nietzsche observes, the most common lie is the lie which we lie to ourselves. I do not, then, interpret resistance in a strictly psychoanalytic or self-referential way but rather existentially, as an avoidance of self. This is a point of fundamental importance, for it emphasizes, once again, the inexorable tension between freedom and destiny and one's ultimate responsibility for oneself.

> Many patients go to psychiatrists as if to psychic surgeons. When such a patient comes to such a therapist a relationship of considerable length may result, but little else. For the job can be done, if at all, only by the patient. To assign this task to anyone else, however insightful or charismatic, is to disavow the source of change. In the process of personality change the role of the psychiatrist is catalytic. As a cause he is sometimes necessary, never sufficient.
>
> —Alan Wheelis (1973, p. 7)

Once this is realized, the therapy proceeds quite naturally as the client *chooses* change supported (now gently, now more forcibly) by the therapeutic relationship within the context and confines of the therapeutic container.

Essentially, then, the psychotherapist needs to let go of her or his own compulsivity—that is, of *the compulsion to act or solve.* This is harder than it sounds but serves to underscore the essential tension between the client's incessant search for answers and clearly delineated techniques of change and the ultimate realization that one, in the end, is responsible for oneself.

> When the Zen master Po-chang was asked about seeking for the Buddha nature he answered, "It's much like riding an ox in search of an ox."
>
> —Fritjof Capra (1975, p. 124)

Like Wheelis, the Zen master understands the futility of the search for magic fluid.

With these thoughts in mind, let us briefly review some of the salient aspects of Ron's course of psychotherapy. Ron has been working with me for over 2 years in weekly sessions, which he is currently in the process of winding down. Early in treatment, Ron was able to recognize that his exaggerated reaction to his fiancée's disclosure belied his own significant impulse to antisocial behavior, an impulse, as we have noted, episodically acted out. With this realization, the client quickly settled into the real therapeutic struggle: that of *a confrontation with self*. He gradually acknowledged that beneath a veneer of bravado he harbored deep-seated feelings of insecurity and a concomitant resentment of authority. Clashes with the law and its enforcers, ambivalence about a rigid moral code Ron had inherited but not chosen, an often judgmental and supercilious attitude toward his fiancée (indeed, toward women in general) all related to the client's unresolved themes concerning a world that was over constricted, limiting, and lacking in nuance and depth.

It is important to note that just as the client's insecurity—his reactive egotism and relentless need to achieve—had its roots in relationship, his authentic confrontation with these themes would likely come about only through a corrective connection, one based on presence and genuine empathy. Once Ron had successfully tested the relationship to his satisfaction (a far stormier affair than I will here elaborate), he was able to settle into the real work of therapy. Although numerous similarities exist between existential approaches to change and so-called Eastern "ways of liberation," this is a way in which the two related approaches significantly diverge: For us, relationship is paramount, the very lynchpin of change.

Gradually, using the therapist as support and guide, Ron was able to move forward in his embracement of freedom. Realizing that his work was not satisfying in any fundamental way, and acknowledging further that what truly interested him was teaching and working with adolescents, Ron began to focus more on dissatisfaction with self and situation, rehearsing in therapy for the possibility of change. Within months, Ron gave up his position as a sales representative, finding odd and temporary employment while pursing his teaching credentials. He did all this, moreover, without the initial support of his parents and risking considerable uncertainty about his future in an economic climate that did not augur well for prospective teachers. Eventually (and here I was as much surprised as anyone), Ron's efforts paid off. He acquired a teaching position in his hometown. The work has been frustrating, challenging, yet ultimately rewarding. It is no longer a fixed endpoint, however, nor does the client any longer tread a carefully planned professional itinerary. He is more willing to live in the moment, as they say, accepting the inevitable pangs of life and death anxiety that will eventually lead yet again to further change. Already, he foresees a time when teaching will not hold so much interest for him, as he looks now into graduate work in administration. Anxiety, no longer circumvented, is now accepted as the way of life, indeed, very much as normal.

Working with adolescents has elicited a periodic return of a moral rigidity that has at times limited Ron's ability to relate to and ultimately help his students. With each new return of the repressed, however, Ron is quickly able to look within and recognize that the source of the struggle is significantly internal. To the extent that he does this, he becomes more self-accepting (of doubt, of passion, of the daimonic) and better able to accept others. Interestingly, Ron has acquired numerous accolades in his 2 years of teaching, though these awards no longer seem to carry the weight they possessed when he worked so "hard at life, at getting to the next step." The emphasis is now on self and genuine relationship, as opposed to external validation.

On the interpersonal front, my sense is that the client has not fared quite so well. About a year after the initiation of psychotherapy, Ron married his fiancée. He and I agree that there have been compromises here insofar as his feelings about his wife have never matched those he once had for a former girlfriend. I tactfully and gently brought up these perceived compromises without any presumption whatsoever of knowing what was best for the client. Respect for autonomy is absolutely essential in effective psychotherapy. Clients will change, if at all, in their own direction and at their own pace.

The marriage has been supportive for Ron yet limiting as well, as his wife also struggles with relentless insecurity. Ron realizes the compromises herein (compromises which bother him more at certain times than at others) but has been less than successful at getting his wife to seriously pursue her own course of therapy. "She's a good person," Ron often sighs, fully aware that this is no longer always enough. Here, as elsewhere, I have maintained a nonjudgmental stance. I understand well the difficulties involving in seeking one's "soul image" (Jung, 1921/1961) and find few individuals who choose relationships for reasons that are entirely unambiguous. Further, compromise, to the extent that it is *conscious* compromise, is still being addressed and need not be taken as failure. It may be acted upon at a future point.

At the very least, Ron seems to have significantly worked through his prejudicial attitudes toward women. He now freely accepts that his wife's insecurities mirror his own, and he understands that his father has, through life, been as utterly dependent on his hero-identity as his mother has been on a more subsidiary role. In this respect, his relationships with his mother and wife have improved, and he is more discerning of his father's shortcomings. Thus, the client's former world of absolutism slowly yields to one of relativity and ambiguity of the human endeavor.

As Ron winds down his present course of therapy, I ponder the relationship and the process of change. Ron is undoubtedly more fulfilled in his work and life than before. He has seized his own rung. Whatever frustrations now ensue, they are, at the very least, a consequence of choosing his own life rather than what we may call "soul murder." This is genuine freedom—freedom that encompasses destiny. In relationship, Ron continues to struggle with feelings of uneasiness, inconsistency. Here too, however, there are signs of real growth as the client is far less defensive and more open to others than was formerly the case. The psychotherapeutic process has separated Ron further from anonymous and everyday relations while heightening an existential loneliness as he searches for others to whom he can more deeply relate. This is, perhaps, the price one pays for increased authentication of one's existence. The client now seeks genuine encounter, hardly something that can be ordered up at will. Further, Ron is presently only 26 years of age. I foresee a future for him that is open, unscripted, and full of possibility.

Although Ron's progress has been impressive in many respects, it is important to note that I by no means contrive of it a trophy for myself. Just as the client is ultimately responsible for himself, so too in the end is he due the real credit for growth achieved. The psychotherapist's role, as Rollo May has often observed, is like that of Virgil in Dante's *Divine Comedy:* The therapist is a guide who eventually is left behind for even loftier heights. (I am well aware of the numerous individuals whom I have not helped and do not choose to shoulder accountability for all that is and isn't accomplished in psychotherapy.) The client's youth and turbulence and perhaps my own lack of pretense all augured well in the present instance, but it was Ron himself who took up the challenge. For psychologists who have spent half their lives in training programs and small fortunes on textbooks and the latest workshops on technique, it may seem rather prosaic to be counted as mere midwives, but it is nonetheless so. And to be sure, it is perhaps no small feat to bring something new into the world that will add neither to the noise nor the folly and just may, in fact, contribute to the ultimate good of a planet that has quite obviously lost its way. Midwifery, we recall, was good enough a career for Socrates.

In a similar vein, I no longer try to be overly objective about the precise means by which change occurs in therapy. The brilliant Otto Rank once treated a patient who, curious about a sudden and uncharacteristic burst of self-assertion on his way to the psychoanalytic hour, later recalled:

And so Rank said, "Well, I will tell you something that you may find rather comforting. I don't understand what happens." He said, "You don't understand, and neither do I." He just simply knew that from experience he could expect that certain things could happen if they were handled rightly and if the person's psyche and personality could be influenced for the better along certain lines. But he wouldn't pretend at all to try to give me a lecture on why it was happening because he said, "I don't know."
—In Lieberman (1985, p. 272)

The sages of old had nothing on Rank.

Finally, Ron's compulsive traits remain in many respects, though certainly abated. Many of his current laments and longings are strikingly reminiscent of early sessions, reminding us of Jung's insight that the fundamental problems in life are never resolved in any final way. Still, there is real joy that Ron and I have experienced in this relationship, one that has enabled the client to open himself further to life in a way hitherto unthinkable. If Rank is right about the human tendency toward "partialization" of the world (and who can doubt that he is?), Ron's purview is now at least broader. He sees further into life as he embraces the joys and burdens of freedom. He is no longer a wheel horse. The result, I am convinced, will be a more fulfilling existence, one in which he does not flinch from life or death or his particular way:

And that's life: it does not resemble a picaresque novel in which from one chapter to the next the hero is continually being surprised by new events that have no common denominator. It resembles a composition that musicians call a *theme with variations*.
—Milan Kundera (1991, p. 275)

Who among us could say more?

REFERENCES

Ansbacher, H. L., & Ansbacher, R. R. (Eds.). (1956). *The individual psychology of Alfred Adler.* New York: Harper Torchbooks.

Buber, M. (1948). *Tales of the Hasidim: Later masters* (O. Marx, Trans.). New York: Schoken Books.

Capra, F. (1975). *The Tao of physics.* Boulder, CO: Shambhala Publications.

Fromm, E. (1941). *Escape from freedom.* New York: Holt, Rinehart & Winston.

Jung, C. G. (1961). *Psychological types* (R. F. C. Hull, Trans.). New York: Bollingen Foundation. (Original work published 1921)

Kaufmann, W. (1961). *Religion from Tolstoy to Camus.* New York: Harper Torchbooks.

Kierkegaard, S. (1939). *The point of view* (W. Lowrie, Trans.). London: Oxford University Press.

Kierkegaard, S. (1944). *The concept of dread* (W. Lowrie, Trans.). Princeton, NJ: Princeton University Press.

Kierkegaard, S. (1954). *Fear and trembling* and *The sickness unto death* (W. Lowrie, Trans.). New York: Anchor Books.

Kundera, M. (1988). *The art of the novel* (L. Asher, Trans.). New York: Harper & Row.

Kundera, M. (1991). *Immortality* (P. Kussi, Trans.). New York: Grove Weidenfeld.

Lieberman, J. (1985). *Acts of will: The life and work of Otto Rank.* New York: Free Press.

May, R. (1958a). Contributions of existential psychotherapy. In R. May, E. Angel, & H. F. Ellenberger (Eds.), *Existence: A new dimension in psychology and psychiatry* (pp. 37–91). New York: Basic Books.

May, R. (1958b). Origins of the existential movement in psychology. In R. May, E. Angel, & H. F. Ellenberger (Eds.), *Existence: A new dimension in psychology and psychiatry* (pp. 3–36). New York: Basic Books.

May, R. (1967). *Psychology and the human dilemma.* New York: Norton.

May, R. (1981). *Freedom and destiny.* New York: Norton.

Milosz, C. (1981). *The captive mind* (J. Zielonko, Trans.). New York: Vintage Books. (Original work published 1951)

Nietzsche, F. (1974). *The gay science* (W. Kaufmann, Trans.). New York: Vintage Books.

Ortega y Gasset, J. (1964). In search of Goethe from within (W. R. Trask, Trans.). In M. Friedman (Ed.), *The worlds of existentialism* (pp. 117–122). New York: Random House.

Pagels, E. (1989). *The gnostic gospels.* New York: Vintage Books.

Rank, O. (1945). *Will therapy* and *Truth and reality* (J. Taft, Trans.). New York: Knopf.

Wheelis, A. (1973). *How people change.* New York: Harper & Row.

Yalom, I. (1980). *Existential psychotherapy.* New York: Basic Books.

Editors' Introduction

In this interesting case reprinted from The International Gestalt Journal, *a Gestalt therapist shares a verbatim segment of her time with a patient and then allows four colleagues to critique her work. One of those four colleagues is Lynne Jacobs, coauthor of the Gestalt therapy chapter in* Current Psychotherapies. *Sally Denham-Vaughan then responds to the four critiques of her work. The case permits the reader to see firsthand the many different ways in which the therapist could have directed the therapy session.*

The therapists reviewing the case were blind to the identity of the therapist providing services, and the therapist whose work was reviewed did not know the identities of the four reviewers. This is why the reviewers sometimes use male pronouns when referring to the female therapist.

Although only representing about 15 minutes of a therapy session, the case illustrates the commitment of the therapist and the isolation and loneliness of the patient, as well as some core Gestalt principles such as field theory, the importance of presence, contact and awareness, contact boundaries, retroflection, and the conceptual limits imposed by diagnostic labels.

How would you have handled this case? What would you have done differently? Read the case a second time to see if you can identify choice points where you might have made different choices rather than those made by the therapist. What are your reasons for preferring different interventions?

9 | FIRST OR NOWHERE?

Sally Denham–Vaughan

> *To avoid criticism, do nothing, say nothing, be nothing.*
> —Elbert Hubbard

What follows is a transcript of part of a session (approximately 15 minutes) that took place in the summer of 2002.

BACKGROUND

Briefly, Louisa has been in therapy with me for some $3^1/_2$ years now, and we have had 143 weekly sessions. I first met her following admission to a psychiatric hospital, where she had been sectioned (an involuntary patient) for treatment of her mental health problems and especially suicidal behavior. She had been in the hospital for some 3 months, and upon being discharged, it was agreed that she should be referred for psychotherapy. Her formal diagnosis is of borderline personality disorder (BPD), with comorbid Axis 1 disorders, including severe bulimia and severe depressive disorder. In terms of her personality disorder, she fulfils all the *DSM IV* features for a diagnosis of BPD, and I have assessed her using the SIDP IV. Within this classificatory system, she can also be described as having avoidant and dependent traits.

In terms of personal history, Louisa is the second born of twins conceived on a honeymoon night. She believes that the pregnancy was unplanned, that her parents were ill prepared for children, and especially that her mother and father had a preference for boys.

The first-born twin, Michael, she describes as having always been "first, quicker, louder, more positive, and more creative." She has great difficulty owning and accepting her identity, feeling that neither her birthday nor even her name truly belonged to her. (If she had been a boy, she would have been called Louis.)

Over time in therapy, we have covered a wide range of areas, including attempting to manage her active suicidal behaviors, which include serious self-harm and severe bulimic difficulties. Both of these problems have been formulated as reflecting a fundamental feeling that she should not exist, but that if she is on this planet, then she should make only a positive contribution to others and have no needs of her own. Just being aware of her wants and desires triggers tremendous self-criticism.

Louisa is single and lives near her parents. She is 35 years of age, does not have a partner, and has never been married. She has very few friends, or indeed even acquaintances,

From *International Gestalt Journal* 2003, 26/1, p. 14–20. Reprinted with permission.

and does describe herself as being profoundly lonely. She lives in a small house with a range of animals, which are her "substitute family," including two dogs, two cats, and a range of hens and geese. She also has two horses.

This transcript comes after approximately 20 minutes of the session. Louisa has come into the session extremely upset having had the experience of reversing her car, hitting an object, and getting out only to discover that she had run over her new kitten. The kitten was killed by this incident and Louisa has been blaming and berating herself for the animal's death. I have been trying to facilitate her staying in contact with herself and me without dissociating or having a "panic attack." (Both these phenomena have occurred in previous sessions.) The main themes so far have been repetitive statements to the effect that this whole incident is certainly her fault and proof that she shouldn't exist.

TRANSCRIPT

Every act of creation is first of all an act of destruction.

—Pablo Picasso

Client (00:00): It just feels that I shouldn't be here . . . and that I shouldn't even bring that up.

Therapist (00:12): Do you believe that I think you shouldn't bring that up?

C (00:21): I don't know, I feel so awful, always harping back to the past. Why was I born? I just feel so awful. You'll think I'm so awful, bringing it all up again.

T (00:39): Sounds like the past has spontaneously arrived here, rather than you having gone looking for it.

C (00:43): No.

T (00:46): It's rather that it's come and found you.

C (00:49): It feels like it's a "come-back" you see that I can't just forget it. It's like it keeps on repeating itself, and it's just going to keep on repeating itself. The memories keep coming back, and it keeps on happening. Something will happen, sooner or later, and the pattern is there . . . all the same.

T (01:21): What is the pattern? What does it look like?

C (01:29): (angrily, hopelessly) I don't know.

T (01:43): I'm wondering then . . . what's the connection? What is repeating? (Pause)

C (02:08): That I should just keep out . . . that there is nothing I can create or get right.

T (02:21): So that's what's being repeated? That's the connection. That's what it means to you.

C (02:27): Well, everything I try to do, I get it wrong. Not just get it wrong . . . I kill things. I do it . . . (Pause)

T (02:53): So there is the connection . . . then this is the pattern you come down to.

C (02:55): Oh God; it's so awful. (Pause)

T (03:15): (reflectively) I imagine a spiral, a vortex; I wonder how it seems to you.

C (03:20): It's all down to me being here.

T (03:25): What's the feeling that goes with that . . . that it's all down to you being here?

C (03:31): Horrible, hateful; . . . that it's all down to me . . . my mistakes. What is the point of me being here? I've always said that I haven't got a function in life; but at least if I haven't got a function, if I don't get things wrong . . . no one gets hurt.

T (03:50): Sounds like you've got back to that very early decision that "I shouldn't be here"; and if I am here, I should have no needs, make no waves, and definitely get nothing wrong.

C (04:06): Well at least then I'm not doing any harm by being here. But as soon as I start taking part . . . Oh.

T (04:20): You look in such pain, physical pain when you say that.

C (04:30): Well, I just can't bear me. I've just had all these things happen to me . . . it's just like something's trying to get rid of me; but it doesn't quite happen.

T (05:05): (*beginning to feel anxious that she is dissociating*) Can you try and make a bit of contact with me.

C (05:15): Sorry, sorry.

T (05:17): I wasn't meaning to criticize you . . . I was just concerned you were disappearing, hating, and punishing yourself.

C (05:28): Self-pity.

T (05:30): No . . . not self-pity . . . self-hatred, that's what I see.

C (05:35): Mmmmmm.

T (05:41): Do you remember when we talked about the early decision; that "I just shouldn't be here"?

C (05:52): Well, it feels like it keeps coming back. It's here right now . . . I shouldn't be here. That's true.

T (06:01): So you think that's the truth . . . and that the pattern you are seeing reflects the truth, which is at the heart of that decision.

C (06:13): Are you saying that I'm wrong?

T (06:18): What I'm trying to say is that this decision is your interpretation of a set of events, but I think you know that I believe something different . . . that your existence is important.

C (06:31): (*slowly and with emphasis*) Maybe I'd believe that if I'd been born a single person. But it's like, when there's twins, it's like a repeat one has been made. Like an afterthought; so in effect, my brother's the one that was meant to be born. You know, he's the one who can create, and I'm the . . . oh . . . I can't explain it . . . a by-product. . . . A repeat, with nothing to make me separate, important. He's the one who was meant to be born. He's the one who is making a contribution, being useful to life, making a difference to life, and it's like I'm looking on.

T (07:56): I notice I feel really sad when you say that.

C (08:01): Well, what is the point to my life? I've just always been there to create problems, to be surplus.

T (08:23): I'm wondering what it's like for you to say that here, with me . . . to say that to me.

C (08:31): Well, I think it's your experience. That I'm just one more . . . there are plenty of clients, I'm just one more, a problem. Not even getting better, just killing things.

T (08:50): Do you know; that is absolutely not my experience of being here with you . . . now . . . or over time. (*Pause*) But I feel very sad when I hear you say that; and I understand and feel . . . I feel it here in my body as well as in my emotions; . . . that that's what you believe. I notice I have a sort of choking; almost like I shouldn't be even breathing . . . and I'm wondering if that is telling me something about how strongly you believe you shouldn't exist.

C (09:14): Well, when you've always been with someone who's so . . . oh, . . . everything that you're not; but he even looks the same; . . . well there comes a time when you just think . . . it's not even that I'm second; I just shouldn't be at all. It's a feeling that just comes up. You know, something happens and it'll bring me back to it. (*Pause*)

T (09:50): So, what is it like for you, that I'm here with you now . . . different from you . . . and with such a different belief about you, and a different experience of you too? I'm just wondering if that makes you feel apart from me.

C (10:23): No, . . . I really want to believe you, to be *with* you.

T (10:30): I feel really moved and pleased when you say that. I'm glad you *want* to believe me. So let's start with that. I'm wondering if you think I'm being genuine, real with you now. If I'm saying my truth or if I'm just trying to reassure you.

C (10:53): I know you wouldn't lie to me; but I know you couldn't agree with me; that's not your role, to agree with me about that.

T (11:09): Well, I neither agree nor disagree. I have a response, a reaction; I have a truth that is based on my own understandings, and my experience of being with you.

C (11:20): (*looking confused*) What?

T (11:27): For example, if I think of being with you, I can recall many times and memories of both good and bad times: successes and failures. So there is contrast and difference. It is not all the same . . . all problems . . . all sad. My view of the pattern does not lead me to your conclusion; I do see and believe there is purpose in your life. I just believe that life, including your life, is purposeful. There are not "mistakes" or afterthoughts. (*Pause*)

C (12:21): I'm just thinking of one of my little dogs. He was born last and almost died. But you know, I really really wanted him to live . . . almost more than the others. And when they got old enough to go to homes, he was the one I kept.

T (12:36): So you chose him.

C (12:41): Oh yes . . . (*Pause*) I suppose I identified with him. Coming last; being a nuisance . . . he wouldn't eat or feed properly so I bottle-fed him for a while.

T (12:58): So why did you choose him if he was such a nuisance?

C (13:07): Well, I loved him: I know he reminded me of me; but I just thought it wasn't his fault, being small. And do you know, he really fought for life . . . and he's grown up; and he's a lovely little dog.

T (13:25): So, is he really a nuisance?

C (13:31): No; not now; and not then really; he just needed a lot . . . well; a bit more than the others; but he was worth it. I mean he had the chance to go either way didn't he? He could easily have died either before he was born, or at birth, or even later . . . but he didn't.

T (14:02): So he really fought for life?

C (14:10): Oh yes.

T (14:15): With a purpose . . . a sense of purpose.

C (14:17): (*smiles*) Well he's a real fighter, even now. (*Pause*)

T (14:31): (*feeling moved*) I'm not surprised you identify with this little dog. So much in common. I'm thinking that even while part of you has found it so hard to take your life; and accept you are alive and have needs; part of you has really fought to stay alive. (*Pause*) I was just really appreciating the fighter in you. Thinking about the struggles you've had . . . the struggles we've had; and I just had a really warm, pleased sense of your aliveness. (*Pause*)

C (15:15): It's still a struggle.

T (15:23): I do know that Louisa, I see that; I really see your struggle; and I've seen and felt it today especially with what happened to your kitten.

C (15:32): I don't know how to cope with that.

T (15:39): Of course not; how could you know . . . it's an awful experience. And: I see you struggling to cope; as I've seen you struggling with many things; and I trust that struggle will bring you through.

The session moves on to a new figure focusing on Louisa thinking about and considering things she might do to support herself at this time. I felt that we had touched a very dark place in her, and one that lies at the center of her issues. I felt relieved that we had come through with a strong contact that was maintained for most of the session. This felt different from previous sessions discussing difficult events.

COMMENT 1: AN INDIVIDUALISTIC OR FIELD-ORIENTED POINT OF VIEW?

Jacques Blaize

First, I would like to thank the unidentified therapist for taking such a risk in publishing this transcript and being willing to be criticized. So I am pleased to accept this opportunity to open some tracks of reflection and not to say what the therapist should have done or not, which would be too simplistic because of the context: a few minutes of therapy, isolated from the whole of the therapy.

POSSIBLE EFFECTS OF THE DIAGNOSIS

My first comment is about the influence of the diagnosis on the therapeutic situation: It seems to me that the therapist is sometimes very careful and, maybe, anxious. (He says himself that he feels "anxious that she is dissociating.") And I cannot help thinking that the diagnosis of "borderline personality disorder, with comorbid Axis 1 disorders" is a determinant factor in the therapist's field organization.

This question is, for me, more general than the present case. A plausible hypothesis would be that the knowledge of such a diagnosis itself contributed to the increase in the therapist's anxiety and that this anxiety itself raised the patient's feelings of insecurity. Also, it is possible to argue that the prior information about a risk of dissociation could increase the probability of such dissociation. This is not to say that the therapist was too careful! Nor do I say that it would have been better not to know the diagnosis. I only want to underline that knowing the diagnosis structures the field in a particular way; not knowing it would structure the field in another, different, particular way.

So the title "First or Nowhere?" could apply not only to the patient's problem but also to the ongoing therapeutic situation: Is it possible to work only with a pure "here and now," or as therapists, have we necessarily to cope with some "first," always present? Here, the "first," or better, the "before" would be the knowledge of the so-called diagnosis.

AN OSCILLATING ATTITUDE: SOMETIMES INDIVIDUALISTIC, SOMETIMES FIELD-ORIENTED

My second remark is about the therapist's attitude. It seems to me that he very often oscillates between a field attitude and an individualistic one.

Thus, at the very beginning of the transcript, when the patient says, "I shouldn't bring that up," the therapist answers: "Do you believe that I think you shouldn't bring that up?" (00:12) This is, for me, a field posture: The therapist here makes the hypothesis that the feeling of the patient belongs not to her as a separate person, but that this feeling is the result of the therapeutic field's organization, and therefore that he has, as therapist, contributed to it. But immediately after, and even though the patient continues addressing him directly ("You'll think I'm so awful . . ." [00:21]), the therapist seems to withdraw, sending back the patient to herself and to her past, contributing so to an individualistic position ("Sounds like the past has spontaneously arrived here . . ." [00:39]).

Another example can be found when the therapist asks the patient to try making a bit of contact with him (05:05). The patient says "sorry," and then the therapist answers that he was not meaning to criticize her. For me it is an individualistic position, referring to therapist and patient as isolated persons. A field position would be to look at the emergence of this theme of criticizing in the therapeutic situation.

For me these examples raise the question: What is the meaning of this oscillation between the individualistic and the field-oriented attitudes? Maybe, when the therapist leaves the field's posture, he is, out of awareness, avoiding the contact with his patient, protecting himself. Maybe also, he chooses this deliberately, considering for instance that continuing the contact would be too unbearable for the patient. Maybe, maybe . . . Here, only the wider context of the whole of the therapy, or the comments of the therapist himself could help us to opt for one or another of these hypotheses.

SUGGESTING POSSIBILITIES OR INTENDING TO CHANGE THE PATIENT?

My third question involves the nature of the therapeutic project: The therapist opens the possibility of different truths (06:18). And it seems to me that it is an important moment, creating a stronger contact between the therapist and the patient. My question is: Is the therapist's aim only to open the field of possibilities or also to lead the patient to change her negative image of herself, to try to convince her she is wrong?

Sometimes it seems clear that the therapist searches only to open the field of possibilities, for instance, when he says: "Well, I neither agree nor disagree. I have a response, a reaction. I have a truth that is based on my own understandings . . . " (11:09). But sometimes it also seems that the therapist tries to influence the patient, especially when he tells her his feelings. So when he says, "I notice I feel really sad when you say that" (07:56), or "but I feel very sad . . . almost like I shouldn't be even breathing" (08:50), it is as if he was asking her to change and to protect him. And a few minutes later, when the patient says, "I really want to believe you, to be *with* you" (10:23), the therapist answers, "I feel really moved and pleased when you say that. I'm glad you *want* to believe me" (10:30). Here also it is as if the aim of the therapist was to lead the patient to another, better, image of herself.

Of course, I am aware that my formulations are excessive, and I imagine that the intentions of the therapist were not so clear, not so obvious. But it is to open the significance of the therapist's self-disclosure. Telling his feelings is a possible way toward the exploration of the field; it can also be a means to influence the patient.

IMPLICIT RETROFLECTED DEMAND?

Another question is about the function of retroflection: If the therapist comes to develop many efforts and arguments to change the patient, it is probably because the patient, through retroflection, and quite massive retroflection, as seems to be the case here, is effectively asking him to try and convince her that she is not so awful! So the therapist has to choose: He can accept such an implicit demand, and it seems that this is the choice of the therapist in our present transcript; he could also work to bring to light the function of retroflection and how it strongly contributes to the field's organization. It is a matter of the therapist's strategies and beliefs.

SUPPORTING THE PATIENT OR THE ONGOING EXPERIENCE?

My last comment will be about the little dog the patient evokes, near the end of the transcript. She says: "He was born last and almost died. But you know, I really really wanted him to live . . . almost more than the others" (12:21). And a few minutes later: "Well he's a real fighter, even now" (14:17). Here, the therapist seems to refer the patient to her own struggle for life, saying, "I was just really appreciating the fighter in you. Thinking about the struggles you've had . . ." (14:31). It could be, once more, an individualistic position, the patient being invited to become conscious of her fighting capacities.

But the therapist adds, ". . . the struggles we've had!" Saying that, he includes himself in the process; he assumes with his patient the role that she has assumed with the little dog, the role of a desiring human being. If the dog has survived, it is not only because of her own efforts; it is above all because of the desire of the patient that this dog should live. And if the patient, sometimes, exhibited suicidal behaviors, I guess it may be connected to a lack of other people's desire for her to be alive, maybe especially from her parents.

So it's possible to imagine that the therapy session here related is, fundamentally, an attempt to supply an archaic loss of attention and desire, which could explain that most of the time the therapist seems concerned with giving support to his patient more than with giving support to the ongoing experience, including the exploration of the here and now process of organization/disorganization of the therapeutic field.

COMMENT 2: THE UNDOING OF A RETROFLECTION

Marie-Claude Denis

> The retroflector abandons any attempt to influence his environment by becoming a separate and self-sufficient unit, reinvesting his energy back into an exclusively intrapersonal system and severely restricting the traffic between himself and the environment.
>
> —Polster & Polster, 1974, p. 71

Louisa's therapy session "First or Nowhere?" relates what must have been a most significant moment in the client's life. A dramatic event, the client killing one of her pet kittens, turned out to be her entry into the "real" world, thanks to the patient and skilful facilitation of her therapist.

I think this excerpt can be considered as a beautiful example of the undoing of a retroflection where the client (a) emerges into the "real" world, out of her self-arranged, closed-in world, (b) gains access to a fuller range of experience, involving her whole person (including physical sensations and affects) instead of returning to her stereotyped cognitive beliefs, (c) contacts the other as a separate and differentiated person instead of falling back to her opinion of the other, and (d) recognizes her identity. This session is very rich and dense in reporting the process of moving from a defensive retroflective position to a contactful experience.

THE RETROFLECTING LOUISA AND HER "TRANSITIONAL" PETS

> In retroflection, the split often creates internal abrasion and considerable stress because it remains self-contained and does not move into the required action. Movement towards growth, therefore, would be to redirect energy so that the internal struggle is opened. Instead of operating only within the individual, energy becomes free to move towards a relationship with something outside oneself. The undoing of retroflection consists of the search for the appropriate other.
>
> —Polster & Polster, 1974, p. 85

While being avoidant, engaging into self-destructive behavior, and refraining from contactful action, Louisa can be said to be a retroflector. She cloisters herself in the belief that she shouldn't exist. She seems to have constructed a world for herself where her personal dilemma of being a twin is repeatedly reproduced with numerous pairs of pet animals. From the story reported, we understand these animals to be genuine transitional objects, as Winnicott and Winnicott (1982) conceived them, one of whom literally catapulted Louisa into "reality." Somehow petrified by the fear of "getting it wrong" if she did anything, she refrained from action. But that day, when she did happen to act inadvertently and commit her most dreaded deed, killing one of her cherished pets, she has been projected through the phobic layer, right into the impasse leading to face the real her.

What or whom did Louisa kill when she hit her kitten? Did the fact of being a twin have anything to do with Louisa's retroflective behavior? Did she unconsciously feel like killing her brother? When hurting herself, was she retroflecting a smoldering anger toward him? Did she need her brother to feel whole? Or on the contrary, did she feel he shouldn't exist in order for her to be?

LIVING IS ENGAGING INTO ACTION

Only hypothesis can be drawn to answer these questions. One can only guess that a link may exist somewhere along that line. But we can witness that, killing her kitten, she broke the walls between herself and the outside world: The catastrophic idea she had of herself has been made real. As awful as the experience could be, it opened the way to genuine feelings that she has been able to express and share with the therapist's help. It also led to recognize her right to exist, just like this little dog of hers who, like her, came last, had been a "nuisance," but whom she nurtured and loved.

This process of coming into the world couldn't have succeeded without the therapist's intervention. How did the therapist facilitate this happening?

THE "APPROPRIATE OTHER"

Though the goal is for the individual to seek contact with otherness, the work-through of the inner struggle must frequently come first. In retroflection, since the impulse to do or be done to in contact with others is severely overshadowed, the interaction within the divided self must be re-energized with awareness. Close attention to the physical behavior of the individual is one way to identify where the battle is taking place . . .

—Polster & Polster, 1974, p. 87

Louisa's therapist must have been good for her since the therapy has been lasting for more than 3 years. How has she been the "appropriate other" to help Louisa come out of her cognitive bound, closed in space? While Louisa was projected into reality by the accident of killing her kitten (one could say by this accidental loss of one of her transitional objects), how did she help Louisa come to acknowledge her feelings and open up to a caring and loving space?

Some indications come out clear in the excerpt showing how the therapist worked through Louisa's emergence into a shared ("real") world, helped her to access a fuller range of experience and gain a sense of her identity. Deeply rooted in an I-Thou dialogue, the therapist asked for projections ("Do you believe that I think . . ."; "I'm wondering if you think I'm genuine"), specifications ("What's the connection? What's being repeated?"), or feeling ("What's the feeling that goes with that?").

At all times, the therapist has been very present and empathic to the client ("You look in such pain"), pointing to retroflective behavior ("I was concerned you were disappearing, hating, and punishing yourself"), specifying feelings or emotions ("not self-pity . . . self-hatred"). She opposed the client's belief with her own ("I believe something different . . . your existence is important"; "it's not my experience of being here with you"). She expressed personal feelings and physical sensations as a reverberation of the client's experience ("I feel sad when you say that"; "I notice I have a sort of choking, almost like I shouldn't even be breathing"). She pointed to the present moment and to the relation between the two of them ("I'm wondering what it's like for you to say that here, with me"), confronting the client on the difference ("I'm here with you now . . . different from you . . . and with such a different belief about you"). She made room for polarities and opposing situations, making for complete and differentiated experience ("I have a truth based on my understanding, and my experience of being with you"; "I recall many memories of both good and bad times: successes and failures"). This altogether opened the way to the expression of love ("I loved him"), understanding ("he reminded me of me"), acceptance of needs ("he just needed a lot"), and recognition of worth ("he was worth it").

Underlying all of the techniques used, I trust that the therapist's capacity to be true and to share her thoughts and feelings have been critical in Louisa's therapeutic progress toward full and genuine contact.

REFERENCES

Polster, E., & Polster, M. (1974). *Gestalt therapy integrated.* New York: Vintage Books.

Winnicott, D. W., & Winnicott, C. (1982). *Playing and reality.* London: Routledge.

COMMENT 3: THE ECOLOGY OF PSYCHOTHERAPY

Joel Latner

Whenever I hear about a patient not my own, I look for something in the description, which brings the person and the situation alive to me. With my thus activated imagination, I can penetrate empathically into some part of their life and know who they are and what is important to them to find my own truth and my version of theirs. This is in principle not different from what I do with my own patients when they talk about their friends and families. If the descriptions have a kernel of the independent life of the person being talked about, the person comes alive and the descriptions can inform my judgment of what I am hearing. In this way, I hear about the person who is talking to me (my patient or, in this case, the therapist) and also the person who is being described.

So I notice the descriptions each person gives: the patient's characterization of his or her life and its distinctive features and the facts that they consider important. In this case, it includes what her therapist refers to as her "serious self-harm," her feeling that she should not exist, and her self-criticism. Similarly, the therapist's description of Louisa's diagnosis, her admission to a hospital, her suicidal behavior, her "avoidant" and "dependent" traits.

At the same time, I remain open to the possibilities that "coming alive" suggests: a unique life lived, distinct from the descriptions, not reported, not understood, not conceptualized.

I know that these stories of the therapist and the patient have their own descriptive and explanatory power, and I take note of the way these are used by each of them. Typically, I find such descriptions and self-definitions mildly oppressive because they are evidently restrictive and categorical, and at the same time ("Holding Both!"—see Latner, 2001) in my mind and my imagination, I take them seriously and also retain my own ability to make my own judgments. So I start out with this tension between what I am given and knowing that we all are desperate to construct a coherent picture of who we are and of what our lives consist. We do this the best way we can, with what we are given: what we are told, what categories of understanding our culture gives us, and what serves to stitch together and hold together a picture of ourselves.

COMING ALIVE

So I had my customary difficulty here until I found my footing in the actuality of the events reported in this transcript. The therapists says he has been "trying to facilitate her staying in contact with herself and me," and I wonder what she is doing to be out of contact (how she achieves this), what she is in contact with, and what contribution he makes to this situation. Asking myself these questions reminds me of my own perspective as I find what is transpiring in the session—in this case, how the therapist works — and also it helps make these two people alive for me.

But then I read further in the transcript, and I see how the therapist does what he says he does: He insists on his presence and his questions, taking her seriously and asking her to be clearer for him and to engage him. He says, "What is the pattern, what does it look like?" (01:21) He is saying, in effect, "What are you talking about? I don't follow you; tell me so that I can understand you." And she answers him, finally, "Oh God, it's so awful" (02:55). This sounds like it could be something uttered from her visceral connection with her life as she knows it. But it is followed by a pause and the therapist's "reflective" comment; he imagines a vortex. It strikes me that this image is perhaps designed to be a characterization of "Oh God, it's so awful," but he is too literal; he is trying to imagine what she means by "patterns," and it comes out too abstractly. Not as the vortex she *is,* or the vortex she is *in.* He offers something mental, too abstract. She can only respond in the same way, abstractly, and in terms of how she thinks, by saying how she thinks about this new incident—killing her kitten—is in the categorical realm of what she knows already, "down to me being here."

The therapist tries again. He asks for what is missing (for him, and for me too), something direct and emotional (03:25), which embodies the self-loathing in the words she uses, "horrible, hateful . . . my mistakes"; to my eyes (and heart), he doesn't get what he asks for. I am sympathetic to his efforts, but he is asking for something she cannot deliver—not the way he is asking it. She does not know how to feel what she is talking about. (And the therapy is not focused on this, on her meaning what she says and on learning how to do this. It is difficult, isn't it, to mean what you say?)

Though he keeps looking indirectly for this, saying that she looks to be in such pain (04:20) when she says ". . . as soon as I start taking part . . . Oh" (04:06). Then he says she makes him more anxious (05:05), saying, "I just can't bear me . . ." (04:30), and he reports that he believes she might be dissociating (05:05). I would agree with him that she is perhaps dissociating, but not more than before. Louisa seems persistently disconnected from what she is saying—though he acts as though she is making sense (!)—but at the same time, paradoxically, the power of what she is saying moves him, "you look in such pain . . ." (04:20).

The therapist then asks for what is lacking, "Can you try and make a bit of contact with me" (05:05). This is a key moment, a key intervention. He is aware of the gap between how stirred up she is and how disconnected she is from herself and also from him. He asks her to come forth. She catches a part of his meaning very well, distorting it through the prism of her self-hate. He is suggesting that she should do something she is not doing, and she apologizes and then asks if he is saying she is wrong (06:13).

Another way to think about what is occurring is that Louisa lives in a world of her ideas, disconnected from a good deal of the actuality of her life, including her therapist. He sees this and attempts to intervene, though there is not much in the transcript which indicates that this is—as it ought to be, for Louisa and for her therapist—the central focus of her therapy. She needs to learn to be contactful, by which I mean open to contacting the other as fully as she does herself and allowing the play of contact, within and without, to be free of her control. This is what we in Gestalt therapy call spontaneity. Instead, she tends toward being self-involved, contacting herself, imposing her preoccupations on her perceptions. How can she do what he is asking? It seems to me she does not know how.

She tries, doing it in her characteristic manner, turning it into what she knows, the ideas she characterizes as "self-pity," and her familiar thoughts about the patterns of her life mistakes. As I read the transcript, I think the therapist could perhaps have broken through her self-involved and self-defining awareness of him if he had said, instead, "When you look like you are in such pain, I feel so sad and worried about you. I don't mind feeling this way—please, I'm not blaming you for your reaction—but I want to help you, and I think if you saw my interest in you and my affection and concern for you, it would make a difference."

I know, of course, there is a potential in saying this that she will feel blamed by him—as she has already—but instead of asking her to do what she cannot do and to do it without specific instructions. (What does "make a bit of contact with me" mean to someone like Louisa? She thinks she is making contact!) Saying what I have suggested creates a new situation: an immediate and compelling reality in which the therapist acts more like a human being, undefined and unique, not a "therapist," the familiar (and classic) role of a passive person who reflects at a remove and does not engage or react.

This role is one of our legacies from our heritage in psychoanalysis, where the analyst wishes to disappear to allow the patient's projections to be played out in the room. But it is anachronistic. We have learned that patients will project, no matter what we do (as will we), and we cannot utilize the actuality of the here and now if we do not attend to it. I think it is also a legacy of our fear of our founder and his putative bad behavior in therapy. We will be beyond reproach (by whom?), but as we recede, we will also take no risks. This part of the transcript is an instance of the risk of taking no risks.

Sure enough, as the meeting continues (06:13–06:18), the therapist takes a more human stance in the therapy. He reflects her at 06:01, and she, asking for his engagement and reading him correctly says, "Are you saying I'm wrong?" (06:13). She says, in effect, where do you stand? And he says, in effect, without denying her beliefs, yes, I think you are not correct in how you see things; I see things from my perspective as well as yours, and "I believe something different."

This is contactful, and he engages her vividly. She reiterates her ideas (are they convictions or just repetitive ideas?), and he strides forth into the room at 07:56, saying, "I notice I feel really sad when you say that," only hedging his daring with "I notice." And he is bolder still at 08:50, "That is absolutely not my experience of being here with you . . . I notice I have a sort of choking . . . telling me how strongly you believe you shouldn't exist." This is the essential contact from the therapist, telling Louisa how it is for another human, the one who has devoted these 143 hours of his professional life to her care, to be with her. He has brilliantly abandoned the safety of his obscurity, his clinical distance, and instead of asking her to meet him, he does it himself. (Who knows? If he continues in this direction, soon he will tell her about himself, his life, his loves, his family, his disappointments, and she will find the actuality of this world unavoidable!)

She responds, arriving in the room with him. He says, directly and engagingly, "What is it like . . . I'm here with you . . . and a different experience of you . . . I'm just wondering if that makes you feel apart from me." (09:50). (Better: What is it like *for you?*) Louisa replies, obliquely, "I really want to believe you . . ." and then, striding forward, "to be *with* you" (10:23).

The next words from both of them circle around this meeting they have initiated. He backs off, "wondering"(10:30), consulting his thought processes, but trying also to find again the pulsing vein he had touched. She tells him something important about the man she has known these 4 years, "I know you wouldn't lie to me" (10:53). He gets didactic—backing off—and she responds with apparent confusion (11:20). The therapist's sentences at this point, explaining his ideology ("So there is contrast and difference. . . . I just believe that life, including your life, is purposeful" [11:27]), show him stepping back from the vitality of their meeting—what is he afraid of?—into ideas and beliefs, reasserting the morass she and he were struggling in previously.

This is a critical moment, where it is clear that he can control the tone of the therapy and the "disease" of his patient. In fact, the form of his statements is not different from the ones he was hearing from her earlier. He says what he believes about life in general, and therefore her life; earlier in the transcript, she was telling him how she sees her life in general. Here he is encouraging a generalized present. At this point, it seems as though he has lost touch with what was important and lively about this encounter and how he can make this occur. He is either not aware of the way he controls the extent of their intimacy, or he is afraid of it. He is again taking the distant and parental benign-teacher–therapist position and telling her his good ideas, in contrast to her bad ones about patterns and self-hate.

But Louisa is a straightforward person (and she seems healthier than we have been led to believe), and her response is refreshingly concrete: "I'm just thinking of one of my little dogs" (12:21). The topics she touches on as she continues, reminiscing about her dog are—not coincidentally—love, acceptance, and the struggle to grow (13:07). But the therapist insists on his teacherly posture with her ("So, is he really a nuisance?" [13:25]). The therapist realizes he is moving in the wrong direction and tosses away this unconstructive stance and says he is moved. "I just had a really warm, pleased sense of your aliveness" (14:31).

Louisa steps back a moment (What's with this guy? He's here and then he's gone!? And then he's back!?!) and takes her familiar infirm position, saying, "It's still a struggle" (15:15). And so the therapist too returns to his kindly role, full of hope and encouragement (15:23 and 15:39), "I see you struggling to cope . . . and I trust that struggle will bring you through." I read into his words his feeling of joy at her spontaneous emergence and his pleasure at his knowledge of his part in it, but this is not the best way to say it.

CONCLUSION

In his summary paragraph, the therapist says they had touched a dark place in her, and they had also maintained a strong contact for most of the rest of the session. I wished he had considered himself more in the course of the therapy and in his final comment, which is misleading. It directs our attention to the wrong place and suggests that this disturbed woman has dark places in her. This term expresses his overly intrapsychic perspective. It is not necessary to ignore the inner world, but he looks too insistently away from himself and to Louisa. Properly, he should embrace them both.

I would say that the place they had touched was the result of the efforts of two people who fail to touch each other because of the ways they encapsulate themselves and blunt their contacting. He does this by his impersonal methods, his intellectualizing interventions, and the way he hides what is distinctive about him. Louisa encapsulates herself by organizing her awareness and her social milieu (her therapist, in this case) to focus on her mental constructions—without regard for the rest of her awareness or her qualities: her capacity for engagement, her emotions, her feelings, her liveliness, her creative resources. But each of them persevered and, because of the daring of the therapist and Louisa's responsiveness—they both have good instincts, a taste for life!—they made something important.

I don't see any sign that he has yet recognized what they did, unfortunately, or how they can repeat it, but I am optimistic that they can again create a life between them that is vital and engaging and that they will each grow in it.

REFERENCE

Latner, J. (2001). Alles einbeziehen—Gedanken über Ganzheitlichkeit [Holism—Holding all]. In F.-M. Staemmler (Ed.), *Gestalttherapie im Umbruch—Von alten Begriffen zu neuen Ideen* [Gestalt therapy in upheaval—From old terms to new ideas] (pp. 117–141). Köln, Germany: Edition Humanistische Psychologie. Also in *British Gestalt Journal 2001, 10/2*, 106–113, as "The sense of gestalt therapy: Holism, reality and explanation"; as "Lo Holistico: Abarcandolo Todo" in *Figura/Fondo, 11*, 2002. The article was accepted for publication in *Cahiers de Gestalt-thérapie* in 2002.

COMMENT 4: BEING A REPEAT, REPEATING BEING

Lynne Jacobs

So much of the therapeutic process is circular. There are the repetitive loops, and then there are the recursive loops, and loops that have aspects of both repetition and recursiveness.

REPETITIVE AND RECURSIVE LOOPS OF EXPERIENCING

The repetitive loops reflect imprisonment in, and also investment in, a closed system of negative expectation, dread, and despair. In general, I believe the imprisonment in dread and negativity is an outgrowth of trauma. On the other hand, the investment in the closed system is a creative adjustment (the creative nature of which has been long forgotten, needing reawakening in therapy), one whereby the negativity, dread, and despair that characterized one's reactions to trauma are used in the service of maintaining a sense of security. One's conviction that the next moment of existence offers no possibility for richness, but only pain and misery, offers a sure and secure guideline about life. Such a conviction removes uncertainty, and uncertainty is messy. Uncertainty leaves one open to rising hopes and crashing disappointments, to loves and losses, to enthusiasms and embarrassments. Uncertainty draws us toward the world and all its vagaries, whereas a firm conviction about the hopelessness of life draws us away from the roller coaster that living inevitably is.

Recursive loops, on the other hand, are the manifestations of the fluidity and movement of present-centeredness, in which one's history and one's future are intermixed oscillating grounds for each other. In other words, a recursive loop is an inevitable outgrowth of contacting. In a recursive loop, one may touch upon very familiar themes and yet do so in a way that casts new light upon the theme, reshuffles the images of one's history into a different Gestalt, or opens a surprising new pathway into the next moment. Every so-called "new" experience, contact with novelty, is only *relatively* new; it is emergent from the ground of our history. "New" experience reorganizes our history as it also becomes our history, the ground for the next moment and so on.

Therapist and patient each bring repetitive loops to their relationship. They also both bring recursive loops or at least an aptitude for their development. And over the course of therapy, they will develop some dance steps together. The ritualized dance steps will draw on the repetitive tendencies of both and will become a unique but still relatively closed system. Both will have to work together to "open up" the dance to greater degrees of improvisation if their relationship is to develop. The development of the patient is an emergent phenomenon of a "recursive loop dance" that draws on the shift, in both partners, from relating in a repetitive loop to relating in recursive loops.

ATTUNEMENT TO REPETITION

Louisa and her therapist[1] have lived through many a repetition. Louisa, with her pronounced tendency to dissociate, probably knows from direct experience what trauma is. This anguished woman who describes beautifully and compellingly the annihilation of being a pointless repetition herself ("Maybe I'd believe that [my existence is important] if I'd been born a single person. But it's like, when there's twins, it's like a repeat one has been made. Like an afterthought; so in effect, my brother's the one that was meant to be born. . . . [I am] surplus." [06:31–08:01]) lives in a very familiar loop that she and her therapist have traveled many times, illustrated by the following exchange:

C (03:31): Horrible, hateful; . . . that it's all down to me . . . my mistakes. What is the point of me being here? I've always said that I haven't got a function in life; but at least if I haven't got a function, if I don't get things wrong . . . no one gets hurt.

T (03:50): Sounds like you've got back to that very early decision that "I shouldn't be here;" and if I am here, I should have no needs, make no waves, and definitely get nothing wrong.

C (04:06): Well at least then I'm not doing any harm by being here. But as soon as I start taking part . . . Oh.

T (04:20): You look in such pain, physical pain when you say that.

The theme of utter negation has had many repetitions in the history of this therapeutic relationship. This theme of repetitive loops is not often addressed in Gestalt therapy literature, with its emphasis on fresh, new experiences, and yet I hazard a guess that we are all familiar with the enervating and demoralizing influence of such repetition.

My belief is that part of the transformative power of the relatively newer moments of contact derives from the shared history of having lived together in the repetitive loop. Further, I believe that the recursive evolution of this therapy session, which moved from heartbreak (of killing her cat), into familiar repeat ("It feels like it's a 'come-back' you see

---

[1] For simplicity's sake, I will write as if the therapist is male.

that I can't just forget it. It's like it keeps on repeating itself, and its just going to keep on repeating itself. The memories keep coming back, and it keeps on happening. Something will happen, sooner or later, and the pattern is there ... all the same." [00:49]), into heartfelt shared engagement with Louisa's darkest thoughts and feelings (the later two-thirds of the transcript), into a newer perspective (reflected in her loving/self-loving discussion of her puppy), derived in large part from the therapist's openness to the repetitive loop. I cannot emphasize this enough: *The therapist's willingness to really know the patient from within her repetitive experiential world was fundamental to making it possible for the patient to emerge, even if momentarily, from that world.*

Our paradoxical theory of change emphasizes the importance for the patient of identifying with his or her immediate, ongoing, moment-by-moment experience. The same is required of the therapist, I believe, although with a twist. The therapist needs to be able to identify with his or her own experiencing and also to attempt to stay in contact with the patient's experiencing at the same time. This is often done through practicing "inclusion" (Buber, 1967, p. 173). One means whereby one might practice inclusion is through emotional attunement. By attunement I mean attempting to find an emotional resonance with the patient's emotional state and perspective.[2] I contrast this notion with the emphasis some other therapists place on focusing on the quality of patients' contacting. Obviously, at various points in our therapeutic work, we will want to experiment with various modes of contacting. But there is a big difference between an exploratory atmosphere that has been built on being well met and respected for your current solutions and one that is built on an atmosphere that suggests there is a right way to contact and a wrong way.

The transcript provides a lucid example of how repetitive loops begin to break out into recursive loops through an ongoing process in which the therapist attempts to really know the patient's experience. There are plenty of examples of the therapist attempting to feel his way into the patient's perspective. Here are some from the first third of the transcript:

T (03:15): (reflectively) I imagine a spiral, a vortex; I wonder how it seems to you.
T (03:25): What's the feeling that goes with that . . . that it's all down to you being here?
T (04:20): You look in such pain, physical pain when you say that.

An important point here is that the therapist's efforts to formulate an attuned understanding of the patient's struggles did not result, as some people fear, in an entrenchment of the patient in her repetitive loop. Rather, his attunement, his emotional resonance, seemed to provide a platform that deepened the conversation, made it more emotional, *and* ultimately more exploratory.

In particular, the therapist also attempts to track the patient's experience of the therapist's impact. This is a special case of attunement, and an interesting effect of his questions about his potentially difficult affect on Louisa is that Louisa's conversation often began to open into the recursive looping following his queries about her experience of being with him.

The patient began by saying she shouldn't even bring up her repetitive pessimistic version of herself. The therapist asks, "Do you believe that I think you shouldn't bring that up?" (00:12). At this point, she does not really explore his question but begins her descent into what the therapist called a downward spiral (might that have been his experience?). At another point, he asks her, "I'm wondering what it's like for you to say that

---

[2] There is some confusion among Gestalt therapists about the concept of "attunement," a concept that first gained wide currency in contemporary psychoanalysis (Stolorow et al., 1987) and in child development studies (Stern, 1985). I think that Gestalt therapists who criticize attunement as a surrender or diminishment of the therapist's phenomenology are mistaken (see, e.g., Philippson, 2001; Resnick, 1995). The practice of attunement in fact requires *exquisite* ongoing awareness of one's own phenomenology. That is why actually practicing inclusion or attunement is so difficult to do!

here, with me . . . to say that to me" (08:23). In response, the patient voiced her *ideas* about the therapist's feelings, which opened the door for them to have a long conversation about their differing *experiences* of being with her. Their conversation about differing experiences of being with her vacillated back and forth between familiar and new and ran through the rest of the session. We can see here the interweaving of repetition and recursiveness that runs through many a therapy session.

The therapist also listened, throughout the session, both with an ear for the emotional tone of her misery but for something that might reach past the immediate moment, something that might provide some perspective. Hence, the references earlier to "patterns," which he elaborates as: "Sounds like you've got back to that very early decision that 'I shouldn't be here,' and if I am here, I should have no needs, make no waves, and definitely get nothing wrong" (03:50).

I think most of us look for such fundamental themes, patterns, and repetitions, and we look to put them into words, in part in the hope that the words will create a slight shift in perspective. Instead of just living from the negative theme, our hope is that labeling the theme might allow for exploration of the theme.

Another important contribution from the therapist is that he offered his own experience as part of the evolution of a recursive dialogue in which they were both implicated. Some of the therapist's statements seem to be an attuned responsiveness to the patient's interest in conversation that is outside the repetitive loop. Other statements seem more reactive to the therapist's distress (as when the therapist was worried about another dissociative episode), and yet they all emerge from the ground of genuine interest in the patient's experiential world (which is the therapist's contribution to living through the paradoxical theory of change). When the therapist reacted to his own anxiety, the exchange did not go well, although they both were able to recover quickly. When he spoke from a more centered state, the patient appeared genuinely interested, engaging in conversation with him.

RECURSIVE DANCE

By the time they were engaged in Louisa's moving story about her puppy, with its obvious parallels to her own story, they were dancing together smoothly, daring to try a few new moves, building the moves out from their original choreography. They were in a recursive loop, still addressing her fundamental themes, but in creative new ways. They weren't throwing away the old steps; they were adding new ones that emerged from their way of dancing the older steps together while being open to experimenting with new steps. The experiments were built upon skill with the old steps, but having new steps puts the old steps into a different context now. The old steps are not the only steps they know.

My guess is that Louisa is just beginning to dance new steps. She is at the edge of her imprisonment, the new steps a beginning breakout. I said at the beginning of my remarks that I thought repetitive loops were both a reaction to trauma and also reflected a self-protective investment in sameness and security. The figure at this moment seems to be her imprisonment. At another moment, it may be her investment. Ultimately, unless her investment is also explored, the new dance steps will be small gains and in fact may be assimilated back into a repetitive loop.

However, at this point, such a focus would seem to me to be ill-timed and might well reimprison Louisa in her sense of worthlessness. There may be moments that emerge later; for instance, she may become aware that she is anxious when she dares to believe her therapist truly does value her, when the investment side of the polarity can become a momentary focus. When that begins to happen, there may be stretches of time when the therapist and patient will go back and forth (in recursive loops!) between imprisonment and investment. Then still newer dance steps will develop again, some uncoordinated, with "who is leading here?" being fought out, and others thrillingly mutually coordinated. But for now, we have all born witness to the tiny but awesome beginnings of a new dance.

What a privilege to have been allowed a glimpse of an intense, moving, therapeutic encounter. I am grateful to the therapist and to the client for letting all of us walk along the way for a bit with them. I was moved deeply by both of you, your courage, and honest dialogue with each other. I wish you both all the best.

REFERENCES

Buber, M. (1967). *A believing humanism: Gleanings* (M. S. Friedman, Trans.). New York: Simon & Schuster.

Philippson, P. (2001). *Self in relation.* Highland, NY: Gestalt Journal Press.

Resnick, R. (1995). Gestalt therapy: Principles, prisms and perspectives. *British Gestalt Journal, 4/1,* 3–13.

Stern, D. (1985). *The interpersonal world of the infant.* New York: Basic Books.

Stolorow, R., Brandchaft, B., & Atwood, G. (1987). *Psychoanalytic treatment: An intersubjective approach.* Hillsdale, NJ: Analytic Press.

FIRST OR NOWHERE?
A QUEST FOR EXISTENCE:
RESPONSE TO THE COMMENTS

Sally Denham-Vaughan

In my response to the comments, I wish to take the opportunity to explore a number of themes. First, I want to write briefly about my process of offering the transcript and then receiving feedback. This is something that was, somewhat to my surprise, remarked upon by a number of the commentators. Second, I shall attempt to explain my process regarding some of the interventions made (or indeed not made) in the transcript. Finally, I wish to highlight one or two key themes that this exercise raises.

MY BASIC ATTITUDE

With regard to my process of offering and receiving, I was particularly struck by the supportive nature of the feedback I have received. I heard the commentators highlighting the risks involved in offering the transcript, their general support and curiosity for the work, and also their appreciation of the opportunity to glimpse an intimate moment in an ongoing therapy. I was struck by the "reaching out" I felt from these unidentified watchers and began to reflect with interest upon aspects in myself that had enabled me to undertake my role in this joint venture.

It was, unsurprisingly perhaps, a risky and scary business for me to reveal my therapeutic work. I had what I imagined to be fairly usual fears of being criticized, shown to be theoretically lacking or methodologically clumsy, and was particularly anxious that the comments were made by "unknown strangers" rather than within the context of a dialogue.

I wondered then in more detail what had impelled me forward! I kept coming up with the phrase "I trusted I would not be annihilated."

I felt moved by these words. I also reflected on the fact that perhaps it is this aspect of my character that is supporting me in working with Louisa, who both fears annihilation and, in this transcript, finds herself to be the cause of it in a very literal sense. I was therefore struck by how central this, possibly naive, trusting in my ability to survive, and indeed finding support for myself in that process, had been in the exercise and also in the therapy.

I wondered if this possibly reflected a basic attitude that underpins my work, which I think is central to many of us within the Gestalt community. It is the belief that growth and change are possible and that the organism orientates itself naturally toward these ends.

I now wish to deal with some of the individual comments.

RESPONSE TO COMMENT 1

I consider myself a fairly classic Gestalt therapist in that I work with elements of field theory, dialogue, and phenomenology. I was delighted that this first commentator picked up on possible tensions between these maps, which I think are often glossed over.

I now wish to talk about this with specific reference to the issue of diagnosis, which is also noted in comment three.

As stated in my introduction, I work in the British National Health Service, where Gestalt therapy is, unfortunately, rapidly disappearing. One of the reasons for this, I believe, has been our ongoing ambivalence regarding the issue of diagnosis and preconfiguration of the field with reference to specific client groups. In particular, Gestalt psychotherapy has little to say about "evidence-based" work with the Axis 1 disorders named in *DSM-IV* and lacks a coherent model of brief therapy that can be reliably agreed upon.

Thus, there are times when I find myself balancing an internal tension between the need to work in a way that recognizes the system within which I work—that is, "field congruence,"—without losing my identity as a Gestalt therapist. Specifically, I experience a "pull" to engage in an "I-it" mode of relating that challenges my commitment to both dialogue and the phenomenological principle of horizontality.

I *am* constantly aware of the potential abuses that can result from rote labeling and psychopathologizing of people. As a trainee (when I was already a practicing clinical psychologist), I was struck by Clarkson's statement, "to label people can be to strip them of the unique way in which they have chosen to give meaning to their existence and their historical context" (1989, p. 23). Within my environment, this process does occur.

Regrettably, however, I have witnessed this same process at work within a range of Gestalt settings. Therefore, I would ask that we attempt to own our shadow rather than comfortably project it onto the mental health system. Any semantic form can be misused if misapplied, including Gestalt psychotherapy language.

I believe I share with Louisa a dialectic tension in experiencing the environment as *both* potentially destructive *and* potentially lifesaving, at times even life enhancing. Perhaps it is no surprise that these themes are also paralleled within Louisa's therapeutic journey and in the brief vignette of our work together that the transcript describes.

Second, I was somewhat confused by some of the examples that this commentator described as expressing an "individualistic" stance. My experience is of oscillating, intentionally, around four key aspects in the current phenomenal field. These include myself as an individual, the client as an individual (both of us with unique intrapsychic structures), the "between" of our relationship, and the environment that frames and configures our meeting. For me, these elements comprise the "total situation" that a field perspective demands we examine (Lewin, 1951, p. 288).

In addition, Parlett (1991) states that therapy "may include the past-as-remembered-now or the future-as-anticipated-now, which will form part of the person's experiential field in the present" (p. 71). Thus, the temporal focus is the present as it combines past and the anticipated future.

I thereby recognize that I may have a different "take" with regard to a field theoretical mode of working from this writer, as mine *includes* attention to individual intrapsychic experience as it emerges in the context of specific field conditions. For example, one aspect that I am alert to with regard to Louisa's process is her tendency to constellate herself as a burden in relationship. My experience is that too intense, prolonged, or intimate contact between us triggers her into initial confluence, followed by intense shame and isolation. I therefore attempt to keep the contact available, but "calibrate" it in line with my previous experiences of her responding with either feelings of abandonment or shame if the contact is either underplayed or overmade.

I judge this way of working as wholly consistent with a "field" paradigm, recognizing her process with me across time and emergent in the here-and-now relational frame. To me, this is not an "individualistic" way of formulating her case but recognition of the self as process model being meshed with a field theoretical stance. As such, both Louisa and I emerge as ourselves at the boundary formed by our meeting. The entire phenomenal field is present in this meeting, shaping and forming not just our relationship but also the selves who are available to the meeting.

I was interested in comments where again this commentator made for me a false dichotomy between my being open to either "the field of possibilities" or "leading the patient." This raises an interesting dialectic tension surrounding work with patients where their current experience of themselves is *truly* unbearable and overwhelming. When I contact Louisa in that place, I wish to validate not only where she is now but also her sense that this place is unbearable and she needs to get out of it as fast as possible!

At these moments, I am questioning the value of us as Gestalt therapists holding too tightly to the notion of the paradoxical theory of change and believing that it is always acceptable to stay with the client and his or her experience in any state that is expressed. My sense is that here we confront a real theoretical tension with very fragile clients, between the phenomenological method and the practice of the dialogic relationship. My reality is that I have now lived with Louisa's wish to kill herself for some 4 years. On the one hand, living with this for that length of time has reassured me that she is unlikely to kill herself. On the other hand, I have also validated her desire to kill herself so frequently and felt the intensity of her desire so strongly that I now hold this as part of my inclusive relational stance with Louisa. I thus have an emotional response to her self-destructive feelings and behaviors, which I see being authentically presented in this vignette. My experience is of attempting to be present with this while also demonstrating my respect for her ultimate decision regarding whether to end her life.

Finally, I was struck by this commentator's last paragraph, where she or he imagines that the therapy session is fundamentally an attempt to supply an archaic loss of attention and desire. It is indeed within my awareness that Louisa carries archaic longings for specific types of contact, commonly known as self-object needs, which were unmet in her childhood (see Kohut, 1971). I would say that my experience is of wishing to give support to these longings, as well as to the ongoing experience of exploring the here and now. I do not see these as an "either–or" that we can follow in therapy. Indeed, Yontef's and Jacobs's "relational Gestalt therapy" (see Jacobs, 1992, 1995; Yontef, 1993, 2002), which combines elements of self-psychology with Gestalt therapy theory, emphasizes the importance of both these activities occurring simultaneously within the therapeutic encounter.

RESPONSE TO COMMENT 2

I appreciated this commentator looking at the work through the lens of moderations to contact. In particular, I resonated with the idea of "creative adjustments" that have been used to survive traumatic field conditions in the past, becoming embedded as "fixed Gestalt" (see Perls, Hefferline, & Goodman, 1951).

With Louisa, I am frequently reminded of how her original needs were often denied or distorted, and continue to be so, due to a danger being perceived in pursuing their satisfaction. Currently, the whole of Louisa's being—physical, emotional, and cognitive—frequently moderates contact in these fixed ways.

I felt especially pleased that this commentator seemed to have so accurately picked up the fears of annihilation/annihilating that emerge from Louisa's work. She does indeed admit to historical feelings of wishing to kill her twin so that she could have been "the only one." In many ways, the dreadful experience of killing her kitten is an incarnation of this most terrible (to her) aspect of her personality. Interestingly, however, this theme manifests itself within the therapy as ongoing dreams consisting of her twin killing her. It is indeed the case that the twins did frequently compete for a range of situations, including both being attracted to a young man who eventually had a relationship with both twins but chose to stay with Louisa's brother! She experienced this loss of an early lover as an "annihilation" of her sexuality and has since been abused and raped twice in other relationships.

I felt very met by this commentator in the work and, although the particular map of moderations to contact is not one that I commonly use, I would agree that retroflection is a key contact style for Louisa and add that it is also key for myself. Thus, my ability to cognitively attune, possibly project, and occasionally miss her through retroflecting my more spontaneous, contactful aspects are all part of our therapeutic journey together.

This has perhaps been most powerfully described when Louisa has equated her fear of people with my current fear of riding horses (an activity which she is a master at). She has on more than one occasion said that if I were willing to get back on a horse under her instruction, she would be willing to attend a social group. These moments provide us with very powerful contact when we can both connect with what feels to be an irrational, but overriding, fear that prevents action. At the current time in therapy, we are using the metaphor of me getting on a horse (and I am experimenting with the notion of this as a reality) as an active way of exploring and supporting her overcoming her fear of relationships and contact.

RESPONSE TO COMMENT 3

I was struck by this therapist's attention to the detail in the work. In particular, I found the section on "coming alive" full of momentum and had a sense of this writer feeling into the "sequential imperative" of the work. The detail of the analysis reminded me of Erv Polster's (1991) notion of "tight therapeutic sequences," where each individual intervention is viewed as either sharpening or diffusing the figure.

I was particularly interested in comments regarding my perception, and anxiety, around Louisa's dissociation. The phrase "Louisa seems persistently disconnected from what she is saying—though he [the therapist] acts as though she is making sense (!) . . ." was fascinating to me because Louisa does indeed make sense to me. Whether this is because as individuals we have similar processes regarding contact style, or whether this is simply because I know sufficient ground of her story to have a sense of coherent narrative, one cannot be sure.

I do believe that here this commentator is highlighting a critical choice point of mine regarding how to "be" in the therapeutic relationship. My dilemmas lie in the realm of how to respond, without, as Beaumont (1993) describes, causing a breakdown of contact by either too much intimacy or too much stress.

In some ways, it is true that as an individual I tend toward retroflection and as a therapist can stay within my comfort zone by making insufficient contact. I can only say that this does not seem to be the reality of the ongoing nature of this particular therapy. Rather, my sense is that I have become more delicate and sparing with contact as I have gotten to know Louisa better. It is easy for her to be overwhelmed by contact, descend into dissociation and then shame, with a clear sense of being a failure at not being able to "handle" relationships. It is true that there are moments of excellent contact between us; however, I do configure her dissociation as a creative adaptation to trauma, and my sense is that Louisa and I carefully calibrate our contact.

My main dilemma is therefore around how *much* contact to offer, given her beliefs that only a "twin" who is with her 24 hours a day will be able to provide enough, that I am paid to do the work, and that any needs for contact on her part are burdensome to the other! She thus experiences a tremendously conflictual situation of feeling insatiably needy and dreadfully ashamed of her needy part.

I am curious that this commentator states that "we cannot utilize the actuality of the here and now . . ." if we do not attend to clients' projections. My way of working with projections, I would argue, is more, rather than less, contactful. I favor the method of initially looking for the "perception" that may be concealed within the projected material but out of my awareness. At these points, therefore, I will tend to examine my own behavior/self-configuration to see what has triggered a particular comment from the client. This work is largely informed by that of Stolorow, Brandchaft, and Atwood (1987, pp. 38ff.) in describing their rupture and repair cycle. This seems to be a path that Louisa and I frequently travel together, with her seeming to find my willingness to take responsibility for my side of the relationship very freeing and supportive of her moving forward into more contact. I have a clear sense of being in the immediate actuality of the present while working in this way.

I found this commentator's curiosity regarding my potential fears of Louisa's neediness in the relationship very interesting. I am sure it will not wholly surprise some readers to hear that I am a child of a twin, who had the experience of a twin dying in childhood. My own childhood thus frequently involved being invited to provide a lost twin relationship.

Through my own therapy, I am well aware of how demanding I found this. While it gives me a fairly unique insight into Louisa's neediness, it also gives me a great wariness of ongoing confluence, or being seen to promise to deliver something that I personally and professionally am unable to provide. I am aware that through Louisa's therapy I stand to learn, grow, explore, and examine this issue again and again. This truly is a case where both of us gain from the meeting, and I am grateful to Louisa for this opportunity.

In retrospect, I can imagine that this piece of information would have enabled the commentators to go far deeper into the relational process between Louisa and myself. I can only say that, having met the commentators through their writing, I now feel able to move forward into more contact regarding my own process. Such is the nature of dialogue and retroflection as a contact style!

RESPONSE TO COMMENT 4

I felt very in tune with this writer's comments regarding trauma, creative adjustment, and security, although the notion of repetitive and recursive loops of experience is not a language that I would use, favoring instead notions of creative adjustment, fixed Gestalts, and needed/repeated relational themes.

There were a number of occasions when I found myself so attuned to this writer's formulation of the case that it left relatively little to write and respond to. This left me musing about the notion of confluence and the basic biological necessity that we ground ourselves in as Gestalt therapists. That is, human neural networks are excited by novelty and change. I agreed with this writer that, historically, the stance of Gestalt therapy theory has been to build upon this fact (perhaps due to the effect of Fritz Perls's personality), and we tend to favor action, differentiation, and newness over repetition, calmness, and stillness. We are traditionally a "libidinous" brand of therapy, tending to suit resilient, explorative clients rather than fragile individuals seeking to enact old patterns and have the therapist fulfill additional ego-functions.

I was reminded of Stratford and Brallier's (1979) classic paper describing Gestalt psychotherapy with "profoundly disturbed" people. These writers employ the metaphors of "solvent" and "glue," suggesting the latter as being more helpful with more fragile clients. With Louisa, I seem to shuttle between the gluepot and the solvent spray, attempting to release old stuck patterns as far as we are able, without destabilizing and dissolving her to an intolerable degree. I found this writer's notion of recursive and repetitive loops forming at the contact boundary provided an elegant form for describing this process, and one which I can imagine incorporating into my work with other clients. I also found myself having a sense of confirmation in my work with Louisa; a notion that although we seem to recycle old patterns for much of our time together, fresh, new, and potentially transformative moments arise spontaneously from the ground of our meeting. Indeed, it is the sense of this possibility that supports me in holding the pole of "life" in our work together, especially in those dark moments when Louisa's hold on this seems very fragile.

Interestingly, as I write this some 12 months after the session described in the transcript, I am impacted by a moment that happened today. It has been a beautiful spring day, and Louisa left a message on my voice-mail. Usually, these signal moments of distress and requests for contact and support. Today, however, the content was different. "Sally, I am just ringing to let you know that I've been out with the dogs and I noticed the colors everywhere. I couldn't believe how vivid everything looked and the strange thing was that as I noticed this, I had a sense of aliveness everywhere around me. I remembered you saying that therapy was one way of discovering a capacity for joy in living and I wanted to tell you that I'd had a brief sense of what that might be like today."

I'm sure it will not surprise readers to know that I have been powerfully affected by that call; I looked up from my writing, glanced out the window, and thought, "It *is* gorgeous out there; she's right." In that instant, I realized that not only had Louisa described a potentially transformative moment for her, but she had also improved the quality of my life in that moment. In doing this, she also powerfully reinforced my ability to hold the "libidinous" pole of the therapy for her. I wondered if this moment was an example of a recursive loop, having the potential to grow, change, and heal both the individuals who are present. It certainly felt like it!

I was particularly pleased that the theme of Louisa being a twin was given a central position in how this writer viewed the relational dance. In addition, I was struck by the attention to the process of attunement, which I regard as an essential part of my practice of inclusion. As I said earlier, my aim here is to be fully present in my own experience while attempting to see the situation as the client has constructed it. I would agree that this practice does require an oscillation between the intrapsychic worlds of two individuals who are together working at an emergent relational boundary.

Finally, I appreciated how this commentator also gave a very elegant description of my tracking of the impact of my presence upon Louisa. This was framed within the notion of the recursive loop of being a burden, but it very accurately attuned to my own struggles to calibrate my contact in a way that Louisa found growthful.

SUMMARY

Having read the four comments on the transcript, I am left with a sense of range and variety between the writers. In many ways, for me this is part of the excitement, creativity, and vitality of Gestalt psychotherapy.

On a more somber note, however, I can feel myself left with some lingering discomfort at quite how much variation there is in the maps and models that have been used to discuss the work. I am reminded of some hot debates that have taken place in various Gestalt conferences regarding "What is and is not Gestalt therapy?" This question has traditionally caused me to bridle, feeling a sense of stultification, control, and judgment being potentially used to erode the spontaneous and vital aspect that is at the heart of our work. I believe that Gestalt psychotherapy is unique in its ability to orientate to growth, health, and change as well as distress, despair, and pain, and I am committed to bringing this work to my more fragile clients within the healthcare system.

I now find myself, however, reflecting again upon what are the essential qualities of Gestalt therapy and Gestalt therapy theory. What precisely is it that enables us to describe a case as one that employs "a Gestalt therapy frame" as opposed to say an integrationist perspective or an intersubjective one?

This process of defining Gestalt therapy is not just of theoretical interest but also of intense pragmatic value. My fear is that if we cannot agree on ways of describing and formulating cases, then we cannot fulfill the fundamental requirements needed to research the validity and efficacy of our approach. Namely, the work should be able to be described and replicated in method if not in practice.

Maybe it is this issue at the heart of our approach that explains why we have failed to respond to the challenge of providing adequate research into the outcome of Gestalt psychotherapy. This lack of validation and empirical support is now proving a serious difficulty for those of us wishing to work in environments where an "evidence-based approach" is called for. I firmly believe that if we are to respond to this challenge, it is only by describing cases and beginning to agree on ways of discussing our approach that we will begin to put forward some key signposts and milestones that we might all be able to converge around.

REFERENCES

Beaumont, H. (1993). Martin Buber's 'I-Thou' and fragile self-organisation: Gestalt couples therapy. *British Gestalt Journal, 2/2,* 85–95.

Clarkson, P. (1989). *Gestalt counseling in action.* London: Sage.

Jacobs, L. (1992). Insights from psychoanalytic self-psychology and intersubjectivity theory for Gestalt therapists. *The Gestalt Journal, 15/2,* 25–60.

Jacobs, L. (1995). Self psychology, intersubjectivity theory, and Gestalt therapy: A dialogic perspective. In R. Hycner & L. Jacobs (Eds.), *The healing relationship in Gestalt therapy: A dialogic/self psychology approach* (pp. 129–158). Highland, NY: Gestalt Journal Press.

Kohut, H. (1971). *The analysis of the self.* New York: International Universities Press.

Lewin, K. (1951). *Field theory in social science: Selected theoretical papers* (D. Cartwright, Ed.). New York: Harper & Brothers.

Parlett, M. (1991). Reflections on field theory. *British Gestalt Journal, 1/2,* 69–81.

Perls, F. S., Hefferline, R. F., & Goodman, P. (1951). *Gestalt therapy: Excitement and growth in the human personality.* New York: Julian Press.

Polster, E. (1991). Tight therapeutic sequences. *British Gestalt Journal, 1/2,* 63–68.

Stolorow, R. D., Brandchaft, B., & Atwood, G. E. (1987). *Psychoanalytic treatment: An intersubjective approach.* Hillsdale, NJ: Analytic Press.

Stratford, C. D., & Brallier, L. W. (1979). Gestalt therapy with profoundly disturbed persons. *The Gestalt Journal, 2/1,* 90–103.

Yontef, G. M. (1993). *Awareness, dialogue, and process: Essays on Gestalt therapy.* Highland, NY: Gestalt Journal Press.

Yontef, G. M. (2002). The relational attitude in Gestalt therapy theory and practice. *International Gestalt Journal, 25/1,* 15–35.

Editors' Introduction

This case was specifically selected by Arnold Lazarus to illustrate his chapter on multimodal therapy in Current Psychotherapies. *It is a clearly presented case history that demonstrates a multimodal assessment using the seven BASIC I.D. dimensions and the flexibility required as new life crises and personal dilemmas present in therapy. There is nothing especially dramatic about this case, but it represents the kind of routine "bread-and-butter" work conducted by most therapists most of the time.*

The case provides a good example of the utility of self-help books and the importance of bibliotherapy. It demonstrates the techniques of cognitive restructuring, modeling, tension release, and role-playing, and it illustrates the practice of technical eclecticism (i.e., using multiple procedures from different sources without necessarily subscribing to the underlying theories associated with the procedures).

Lazarus makes a distinction between "boundary crossings" and "boundary violations," and he argues that the former can often be helpful in therapy. In this case, he felt comfortable attending his patient's wedding reception and sharing meals with him outside therapy. Many therapists from other schools of thought would feel very uncomfortable with these practices. What are your own thoughts about when it is acceptable to socialize with a client outside the therapy setting? How do the ethical codes of professional organizations address dual relationships?

10 | THE CASE OF BEN: A FLEXIBLE, HOLISTIC APPLICATION OF MULTIMODAL THERAPY

Arnold A. Lazarus

CASE CONTEXT AND METHODS

Rationale for Selecting This Client

"Ben"—a White male executive who was 50 years old at the beginning of therapy—initially presented with anxiety and relationship problems. The main reason for selecting Ben for a systematic write-up is because this case illustrates a variety of "choice points" that emerged when matters went off track. Several events derailed the ongoing therapy and called for interventions and strategies that had not been part of the initial plan. A case study that describes a smooth monotonic progression from intake to discharge would leave the reader shortchanged when confronting the many issues that often tend to arise and call for tactical and strategic shifts and rapid revisions of the initial treatment plan.

Methods

It would have been far better methodologically if this case had not been taken from my routine clinical practice but had been audiotaped, or preferably videotaped, and subjected to independent assessors. Also, the services of an independent researcher to assess the client before, during, and after the therapy and render an independent report would have been of enormous methodological value. Although this was not feasible in the context of my routine practice (nor is it usually practicable in typical clinical practice), it should be noted that my work environment has prompted me to publish numerous case studies over the years that have evoked critical observations from a number of sources, all of which have enhanced my own critical self-awareness about my ongoing work. In addition, it is my custom to present various cases to two postdoctoral groups with whom I meet regularly in Princeton and in New York and where astute feedback helps keep me on track. The case in point benefited from this process.

Clinical Setting

Ben had called for an appointment shortly after reading one of my self-help books (Lazarus & Lazarus, 1997). He was feeling "down in the dumps" at the time and gravitated to the self-help section of a bookstore where he spotted *The 60-Second Shrink* and browsed through parts of it. He said, "It offered an approach that I did not know existed." He was seen in my professional office, and he paid a prearranged fee for service after each session, for which he received partial reimbursement from his insurance company.

Reprinted by permission of the author, Dr. Arnold A. Lazarus, and *Pragmatic Case Studies in Psychotherapy*. "The Case of 'Ben': A Flexible, Holistic Application of Multimodal Therapy" originally appeared in *Pragmatic Case Studies in Psychotherapy* [Online], Vol. 1(1), Article 1, 2005, pp. 1–15. Available: http://hdl.rutgers.edu/1782.1/pcsp_journal.

Client Data Sources

With Ben's written permission, I called and discussed him with his previous therapist, who said that she had made little headway. She said she was trying to help him with his overall ambivalence, dependency issues, and saw him as having several features of an avoidant personality disorder. She mentioned that two other therapists whom she knew quite well, both women, had also been unable to make much progress with him and opined that a male therapist might be better able to help him.

Ben's history of psychotherapy went back about 20 years. He sought help from several therapists for "various crises and commitment problems." Most of the clinicians he had seen were psychodynamic, except for a Gestalt therapist who "gave me permission to be angry" and an "existential therapist" with whom he enjoyed discussing philosophy. He stated that usually after 3 to 6 months he would terminate the therapy either because he was feeling less stressed or because the process had become circular and unhelpful. Ben mentioned that he was attracted to the cognitive-behavior therapy (CBT) orientation described in *The 60-Second Shrink*. (The book is a popularized version of personal change ideas that flow from the CBT model, organized as 101 "tips and strategies" to help readers handle key life issues and common mental health problems, such as how to deal with anger, depression, stress, and anxiety or the vital elements of a successful marriage and effective parenting.)

Confidentiality

Toward the end of the therapy, the client was told that I was considering writing up his case for publication, and he willingly signed a permission form. His name and other identifying details and places have been changed to maintain confidentiality.

THE CLIENT

Ben headed up the editorial department of a large publishing house. Twice divorced with a son and daughter in their early twenties from his first marriage, he had recently become involved with Holly, a talented advertising copywriter who worked for the same publisher. She was some 8 years his junior and had recently ended a turbulent 2-year marriage. Although Ben had been "in and out of counseling for the past 20 years," he insisted on reviewing his family of origin, his two failed marriages, and his past and present relationship with his children in considerable detail. I had endeavored to educate him as to how my therapy was similar in some ways and yet basically very different from all the others he had experienced. I was able to expedite matters, to some extent, by explaining that a therapist's understanding of historical antecedents was often necessary and helpful in formulating a treatment regimen but that it was usually not beneficial to dwell on the past. I quipped that it was like driving a car while looking only in the rear-view mirror. I also emphasized that for efficiency sake, thorough completion of the Multimodal Life History Inventory (MLHI) (Lazarus & Lazarus, 1991) would provide sufficient background information and help to pinpoint specific areas of his life that were troublesome.

At the end of the initial interview, Ben was handed an MLHI and asked to complete it at home and bring it with him to his second session. On the MLHI, he described his problems as follows:

> Restless, uptight, rarely feel fulfilled or satisfied; relationships with women don't last (I bail out)—fear intimacy; seem to have (still) lots of anger not successfully dealt with; still feel somewhat insecure (much better than before, though); fear speaking up and out.

The initial diagnosis appeared to be a generalized anxiety disorder, although as therapy continued an adjustment disorder with mixed anxiety and depressed mood seemed more apt, as themes of depression and situational stress also surfaced. He attributed many of his problems to the fact that he felt "displaced," having been an only child for 4 years, after which his mother gave birth to another three sons in close succession.

As already mentioned, before coming to see me, Ben had received several years of insight and exploratory therapy without significant change. In line with my guiding conception of therapy (see below), the first step was to discuss with him the observation that therapy, when viewed as education, using social skills learning strategies rather than insight as a major method, calls for didactic methods, homework assignments, with an emphasis on "doing things differently and doing different things." He was told, for instance, that he might require training in anger management and assertive expression and that he may be urged to take certain emotional risks (e.g., expressing his true feelings). "Sounds good to me," said he. He also expressed his positive reaction to the notion of seeing the therapist, not as a sounding board, but as a good listener and an active trainer.

GUIDING CONCEPTION, WITH SUPPORT FROM RESEARCH AND CLINICAL EXPERIENCE

As I will now underscore, the multimodal therapy (MMT) approach that I have developed provides a framework that facilitates systematic treatment selection in a broad-based, comprehensive, and yet highly focused manner. (For a detailed exposition of multimodal therapy and some of the research and clinical experience that underlie it, see Lazarus, 1976, 1985, 1989, 1997, 2005a, 2005b.) The model respects science and data-driven findings, and it endeavors when possible to use empirically supported methods (Nathan & Gorman, 2002). Nevertheless, it recognizes that many issues still fall into the gray area in which artistry and subjective judgment are necessary and tries to fill the void by offering methods that have strong clinical support. By "artistry and subjective judgment," I am alluding to issues and questions that are encountered for which there are no answers from controlled research. "Should I tell my new boyfriend about the abortion I had 4 years ago?" "I wonder if I should tell my friend Clarice what her husband said about her." "Do you think I should accept that job offer in Ohio?" "I wonder whether it will help or make matters worse if I discuss what really happened at the party." Examples are almost limitless. Some therapists never directly answer questions but only reflect back to the client what she or he is saying. This seems to be a masterful evasion of a clinician's duty to educate, provide assistance, clarify, and illuminate options for the client. In the management of some of Ben's choices, the reader will see the precise decision-making processes that were applied.

The MMT approach emphasizes that, at base, we are *biological* organisms (neuro-physiological-biochemical entities) who *behave* (act and react), *emote* (experience affective responses), *sense* (respond to tactile, olfactory, gustatory, visual, and auditory stimuli), *imagine* (conjure up sights, sounds, and other events in our mind's eye), *think* (entertain beliefs, opinions, values, and attitudes), and *interact* with one another (enjoy, tolerate, or suffer various interpersonal relationships). By referring to these seven discrete but interactive dimensions or modalities as **B**ehavior, **A**ffect, **S**ensation, **I**magery, **C**ognition, **I**nterpersonal, **D**rugs/Biologicals, the convenient acronym "BASIC I.D." emerges.

Many psychotherapeutic approaches are trimodal, addressing affect, behavior, and cognition—ABC. The multimodal approach provides clinicians with a comprehensive template. By separating sensations from emotions, distinguishing between images and cognitions, emphasizing both intraindividual and interpersonal behaviors, and under-scoring the biological substrate, the multimodal orientation is most far reaching. By assessing a client's BASIC I.D., one endeavors to "leave no stone unturned."

MULTIMODAL ASSESSMENT AND FORMULATION

The elements of a thorough assessment involve the following range of questions:

B: What behaviors is this individual engaging in that are getting in the way of his or her happiness of personal fulfillment (self-defeating actions, maladaptive behaviors)? What does the client need to increase and decrease? What should he or she stop doing and start doing?

A: What emotions (affective reactions) are predominant? Are we dealing with anger, anxiety, depression, combinations thereof, and to what extent (e.g., irritation vs. rage; sadness vs. profound melancholy)? What appears to generate these negative affects—certain cognitions, images, interpersonal conflicts? And how does the person respond (behave) when feeling a certain way? It is important to look for inter-active processes—what impact do various behaviors have on the person's affect, and vice versa? How does this influence each of the other modalities?

S: Are there specific sensory complaints (e.g., tension, chronic pain, tremors)? What feelings, thoughts, and behaviors are connected to these negative sensations? What positive sensations (e.g., visual, auditory, tactile, olfactory, and gustatory delights) does the person report? This includes the individual as a sensual and sexual being. When called for, the enhancement or cultivation of erotic pleasure is a viable thera-peutic goal. The importance of the specific senses is often glossed over or even bypassed by many clinical approaches.

I: What fantasies and images are predominant? What is the person's "self-image"? Are there specific success or failure images? Are there negative or intrusive images (e.g., flashbacks to unhappy or traumatic experiences)? And how are these images connected to ongoing cognitions, behaviors, affective reactions, and the like?

C: Can we determine the individual's main attitudes, values, beliefs, and opinions? What are this person's predominant shoulds, oughts, and musts? Are there any def-inite dysfunctional beliefs or irrational ideas? Can we detect any untoward automatic thoughts that undermine his or her functioning?

I.: Interpersonally, who are the significant others in this individual's life? What does he or she want, desire, expect, and receive from them, and what does he or she, in turn, give to and do for them? What relationships give this individual particular pleasures and pains?

D.: Is this person biologically healthy and health conscious? Does he or she have any medical complaints or concerns? What relevant details pertain to diet, weight, sleep, exercise, and alcohol and drug use?

The foregoing assessment methods clearly make known the client's presenting prob-lems, the modalities involved, and the cluster of interconnected issues. These findings, often in concert with additional input and evaluation from the client, point to the goals of therapy and the methods, strategies, and procedures that are most likely to help the client meet his or her goals. These methods and strategies are drawn from those that have been empirically found to work in a variety of different therapy approaches ("technical eclecticism," e.g., see Lazarus, 2005b), although all of them are conceptualized within a cognitive-behavioral framework (Lazarus, 1997, 2005a). All of this should become appar-ent as we discuss the initial formulation and subsequent changes of Ben's proposed treatment trajectory. The client's motivation and resilience will determine how rapidly one may proceed, the order of problems that require consideration, and the manner in which homework assignments and between-session activities can be implemented. The reader is referred to Lazarus (2005a, 2005b) for more detailed information that goes beyond the scope of this case history.

It is important to underscore that the multimodal model does not deal specifically with shifts and revisions that can occur in therapy. The model assumes that these psychological dances and flexible maneuvers are part of the artistry and should be in the repertoire of any competent clinician. In line with this, I believe it is particularly important to document in specific cases how this artistry takes place so that it will later be possible to inductively derive guidelines that capture the various patterns by which this artistry can be effective.

Another dimension of flexibility in my guiding conception—and one reflected in the specifics of Ben's case—is the assumption that while generally the therapist encourages clients to develop their own goals and life choices so that they might fully own them, there are times when clients can make wrong choices without realizing the consequences for their mental health and well-being. In my view, these instances call for the therapist to try to persuade the client to make a decision that seems in his or her best interests. This might be seen as consistent with the behavioral idea of "stimulus control," in which the therapist helps to create an environment that facilitates positive responses and consequences for the client.

A final issue contained in my guiding conception is flexibility with regard to the patient–therapist relationship. With some clients, strict and formal boundaries are necessary, whereas with others, a much more open and reciprocal relationship may ensue. There is a vast difference between "boundary crossings," which are often helpful, and "boundary violations," which are detrimental. (Examples of such boundary crossings are in-office strategic therapist self-disclosures, nonsexual touching, and out-of-office encounters such sharing a meal at a restaurant, attending a client's graduation, or teaching a class that a client attends. Examples of boundary violations are sexual activities with clients or obtaining "inside" stock tips from a client who is a stockbroker.) To my mind, the two major ethical concerns are the avoidance of any form of exploitation and respect for confidentiality. But such matters as selective self-disclosure and nonsexual dual relationships are part and parcel of the emphasis on flexibility. These issues are discussed in great detail in Lazarus and Zur (2002).

ASSESSMENT OF THE CLIENT'S PRESENTING PROBLEMS AND GOALS

Initially, it seemed that the therapy would follow the well-researched pathway of cognitive-behavior therapy in which each significant problem would be addressed, whenever feasible, by an empirically supported method and in an appropriate and suitable solution-focused manner (e.g., Nathan & Gorman, 2002). In his responses to the MLHI and in our sessions, Ben elaborated that he felt "generally unappreciated" on the job, by his children, and by Holly. He reiterated his basic dissatisfactions and insecurities, his fear of intimacy and his specific relationship with Holly, his anger, and his unassertive proclivities. Consequently, a standard series of cognitive-behavioral procedures was embarked on: relaxation training (for his overall tension and anxiety), role-playing (to acquire a better way of discussing matters at work and with Holly), cognitive restructuring (Ben was apt to have too many "shoulds" and self-downing cognitions), and assertiveness training (to deal appropriately rather than evasively with his children, with Holly, and to be able to express his anger nonaggressively). This course of therapy flowed naturally from the guiding conception that initiating specific CBT procedures was the best way to deal with the type of problems with which he presented. This stemmed not only from the research and clinical literature but also meshed well with my prior experiences with similar cases.

FORMULATION AND TREATMENT PLAN

As mentioned earlier, my guiding conception stipulates that the speed at which one may proceed, the order of problems that call for attention, and the level at which homework assignments and between-session activities can be implemented depend largely on the client's motivation and resilience. Initially, it seemed advisable to divide session time among methods of "cognitive restructuring" (in which Ben's faulty cognitions would be replaced by adaptive thoughts and valid perceptions) and various forms of role-playing to contain his irrational anger, enhance specific social skills, and encourage assertive expression. At this juncture, it was anticipated that a five- or six-session trajectory would be sufficient. By the third session, it was necessary to put the plan on hold.

In general, it is not uncommon to find therapists who continue with their initial plans even when they should be deferred. They often assume that if the initial objectives are achieved, other matters may fall into place. If not, these other tribulations can then be examined and treated. Usually, the failure to be sufficiently flexible—to ignore and disrespect the client's priorities—can derail the relationship. The inability to recognize when preemptive adjustments in the treatment plan are called for may totally undermine the therapy. Some therapists have argued that they must demonstrate who is in charge and not permit the client to take control. From the perspective of my guiding conception, this type of dismissal is viewed as only leading the client to feel unheard, disrespected, and misunderstood.

COURSE OF THERAPY

During the first three sessions, I managed to apply some "cognitive restructuring" in which I pointed out Ben's proclivity to think dichotomously and his penchant to denigrate himself, especially when discussing past mistakes. Most of these sessions, as previously mentioned, were devoted to his recounting his family background, and my active listening at this stage seemed a necessary rapport-building process. Nevertheless, in addition to identifying his faulty cognitions, I also managed to do some role-playing to contain his irrational anger and encourage assertive expression. For example, when he dwelled on some strong resentment to various family members because of what he considered their unfair treatment of him, I invited him to try a role-playing scenario. I would model some assertive comments, and he could "try them on for size." He complied, saying, "I guess this will enable me to put up with less of their crap in the future."

By the end of the third session, it became clear to me that several significant events called for the treatment plan's deferral. Ben and Holly kept on ending and resuming their relationship, which precipitated various crises. Consequently, I tabled the individual CBT approach and paid exclusive attention to their relationship. I began seeing Ben and Holly regularly for CBT-oriented couples counseling (e.g., Lazarus, 2001). A clear pattern emerged. They had specific points of disagreement, and when any one of these came into play, Ben would go on the attack and Holly would withdraw but retaliate passive aggressively. Here again, I selected role-playing as a viable means for promoting rational discourse. I also used the standard CBT procedure wherein a comment would be made or a request would be stated, and the listener would seek clarification. For example:

Ben: You are saying that I am too critical and that I never do anything around the house.
Holly: No, I didn't say that. You do a lot to keep the yard up, but you seldom help me with stuff inside the house.
Ben: Oh. You'd like more help with stuff like the dishes?
Holly: Right.
Ben: Fair enough.

These sessions enabled Ben and Holly to reach various points of agreement so that their relationship became less contentious.

After 11 months of therapy, Ben, rather preemptively, in my clinical opinion, quit his job and decided to become a freelance journalist. Ben's own framing of this was that "office politics" were wearing him down, that the job was basically a "dead end," and that "freedom" might inspire him to do some really creative writing. This too required considerable therapeutic attention. It took a few months for him to realize that his income would continue to be drastically diminished. I regarded his avoidance of committed employment as part of his irrational, "I can't stand it" proclamations. I agreed that he might not like it but stressed that he needed the money and was able to withstand the demands. As mentioned in the Guiding Conception section, this was an instance in which I decided to take a stand for what I strongly viewed as in the client's best interest. I was quite outspoken about my view that a structured milieu would be far better than freelancing, and I encouraged him to find a job with a different publisher. He also continued to search for additional sources of income from freelance journalism.

The unexpected demise of his mother further derailed the initial treatment trajectory. We embarked on a necessary course of grief counseling. In multimodal vernacular, the interpersonal modality took precedence. His desires to vent his feelings, reminisce about his mother, and relate aspects of their relationship to other issues and problems were respected (e.g., he decided that his choice of women was predicated on his desire to find someone very much like his mother—minus her bad points). He discussed his feelings toward his brothers and the way the big-brother role had been foisted on him. He also became intent on drawing up "balance sheets" comparing his late mother's pros and cons with those of Holly. It became obvious that Ben was no candidate for brief psychotherapy.

A year after our initial interview, I did some "stock taking." Although he had weathered the various crises alluded to earlier—the ups and downs in his relationship with Holly, his job changes, and the death of his mother—he had not made much headway in resolving many of his presenting problems, such as his level of anxiety, his penchant for unassertiveness, conflictual relationships, and dysfunctional cognitions. Consequently, we embarked once again on a series of standard cognitive-behavior therapy procedures. Relaxation methods, assertiveness training, and the implementation of several mental imagery methods that revolved around pictures wherein he perceived himself able to cope with various adversities all proved helpful. After some 10 to 12 sessions of individual CBT procedures, he appeared less angry and resentful (which Holly confirmed), he reported feeling more secure and self-accepting, and he was somewhat happier about his relationship with his children. Nevertheless, he was using alcohol to excess (he had started having at least three glasses of wine with dinner every evening), and his relationship with his children remained strained (he avoided calling them and Holly said that although he had stopped bring critical of them, he complained that he felt uptight around them).

THERAPY MONITORING AND THE USE OF FEEDBACK INFORMATION

After about 15 months of therapy, Ben and I systematically discussed the gains that had accrued and the areas that now required specific attention. I asked him to take home a copy of the Multimodal Life History Inventory (MLHI) he had completed when we first met and to indicate thereon (a) issues and areas that had been successfully treated, (b) those that still needed to be modified, and (c) any new problems that had arisen. When he returned a week later for his next session, we perused the MLHI. It became clear that his main problem at this point was his disenchantment with his work. For example, he felt that editing and critiquing other people's work prevented him from fulfilling his own literary ambitions. In line with the BASIC I.D. model discussed in the Guiding Conception section, we then focused on the following questions: What behaviors might diminish his current work pressures? How might he generate positive feelings about his work? What sensory pleasures might be tapped into to offset his tensions? What mental images came to mind when picturing a highly satisfying work environment? In thinking through a balance sheet of pros and cons, which items stood out most clearly? What steps could be taken to counteract some of the aversive encounters he reported? From a health standpoint, was he getting sufficient rest to maximize his performance level?

These inquiries opened up a sequence of events pertaining to certain childhood and adolescent memories that seemed pertinent. For example, he felt that he had been victimized by strict and highly critical teachers, often bullied by older children, given insufficient parental guidance or help, and left to flounder through life. He concluded that these formative experiences resulted in his feeling needlessly hypervigilant and played directly into his generalized anxiety and avoidance responses.

Ben also concluded that he had not grieved sufficiently for his mother. Regarding Holly, he stated that despite her many positive attributes, she was too hypersensitive, too critical, and less accepting than he desired. He termed her "a quintessential nitpicker."

Concerning unresolved feelings about the loss of his mother, I urged Ben to join a self-help support group in the community that dealt with loss and grief. Somewhat reluctantly, he followed through and attended a weekly group that was held at a local church. He went to about six or seven meetings and said they had been "fairly helpful." When I recommended further couples counseling, Ben said he'd think about it.

I also suggested that a few sessions with Ben and his children might prove useful to deal with his feelings. He agreed, and Ben and I met with his adult son and daughter on two occasions and then, at her request, Holly joined us for a third family session. These meetings proved effective in clearing up several misunderstandings and misperceptions. I carefully commenced these family sessions by emphasizing that as a clinical psychologist, I do not take sides but endeavor to be of genuine help to all the members of a family. I set the agenda by saying that the goal of getting together was to come up with and implement a plan that would result in a constructive and satisfying solution for all. My main consideration was understanding exactly what had caused problems in the past and what was preventing them from having a close and caring relationship in the present. The meetings gave them all an opportunity to (a) vent their feelings, (b) make some necessary apologies, (c) clarify misunderstandings, and (d) express their mutual feelings of love for one another.

Ben's first wife (the mother of his children, who lived too far away to be included in the family process) initiated a call to me saying that she was pleased to report that her son and daughter had overcome needless resentments toward their father. But she urged me to impress upon Ben that parenting is a two-way street and that he should make overtures to the children from time to time rather than always waiting for them to contact him. I promised to convey this message, and Ben was receptive to it. (Since I had not obtained

Ben's specific permission to speak to his first wife, I structured my role in the conversation as merely a listener and a conveyer of her message.)

It was now almost 2 years since Ben had first consulted me, and he reported that despite the considerable progress made on several fronts, he had been feeling "down." Further inquiry revealed signs of a clinical depression, a significant problem that had eluded all previous avenues of inquiry. Although from time to time Ben had said he was feeling "depressed," he presented his frame of mind in terms of "normal ups and downs." Indeed, his reason for reading the book (Lazarus & Lazarus, 1997) that had led him to call me was that he had perused it when he was "down in the dumps." I had tried to delve into the nature of his dysphoria several times over the course of the therapy, but he always brushed it aside as "no big deal." At this juncture, perhaps because so many other issues had been resolved, he put a very different spin on his melancholia, and this became the focus of some three or four sessions while we tried to ascertain the forces and factors responsible for it. One can always discern possible psychogenic "reasons" behind dysphoric affect, but given Ben's family history (a father who had received ECT and a mother who was clinically depressed most of her life), the most parsimonious diagnosis was that of a biologically based depression.

It should be noted that when dealing with a biological depression, a multimodal therapist does not lose sight of the fact that in addition to antidepressants or other medical treatments, certain behaviors can prove helpful (e.g., exercising and keeping active), as can sensory responses such as pleasing music and tactile pleasures, as well as positive images, self-affirming cognitions, and various interpersonal activities. Thus, in addition to recommending medication for Ben, as described below, I also employed a number of these modalities, such as persuading him to join a gym and work out with a personal trainer (behavior); to have full body massages twice a week, which Ben had suggested himself (sensation); and to spend time with congenial friends, with or without Holly (interpersonal).

Ben then mentioned that he had suffered similar bouts of depression. He said that he had dealt with these events by "toughing them out," although on one occasion he saw a psychiatrist who prescribed medication that made him worse. (He could not recall the name of the drug, but it was clear that this experience had made him suspicious of psychiatric medication, which was mainly why he kept downplaying and denying the true degree of his depression.) I had given him the Beck Depression Inventory (Beck, Steer, & Brown, 1996) shortly after he started seeing me and his score was only 11, which indicated a mild mood disturbance at worst. At this juncture, I asked him to fill out the Beck Depression Inventory again. He scored 25, indicating a significant depression. It is my belief that he was "faking healthy" the first time. I think he did so for two reasons. (a) He did not want to appear too needy for fear that I may not accept him as a client. (b) He also probably did not want to admit to the full extent of his problems himself. When I said that I would like him to see a psychopharmacologist, he refused, and it took considerable persuasion before he believed that new medications exist that have minimal side effects. He saw the person I recommended, who prescribed Effexor. It proved helpful, with minimal side effects, and Ben took this medication for over a year.

Holly entered into therapy with a female psychologist who requested to see Ben. I had not been contacted or asked to have any input in this. I felt that it was probably best for Holly and Ben to do this on their own. My rationale for staying out of it was so as not to be seen as too controlling or perhaps as needlessly defensive or territorial. Ben saw the therapist alone and then together with Holly for a few sessions. He had feared that Holly and her therapist would gang up on him, but he reported to the contrary that Holly had been mildly rebuked for her unrealistic expectations. Ben reported, "Things between Holly and me are much better these days." He and Holly bought a house and moved in together. Up to this point, they had separate abodes, although Ben had spent most of his time in Holly's house. "I just love this house we bought," Ben reported. "Just being in that home, looking out into the magnificent garden, gives me a natural high. It's even better than Effexor!"

CONCLUDING EVALUATION OF THE THERAPY'S PROCESS AND OUTCOME

At this point, about 2 years and 2 months had elapsed since Ben and I first met. Initially, I had seen him on a weekly (sometimes twice weekly) basis. After around 14 months, our visits were spaced at 10-day to 2-week intervals, except when certain crises had emerged and we would meet as often as needed. Over the previous 6 months, we had met on an average of every 3 to 4 weeks. Ben suggested that we might now consider meeting only if and when needed. I agreed. He emphasized that we had achieved most of our goals: (a) He felt more secure. (b) His anger had diminished significantly. (c) He was inclined to assert his feelings. (d) He was pleased with his children. (e) His work situation was satisfactory. (f) He had come to terms with his mother's death. (g) He was no longer abusing alcohol. And (h) he was not feeling depressed.

Two months later, Ben made an appointment. Holly had changed jobs and was now commuting to work over 2 hours each day. Their relationship had become strained. One of his cousins with whom he was very close had died unexpectedly. "I was tapering off the medication, but I hit a down," he said, "and now I am back on a time-release Effexor and take 225 mg at night. I am also taking Buspar." We had five additional weekly sessions devoted mainly to the exploration of his relationship with Holly. Ben and Holly were both questioning the viability of their relationship. The three of us drew up individual "balance sheets" as to the pros and cons of their staying together or going their own ways. When we compared notes, it seemed that we all leaned in the direction that too many differences (especially concerning their respective expectations of a relationship) and too much resentment made it unlikely that they could sustain a loving and noncontentious relationship

Ben then sent me the following e-mail: "It is crystal clear that Holly and I cannot make it. To be perfectly honest, living with her has been tepid at best. So guess what? She has decided to move into New York and I will buy her share of the house." I sent back an e-mail inquiring if this implied that he and Holly would now definitely be separating and going their separate ways. He wrote back that nothing definite has been decided, but it was certainly heading in that direction.

Several months later, again on e-mail, the following note arrived:

It is now fait accompli. Holly is in New York. I have bought the house—and I love it more than ever. But the best news of all is that I am seeing a woman I dated before I married my first wife. Did I ever mention Jean to you? I was nuts about her back then, but unfortunately for me, her childhood sweetheart appeared on the scene and they got married. A friend mentioned that she was divorced and living in this area. I called her, got together a few times, and things really clicked. I may want to set up an appointment so that Jean and I can discuss the pros and cons of her moving into my house with a view to getting married by the end of the year.

POSTTERMINATION SYNOPSIS AND REFLECTIONS

Instead of a formal appointment, Ben and I exchanged more e-mails. Five months later, I received a wedding invitation and met Jean for the first time at the reception. As mentioned in the section on the Guiding Conception behind multimodal therapy, this approach is very flexible when it comes to selective extratherapeutic activities with certain clients. There was no reason to turn down Ben's wedding invitation. At a suitable moment, I took Ben aside and said, "I think you've hit the jackpot!" Subsequently, Ben and Jean met with me to discuss minor problems between her adult daughter and Ben's son and a daughter. As I write this, it is now almost 4 years since they got married. We have kept in touch via e-mail, and I have met Ben for lunch a few times. Again, I want to emphasize the benefits that can accrue from certain "dual relationships," and with some clients, an expanded therapist role can have a positive effect. Ben stated that it meant a great deal to him to meet up with me more informally in a luncheon setting. These meetings have not been tantamount to free therapy. Ben and I have reacted like two friends catching up on one another's lives. In my view, this change in my role helped to solidify Ben's image of himself as a successful human being rather than just as a perpetual "therapy patient." He has described himself as "happier than I ever thought I could or would be."

In thinking back over the treatment trajectory with Ben, it has the quality of the proverbial roller coaster. This case illustrates the importance of flexibility, a willingness to shift gears and change direction, and the value of a broad-based CBT approach. The client received standard, individual cognitive-behavior therapy to begin. The use of empirically supported methods is a first choice whenever clients' problems lend themselves to specific and well-established interventions. Nevertheless, this initial treatment plan was soon changed to cognitive-behavioral couples therapy, given that dyadic issues had come to the fore with the prominence of the conflict between Ben and Holly. Although Ben's attitudes, feelings, and strategies with Holly could have been dealt with in individual therapy, moving to a couple's model allowed for a more direct dealing with the interactive and transactional components of their problems. The theme throughout this paper is that a clinician must always be ready to address unexpected events. The death of the client's mother also called for immediate changes in the treatment protocol.

The resumption of individual cognitive-behavior therapy for Ben's initial presenting problems then proved effective, but it was also necessary to reassess Ben's range of problems to shed further light on issues that needed to be considered and treated. Thus, family therapy sessions were deemed advisable, and the client was seen together with his children, again viewed as preferable to dealing with these issues only in Ben's individual therapy. Note how the focus swung back and forth between Ben and his personalistic issues to the broader interpersonal context. The use of extratherapeutic resources is also demonstrated by the fact that he was encouraged to join a self-help grief-counseling group, and a referral was made to a psychopharmacologist. Ben seemed to derive benefit from the self-help group, and he certainly benefited from seeing the psychopharmacologist. He said that the grief counseling assuaged his sense of isolation and helped him put the loss of his mother into a realistic perspective. And the medication that had been prescribed for his depression was extremely helpful.

I selected this case not because it is especially noteworthy or filled with pristine insights but because it exemplifies an analogy I use quite often—that of the therapist acting like a heat-seeking missile that pursues problem after problem as they arise in real time and blows them out of the sky. As mentioned earlier, in Ben's case, this involved multiple modes of individual, couples, and family therapy together with the use of outside resources and moving at the end from a more formal therapist role to one of a type of friend. Moreover, the therapy had to be responsive to important changes taking place in the client's life, such as the potentially harmful change in his job situation, the death of his mother, the ups and downs of his relationship with Holly, and the fortunate timing of his meeting with Jean. Over the years, Ben has referred several relatives, friends, and associates to me for therapy. They all reported that he had told them that I had succeeded in turning his life around.

During the years that I treated Ben (and the 4 years I followed him after therapy), I was the one consistent, supportive figure in his life as he grappled with an unhappy work situation, a stormy relationship with Holly, the loss of his mother, and his ungrateful kids. (Ben's father had died from a heart attack at age 69, a few years before Ben consulted me. His relationship with his father was basically good, and the only untoward remarks he made about him were: "As much as I liked him, I think he wanted me to be certain things and behave in certain ways that weren't me." We had discussed this a few times, but it did not seem that these issues were especially relevant to the case.) My encouraging relationship with Ben was designed to provide stability and strengthening for his self-acceptance, while providing encouragement for him to take new directions to address the unhappy parts of his life. My attending his wedding reception and continuing to see him occasionally during the 4 years of his marriage to Jean also provided continuity with his past and the message that I cared about him as a human being, not just an "office client."

REFERENCES

Beck, A. T., Steer, R. A., & Brown, G. K. (1996). *Beck Depression Inventory: Manual* (2nd ed.). San Antonio, TX: Psychological Corporation.

Lazarus, A. A. (1976). *Multimodal behavior therapy.* New York: Springer.

Lazarus, A. A. (Ed.). (1985). *Casebook of multimodal therapy.* New York: Guilford.

Lazarus, A. A. (1989). *The practice of multimodal therapy: Systematic, comprehensive, and effective psychotherapy.* Baltimore, MD: Johns Hopkins University Press.

Lazarus, A. A. (1997). *Brief but comprehensive psychotherapy: The multimodal way.* New York: Springer

Lazarus, A. A. (2001). *Marital myths revisited: A fresh look at two dozen mistaken beliefs about marriage.* Atascadero, CA: Impact Publishers.

Lazarus, A. A. (2005a) Multimodal therapy. In R. J. Corsini & D. Wedding (Eds.), *Current psychotherapies* (7th ed., pp. 337–371). Belmont, CA: Brooks/Cole.

Lazarus, A. A. (2005b). Multimodal therapy. In J. C. Norcross & M. R. Goldfried (Eds.), *Handbook of psychotherapy integration* (2nd ed., pp. 105–120). New York: Oxford University Press.

Lazarus, A. A., & Lazarus, C. N. (1991) *The Multimodal Life History Inventory.* Champaign, IL: Research Press.

Lazarus, A. A., & Lazarus, C. N. (1997). *The 60-second shrink: 101 strategies for staying sane in a crazy world.* Atascadero, CA: Impact Publishers.

Lazarus, A. A., & Zur, O. (Eds.). (2002). *Dual relationships and psychotherapy.* New York: Springer.

Nathan, P. E., & Gorman, J. M. (2002). *A guide to treatments that work* (2nd ed.). New York: Oxford University Press.

Editors' Introduction

With family therapy there is the same dilemma we faced with behavior therapy: Dozens of good teaching cases are available, but it is virtually impossible to select a single case that will adequately illustrate the multiple and variegated techniques used by most family therapists. Ultimately we elected to use a strategic therapy case to serve as an exemplar of family therapy.

We feel fortunate to have been able to locate the following case by Peggy Papp. It demonstrates the effective treatment of the family of a young anorectic woman and demonstrates the use of a "Greek Chorus"—a group of observing therapists who remain behind a one-way mirror. The Greek Chorus is always available to consult with the therapist, and the group will periodically make recommendations about treatment. Family therapists, more than any other group, have used such procedures to good advantage. Would you feel comfortable having your own work scrutinized this closely?

The case describes the treatment of a young woman with anorexia nervosa. The longer this life-threatening disorder remains untreated, the more intractable it becomes. How would this client have been treated differently if seen by a psychoanalyst, a behavior therapist, or someone practicing rational emotive behavior therapy? Would a person-centered therapist, committed to authenticity in the therapeutic relationship, feel comfortable with the manipulation inherent in the use of paradoxical intention? How do you feel about this therapeutic tactic? How do the values of a therapist affect decisions about which tools in the psychotherapist's armamentarium are appropriate in any given case?

11 | THE DAUGHTER WHO SAID NO

Peggy Papp

This case illustrates the step-by-step process of putting concepts into practice over time. It describes the treatment of a 23-year-old anorectic daughter and her family who present the classical pattern of an anorectic family: a high degree of enmeshment, covert alliances between the generations, subverted conflict, and power struggles fought with guilt and martyrdom.

The parents, in rigidly symmetrical positions, are in constant conflict and divert this conflict through Rachel, the anorectic daughter, hence isolating her from her siblings and the world of her peers. The therapeutic dilemma centers around what will happen to Rachel and the various members of her family if she gives up her symptom and becomes a full-blown woman. The consultation group is used to debate this dilemma, and the sibling subsystem is enlisted to free Rachel from her involvement in the parental generation.

Twenty sessions were held over the period of one year with a one-, two- and three-year follow-up. All sessions were videotaped and observed behind a one-way mirror.

For the purpose of clarity, the case is broken down into stages according to the following outline.

Stage I: *Forming a hypothesis*
    Step 1: Gathering information
    Step 2: Connecting the symptom with the family system

Stage II: *Setting the terms for therapy*
    Step 1: Defining the therapeutic dilemma
    Step 2: Setting the terms for change

Stage III: *Putting the therapeutic contract into operation*
    Step 1: Involving father in the therapeutic dilemma
    Step 2: Dramatizing the therapeutic dilemma

Stage IV: *Coping with the forces of change*
    Step 1: Defining change within the therapeutic contract

Stage V: *Coping with the fallout from change*
    Step 1: Defining resistance within the therapeutic framework
    Step 2: Shifting the definition of the problem
    Step 3: Prescribing enmeshment

Stage VI: *Enlisting the sibling subsystem*

     Step 1: Forming a coalition with the sisters

     Step 2: Differentiating from the sisters

Stage VII: *Saying no to therapy*

     Step 1: Pushing the prescription to the breaking point

     Step 2: Escalating the therapeutic triangle

     Step 3: Opposing the group

     Step 4: Supporting autonomy

Stage VIII: *Solidifying change*

     Step 1: Anticipating and rehearsing a regression

     Step 2: Redefining the marital relationship

Stage IX: *Prescribing a farewell ritual*

Follow-up

STAGE I
FORMING A HYPOTHESIS

Step 1: Gathering Information

The information I obtained from the first session is summarized here since information gathering tends to make tedious reading. Rachel, 23, requested therapy for herself, and her sisters, Clare, 31, and Sandy, 26; her mother agreed to participate in therapy, but her father emphatically refused. Having been pushed into various kinds of therapy by his wife for the last five years, he told Rachel in no uncertain terms she would have to solve her problem herself.

I agreed to see the family without him, believing I could involve him later. Some therapists will not see the family unless everyone is present for the first session. Since my way of dealing with resistance is indirect rather than direct, my decisions are based on an evaluation of each case. In this situation it seemed important to go along with father's resistance since it was obviously a reaction to his wife's pressure. Also, the intensity of his feelings was a good indication he could be involved at a later date.

Only mother and Rachel appeared for the first interview as Sandy was in the hospital having her first baby and Clare refused to come after a fight with Rachel.

Rachel appeared frail and flat-chested, but animated, with huge dark eyes and a thin face. She was exceptionally articulate, expressing herself in colorful language and sometimes adding a comic delivery. Her mother, a large, handsome, robust woman with short, white hair, stylishly cut, possessed the style and flair of a seasoned actress. With the exuberance of Lady Bountiful she embraced family therapy, saying she "believed" family members should help one another and she would do anything to help Rachel. She tempered each criticism of her with "there's really nothing wrong with you, you're a wonderful child, but—."

Rachel had begun dieting four years ago during her second year at college. Since that time she had slowly but steadily lost weight until she finally weighed 89 pounds. She had not menstruated for a year and a half. During the last three years she had made several attempts to leave home but failed, each time feeling depressed, isolated, lonely, and coming back home. She now had an interim job as a secretary but was dissatisfied with it. Although living at home, she was talking about moving into an apartment of her own.

The primary concern of Rachel and her mother was not her weight loss or her diet, but the psychological implications, which they saw in terms of Rachel's intrapsychic problems. Rachel's previous individual therapy of one year had focused on the classical individual symptoms of anorexia—high expectations, overachievement, perfectionistic attitudes, obsessions, and control over the body—but had not connected these in any way with the family system.

The mother was interested in our helping Rachel with her high expectations of herself, describing her as being "obsessively and rigidly perfectionistic." She also stated Rachel had been a rebellious child all her life. "I have been worried about Rachel since she learned to say no. It has been no and no and no and no and no and no and no ever since then. She has not wanted to adopt any of our standards, and I question her judgment." She gave as an example of this Rachel's not wanting to join B'nai B'rith or date Jewish boys, and her tendency to pick a boy up off the street and make a date with him. Rachel accused her mother of matchmaking. "I feel like it's mating season. I'm in heat and it's time to find a male for me quick before I'm not eligible anymore. I don't enjoy that." Mother then mentioned drugs, and Rachel admitted she had experimented in college with pot, speed, LSD, and mescaline and ended with, "I don't regret anything."

Mother had kept everything away from father over the years to protect Rachel and to avoid a conflict. When asked what he would have done had he known about these things, she stated "I don't know. I wasn't going to give him a chance! The girls have accused me of being manipulative and maybe I am but I have to be." She spoke of the many disagreements between her and her husband, describing a longstanding conflict because of her closeness with her parents.

At the end of the session, after consultation with the team, I told Rachel and her mother we felt we did not have enough information at this point to make any suggestions and would like to delay our comments until we had met with other members of the family. Rachel agreed to try and get Clare to come to the next session but Sandy was still recuperating from the birth of her baby.

In the following session, Clare, a thin, attractive woman, fashionably dressed, was more than happy to give her impressions of Rachel and other family members. She described Rachel as being "very difficult" and her family as being one in which it was difficult to become independent, as her mother was controlling and "throws guilt around a lot." Both she and Rachel had rebelled against her mother's control, but Sandy "is the model daughter, model sister, model grandchild and, now having had a baby, will be the model mother. She never displeases anyone. She is the buffer, the peacemaker."

Both Rachel and Clare spoke of their being afraid of their father when they were growing up. He was very conservative and strict about dates, two-piece bathing suits, boyfriends, hours, and so on. The mother, more lenient, took this opportunity to say that she was also afraid of his wrath and stated pathetically, "Thank God he never hit me." She compared him unfavorably with her own father and started to cry. "I tried very hard to get my family to help me, and my father would talk to my husband in a gentle manner and say how precious a wife is, how nothing really was as precious as a wife, and really she's the only one who is most important in life. But my husband would become antagonistic toward such conversations." She went into individual therapy at the recommendation of her doctor when she developed stomach trouble, and her doctor put pressure on her husband to go with her. Both blamed him for her physical problems.

Rachel and Clare defended their father and accused their mother of being overly close to her family and rubbing the father's nose in it. Rachel then spoke of her father and her as being the "underdogs in the family. We're ostracized by the rest of them." Rachel had given me the first clue as to how she fit into the power struggle between her parents: She identified with the father's underdog position. I now wanted to know the function of this identification: how it was used in the ongoing day-to-day battle between the parents and how the sisters responded to it. The following dialogue was included to demonstrate how these questions were explored.

Peggy: So you feel you're the bad guy and your father is the bad guy in the family. In what way do you feel you can bring comfort to your father?

Rachel: Because I can understand his viewpoint.

Clare: If there are two bad guys, then you both share the burden?

Rachel: There's company.

Peggy: How do you go about giving him company?

Rachel: We have a lot of common interests, we both like cars and nature and the Bronx Zoo, and we have a good time. We go across the country together.

Peggy: What do you think his life would be like if you weren't around?

Rachel: I don't know—I guess he'd survive.

Peggy: Do you think he'd be lonely?

Rachel: Maybe, sometimes—I'm nice company for him.

Peggy: Then who would there be around to really understand him?

Rachel: (*Long pause.*) I don't know.

Peggy: You don't think your mother could understand him?

Rachel: She will never ever. I shouldn't say that, but as far as I can see, it'll be a very tough thing for my mother to ever understand how my father feels about her family. She will never ever see how he feels about her.

Mother: But who do I think of when I want somebody to make nice to me? I go right back to the womb. On Tuesday I spent the day with my mom and dad and it was a good day. It was a hard day. I took them shopping. They're very old.

Peggy: Do you feel they're the only ones who nurture you?

Mother: (*Nodding.*) Who really take care of me. I don't want anyone here to feel bad, but Sandy also takes care of me.

Rachel: But you demand too much. You're very hard to give to when you demand.

Peggy: Let's see then. When you feel ganged up on by Rachel and your husband, you then go for nurturing to your parents. And who does your husband go to?

Mother: There's always been a young man in his life who treats him like God. Now it's Roy.

Peggy: You're saying that he always finds someone who is like a son to him?

Mother: Yes, Roy is like a son.

Peggy: Was he disappointed he didn't have a son?

Mother: (*Whispers.*) Very.

Peggy: You whispered that "very." You don't want the girls to hear that?

Mother: (*Emphatically.*) Very displeased that he didn't have a son.

Peggy: Do you think they don't know that?

Rachel: I'm daddy's son.

Peggy: In what way have you been his son?

Rachel: Just—my interest in things which aren't typically feminine. I'm not scared of bugs, little things like that. Cars. Daddy asked me to cook hamburgers on the barbecue pit because I can handle it. (*She imitates a boy.*)

Peggy: What's that like for you to be his son?

Rachel: I kinda like it. (*She laughs and acts like a boy again.*) I don't mind, but I don't think he thinks of me as a boy.

Peggy: Do you think of yourself as a boy?

Rachel: No. I was saying that I felt so independent on this move. It always bugs me to depend on people.

Peggy: What do you think it's going to be like for him, your moving out?
Rachel: I think it's going to be all right for him. Already they're talking about switching homes with me.
Peggy: Do you think he's going to miss you?
Rachel: Maybe. He said he was going to miss some things but not others.
Peggy: Well do you think your mother's going to be able to take care of his loneliness?
Rachel: Not unless she starts to look at him from a more objective point of view.
Peggy: Do you think you can teach her?
Rachel: I try, I really try. Then she accuses me of ganging up on her.
Clare: (*Defending mother.*) Daddy's not nice all the time, either.

Step 2: Connecting the Symptom with the Family System

After this exchange, the therapist left the session to have a consultation with the group. We formed a hypothesis based on answering the following questions:

What function does the symptom serve in the system? We speculated that Rachel was starving herself in order to remain a son to her father and fill up the emptiness in his life that she perceived was left by her mother. By not eating, she kept herself looking like a boy, prevented herself from maturing into womanhood, and implicitly promised to remain the guardian of her parents' marriage. The symptom served to keep her at home where she could continue to serve as her father's ally in his battle with her mother and to give her mother a reason for remaining close to her family. By identifying with her father as the underdog in the family, she formed a coalition with him in the service of fighting against her mother's control. The symptom also served the function of freeing the other sisters to establish independent lives outside the family, since Rachel had accepted the responsibility of mediating the parents' marriage.

How does the family function to stabilize the symptom? When mother and father became involved in a power struggle that they could not resolve, mother moved closer to her parents and compared father unfavorably to her own father. Father retaliated by siding with Rachel against his wife, and Rachel joined him to get back at her mother. She became involved in masculine activities to please her father, knowing he felt alienated in a family of women. She cannot give up the symptom as long as she believes she is needed to be a son to him. The power struggle between mother and Rachel has taken many forms over the years, including Rachel's taking drugs, quitting jobs, leaving school, dating non-Jewish boys, and disassociating herself from the family religious beliefs, as well as her present symptom of self-starvation.

What is the central theme around which the problem is organized? The central theme in this family seems to be control—who is going to control the beliefs and values of the others. This is a conventional family that places high value on conformity, respectability, achievement, duty, and family loyalty. Mother is less concerned about some of Rachel's other activities than she is about her not accepting the tenets of the Jewish faith. She complains that her husband rejects her father's value of a wife as being something "precious."

Since we have not yet seen father and Sandy, we are unable at this point to obtain a complete picture of the way each individual operates to maintain control around these central issues.

What will be the consequences of change? If Rachel stopped being a son to her father, she would have to abandon him to what she perceives to be an unloving wife, and she would also be robbed of her major weapon against mother. If she left home, mother and father would have to face their conflicts alone and would probably create a triangle involving Sandy or Clare. Mother might move even closer to her own parents and father closer to his surrogate son, Roy. This would widen the breach between the parents. If father agreed to come for therapy in order to try and resolve these issues, he would lose a major battle with his wife regarding the value of therapy.

Rachel would have to confront the outside world and its relationships rather than centering her life on the family. This would mean her taking responsibility for becoming an adult woman sexually, professionally, and socially.

What is the therapeutic dilemma? The family must decide between Rachel continuing to be symptomatic or facing the above consequences.

STAGE II
SETTING THE TERMS FOR THERAPY

Step 1: Defining the Therapeutic Dilemma

Our first intervention consisted of setting the terms for the therapeutic contest that was to follow by defining the problem as a family dilemma. The family had defined the problem as an individual one—Rachel's rebelliousness, her obsessions, rigid expectations, and self-starvation all were seen as being disconnected from the family. In defining the problem as a dilemma, we connected the symptom with the system.

Peggy entered the session with the following message:

Peggy: (*Sighs.*) We are stuck.

Mother: So are we.

Peggy: We are in a bind and I don't know what to do about it except just be very honest and open and tell you what we're stuck with. Rachel, we are very hesitant to help you in the way we were planning therapy to take, which would be to help you think and feel more like a woman, to gain weight, to have curves, to menstruate, to go out with boys, and to just be yourself. Because, you see, we are concerned about what will happen to your father, that he will become more isolated in a family of women, that he will turn more to his surrogate son, Roy, leaving your mother more alone, so that she will turn more to her own family. We are worried this will create an irreparable distance between the two of them.

Clare: It's a vicious cycle, isn't it?

Peggy: And, you see, we are concerned about all the members of your family, and when one person in the family changes, that changes the relationship of everybody.

Rachel: (*Long pause.*) I don't think I want to sacrifice myself for my parents. I don't think I care that much. I want to help myself right now.

Peggy: (*Still posing the dilemma.*) I can understand how you feel. I just want to make sure you are aware of the effect it will have. . . . Well, think about these things and decide what you want to do.

Clare: (*Suddenly becoming aware of the implication of the terms I have set.*) I want to say that I got very angry about what the group said. That you decided to change your tack. I think that is wrong. (*She bursts into tears.*) I'm worried about Rachel and that's not the thing to do for her.

Peggy: You feel that we should help her—?

Clare: Yes, that's terrible! How can you say because it will affect other members of the family—what should she do—starve herself?

Peggy:	(*Puzzling over the dilemma.*) Well, you know, I think that has to be Rachel's decision and all we can do is—
Clare:	But you function in that decision. You are here to help her.
Peggy:	Well, you see, Rachel is so close to her family that—
Clare:	I think that's terrible! (*She strides across the room and grabs a Kleenex.*) I obviously don't understand what's behind it. I think it's awful.
Peggy:	We feel responsible—we feel obligated to let you know what we think the consequences of change will be and to prepare you for them.

There was a knock on the door and the group summoned me out for a brief consultation.

Step 2: Setting the Terms for Change

Rachel and Clare had reacted against the therapist's homeostatic position and were pressing for change. We decided to use this as an opportunity to bargain with them over the conditions of change and set the price as Rachel's agreement to turn the burden of her parents' unhappiness over to me. We were aware that the father might not agree to do this since he was boycotting therapy. However, it was our way of dramatizing the connection between Rachel's problem and her parents' unhappiness.

Peggy:	(*Entering the session.*) The group wanted to let you know that they heard what you said and that they take it very seriously, and perhaps there is a way I can help you. (*Turning to Rachel.*) If you would be willing for me to see your parents together and for me to take on the responsibility of what will happen to them if you change, then perhaps you could begin to eat. Could you allow me to take on that responsibility rather than your shouldering it?

Rachel agreed to do this and mother was more than willing to have her husband brought into therapy.

Peggy:	My group feels that then it would be safe for you to become a woman. And I will handle the consequences of that with your father and mother.

I informed them I would call father and ask him to attend the next session. To summarize the terms of therapy:

1. We defined Rachel's symptom as her remaining at home and failing to become a woman in order to stabilize the relationship between her parents.

2. We defined the relationship between her parents as not being able to tolerate her absence.

3. We defined the therapeutic dilemma as having to choose between helping Rachel to become a woman and preserving the stability of her parents' relationship.

4. We defined the solution and therefore the terms for change as Rachel's agreeing to pass the responsibility for preserving her parents' relationship to us. This set up the following situation: If the parents allowed us to help them with their relationship, thus releasing Rachel, she would be relieved of her burden and able to leave home. If they did not, we would ask someone else in the family to take on the burden, or else pass it back to Rachel. By making a hot potato of the parents' unhappiness and passing it around to various members of the family, we would dramatize the therapeutic dilemma.

STAGE III
PUTTING THE THERAPEUTIC
CONTRACT INTO OPERATION

Step 1: Involving Father in the Therapeutic Dilemma

After this session I telephoned Sam, the father, and told him I respected his wish not to be involved in family therapy but since his wife had probably given me a one-sided view of the family situation, I would like to get his impressions over the telephone. He was more than willing to share these and spent the next half hour talking about how his wife put too many expectations on Rachel at too early an age, pushed her to leave home and go away to college at 16, and how he had nothing to say about it because his wife controlled the children and paid no attention to his opinions. He ended the conversation by saying he would be willing to come in for a session if it would help Rachel. I told him I would let him know when I thought it would be helpful, not wanting to seem overly eager about his becoming involved.

A week later Rachel moved away from home into her own apartment and I asked the father to come in for a session. He agreed, but only if Rachel and his wife were present, as he didn't want to be in a session with four women. His terms were accepted, and I began by informing him that we had discovered that Rachel was reluctant to leave home for fear he might be lonely if left alone with his wife. He initially scoffed at this idea, but as I began to discuss the family dinners in which Rachel sided with him against mother and her family, he validated the hypothesis. He admitted that he and Rachel had a lot in common. "We identify in certain ways, we understand each other." Rachel agreed with this.

Peggy: What else do you understand about each other?

Father then described a family dinner held with his wife's family at which he sat next to Rachel for comfort and mother had commented, "Like Robin Hood and his men, they gang up and snicker."

Peggy: What will happen at these dinners when Rachel is not there anymore? I worry about what will happen to your father when you're not there. He will be losing an ally.
Rachel: He won't assimilate.
Father: I don't understand what's going on. I don't think she's worried about me in every situation. Do you think about me when there's a party?
Rachel: Of course I'm concerned about you. It makes me feel bad when you're both unhappy.
Peggy: How do you know when either of them is unhappy? What are the signals?
Rachel: When I speak to mother I hear about things that aren't happy in her life, and vice versa. I don't think either of you should keep me out of it, though. You shouldn't try to hide it.
Peggy: Do you think you can be helpful to them?
Rachel: I could be—I don't think they think I care.
Mother: I don't think she doesn't care about us. She cares desperately. She's been very helpful, she picks up my spirits, talks to me when I'm feeling down.
Peggy: I guess you're not only worried about what will happen to your father when you're not there, but to your mother also.

Rachel agreed with this, and mother and father began to quarrel about their respective needs and sensitivities.

Peggy: (*Again using parental conflict as an opportunity to define why Rachel cannot leave home.*) What will happen when Rachel is not there?

Father: She's not there now.

Peggy: What is happening?

Father: We're having a bad time the last few months.

Peggy: Maybe you'd better go back home, Rachel.

Rachel: I'm not going home.

Mother: I don't want her home. We can straighten out our lives better without her there.

Peggy: Can you? Can you do it?

Father: But if she wanted to be home—I don't think we would—I don't—right, Helen?

Peggy: (*To Rachel.*) It's a tremendous temptation, isn't it?

Rachel: No. I don't really want to go back there. I don't.

Mother: I'm glad.

Peggy: I don't know. How are the two of you going to make it on your own?

Mother
and Father: (*Together.*) I don't know.

Rachel: Do you think it's going to go on like this forever?

Father said again that it was no concern of hers, but Rachel kept insisting it was and that they try and work it out.

Rachel: I'd like it if you could both be happy.

Father: How could we do that?

Rachel: I don't know, but you're certainly not trying.

At this point I explained to father that during a previous session the group had counseled me not to help Rachel unless she agreed to release the responsibility of their unhappiness to me. I asked if he would be willing for me to take on that responsibility and he refused my offer. Mother then put pressure on father.

Mother: You see how Sam calls the shots? When you say you won't come here to help us, I'm at your mercy.

Father: I didn't want to start in the beginning. I've been through this and it didn't help.

Peggy: Yes, you told me that.

Mother: What bothers you? Do you feel vulnerable? Do you feel it is an undue expenditure? What is more important—an undue expenditure or our happiness?

Father: Why do I have to be put in the position of choosing on the basis of what is important?

Mother: There we are!

Father: So it's therapy or nothing?

Mother: Of course. It's not important—we're not important.

Peggy: You may be able to work it out without therapy, but what concerns me is are you going to be able to work it out without Rachel?

Mother: We should be able to go hang ourselves and have it not affect Rachel.

Peggy: But how are you going to keep Rachel out of it?

The parents argued and Rachel tried to mediate. The therapist took a break to have a consultation with the group.

Step 2: Dramatizing the Therapeutic Dilemma

The group agreed that if I continued to pressure father to come into therapy I would be siding with mother and he would resist more and more. We decided the group should support his autonomy and recommended that the burden of the parents' unhappiness should be passed to Sandy. Since Sandy was considered a superhuman being and this was a superhuman job, she seemed the appropriate person. I read the following message:

> The group, not having met Sam before, is impressed with his ability to take care of himself. Somehow, the family mythology had led us to believe otherwise. We trust mother has the strength to do the same. As for Rachel, she has carried the burden of her parents' unhappiness long enough and should now pass the burden to Sandy.

All three burst into laughter. Father asked if I had met Sandy, and I replied, "No, but I'm looking forward to it." Rachel said they were just talking about what a super person she was, and I replied, "Then we've chosen the right person for the job."

Father offered to keep coming to the sessions on the basis of helping Rachel but not to work on his relationship with his wife. Sandy accompanied the family to the following session.

STAGE IV
COPING WITH THE FORCES OF CHANGE

Step 1: Defining Change Within the Therapeutic Contract

Rachel began the session by reporting a sudden and unexpected change. She had started menstruating for the first time in a year and a half and gained several pounds. Following through on my definition of the problem, I gave father credit for convincing Rachel he could manage his life without her.

Rachel: I have to tell you something exciting that's happened. I got my period. It's very exciting.

Peggy: You did?

Rachel: Yes, at my sister's surprise party. (*Much laughter.*)

Peggy: Is this the first time?

Rachel: In a year and a half. I stopped expecting it.

Peggy: You've decided to become a woman?

Rachel: (*Laughingly.*) I'm considering it.

Peggy: You'd better think this over carefully.

Rachel: I know it's a big step.

Peggy: (*To the parents.*) Well, how do the two of you feel about what's happening to her?

Father: Very much relieved that she's on her own path. Things are becoming more normal—not altogether, but approaching it.

Peggy: You're not afraid you're going to lose your companion?

Father: No, I'm praying for it. (*Laughter.*) I was pleased that Rachel is approaching normalcy. She also said she gained three pounds. She is very happy about it. Didn't seem to worry about the three pounds.

Peggy: I think you did a very good job.

Father: I did?

Peggy: Yes, I think you did a very good job. Last time you were here you convinced Rachel you could manage your life without her, that you would be okay, that even if your marriage wasn't the greatest or if you didn't stay together that—

Father: Well, we didn't tell these kids that yet. (*Referring to the other sisters.*)

Peggy: Well, but you told that to Rachel and I think you did an excellent job in assuring her you're going to be okay and that it's okay for her to become an independent woman.

Father: And in the last two weeks things are even better between Helen and me.

Sandy was informed of our having designated her to relieve Rachel of the burden of the parents' unhappiness. Everyone reacted with amusement. Sandy refused, saying she had a new baby and besides the parents seemed to be handling their own burden now.

STAGE V
COPING WITH THE FALLOUT FROM CHANGE

Step 1: Defining Resistance Within the Therapeutic Framework

Neither Rachel nor her family were prepared for this amount of change and Rachel suffered a relapse. We immediately realized our mistake in not anticipating the consequences of change and predicting a relapse to lessen the chance of its occurrence. The family used the Jewish holidays as a way of recreating the family turmoil, with Rachel at the center. By refusing to go to synagogue on Passover, she created a minor crisis. Mother reacted in her characteristic fashion by provoking guilt, father tentatively supported Rachel, and Rachel became depressed to keep attention focused on her. She tearfully complained about her apartment, her job, the classes she was taking, and ended with: "There's nothing good about my life right now."

The whole family became involved in trying to analyze Rachel's depression and giving her helpful advice about how to pull herself out of it. Father brought up the inflammatory subject of Rachel not having gone to temple on Passover and asked if her depression was related to her feeling guilty. She denied this, and father stated: "That's good." Mother vehemently disagreed with him. During the following exchange they spoke simultaneously.

Mother: I don't think that's good, that's my problem. I see it as bad that Rachel, who loves us and whom we love, can do something to make us feel badly continuously and continuously—

Father: That's something for us to get used to—

Mother: When it would be good if she would do something to make us feel good.

Father: Helen—no—that's—(*Indecipherable.*)

Rachel: How can you expect me to do something I don't believe?

Father: Helen, that's something—(*Indecipherable.*)

Mother: But you do believe. You've told me you believe.

Father: Helen, she believes in a different way.

Rachel: But I don't. I believe in my fashion. I don't believe in keeping kosher, I don't believe in going to temple, I don't believe in dating Jewish boys, I don't believe that!

Mother: All right. And I believe, Rachel, that it is a sign of not quite loving us enough! I see it as a very selfish kind of act. You have no consideration. She's liable to do exactly what she wants to do because she doesn't want to please us. She's very rebellious.

Mother then went into a long harangue, giving a history of Rachel's rebelliousness. She ended up talking about how important the Jewish tradition was to her.

Mother: I've cried about the continuation of our Jewish tradition.

Rachel: I'm sorry, Mommy; you can cry and cry, but I'm not going to become more Jewish because you cry.

Mother: Therefore, then I don't think that you love us very much.

Rachel: Well, Mommy, if that's your criteria, then I really can't help you.

Mother: Okay, these are my feelings. That's my criteria. Yes.

Peggy: If she really loved you enough, she'd believe what you believe?

Mother: No, dear, no; because I know she believes. She's told me she believes. She believes in God. She says the most important prayer in our religion every night of her life, which I don't do.

Rachel: Why not? Don't you love me?

Mother: Rachel, stop shouting at me.

Peggy: You didn't answer her.

Mother: Why don't I say that prayer? Have you ever asked me to join you in that prayer?

Rachel: No, it's a private prayer. You're supposed to say it by yourself.

Mother: So why are you shouting at me?

Rachel: Why don't you say that prayer? You love me?

Mother accused Rachel of being sarcastic. I asked father if he felt the same way as mother about Rachel's not going to temple. He said he would like her to attend but didn't feel as intensely as his wife. I then asked Clare and Sandy if they had a problem becoming independent in this family, and both answered in the affirmative, describing the pressure and guilt that were applied to them throughout their lives. Asked how they dealt with this, Clare replied she didn't let her parents know about half of what she was doing, and Sandy said she always did what she wanted to do. Both parents were attacked for their rigidity, and the session ended with everyone quarrelling over who was most to blame.

The group was not present during this session and the family was told they would receive a message from them after they had seen the tape. In a consultation with the team, I defined the relapse as a systems problem rather than an individual one and sent the following message:

> It is the conviction of the group that Rachel has wisely decided she has not yet finished her job of diverting her parents from their unhappiness. Since Sandy and Clare have refused to accept this job, she should return home until it is completed.

It was then agreed that at the next session I would take a more lenient position regarding this message, encouraging Rachel's independence in opposition to an adamant position from the group, thus intensifying the triangle between therapist, family, and group.

Step 2: Shifting the Definition of the Problem

In the following session, Rachel adamantly refused to return home and the parents insisted they did not need her anymore to solve their marital problem. Rachel reacted to this exclusion by complaining about every aspect of her life—her job, her apartment, her boss, her feelings of isolation and loneliness. As she enumerated her complaints, the family, following their characteristic pattern, gave her "helpful" advice replete with platitudes about how to pull herself up by her own bootstraps.

We saw Rachel's litany of complaints as a reaction to giving up her important job of repairing her parent's marriage and decided to ask the family to allow her to mourn her leave taking rather than trying to cheer her up. This was impossible for them to do.

Peggy: The group has observed that Rachel's unhappiness seems to be a reproach to you and you're not allowing her to be unhappy. Rachel, they want to say that it's very important that you are unhappy and that your family allow you to be. How can you get them to allow you to be unhappy?

Rachel: I'll just have to keep away from them, I guess.

Father: Then we would worry about her.

Mother: I worry about my children, especially when they're alone.

Peggy: This is supposed to be a happy family, so it's difficult for you to allow anyone in the family to feel unhappy.

Mother: Are you speaking about a facade, Peggy?

Peggy: All families are supposed to be happy. This is a very close family, so it is very important for you to feel that everyone's happy. And when anyone is unhappy (*Mother sobs*), it's really hard, isn't it? How can you get mother to allow you to be unhappy?

Rachel: I don't know. I can't reassure her.

Mother: (*Sobbing.*) I worry about you every day.

Clare then jumped in to say she never told her mother her problems because she didn't want this kind of reaction. Mother and Clare became involved in a heated argument. Mother stated she couldn't help crying over her children's problems. I then focused the issue between the parents.

Peggy: Do you also cry over Sam's unhappiness?

Mother: Yes, a little bit. I do. He doesn't even know it.

Father: I don't believe it. I really don't believe it.

Mother: So I don't tell him.

Father: I don't believe it. (*The parents begin to argue.*)

Peggy: When do you cry over his unhappiness?

Mother: When I see that he is unhappy in his business, that he's unhappy with his partners, if I see he's unhappy in community situations, when he's hurting himself and feeling terrible about it. When I see he's unhappy in relation to Clare's husband and himself, when I see he's unhappy about his mother and sick brother-in-law, my heart hurts—and it's very hard for me to let him know it bothers me, and so I do it in my own little corner.

Peggy: (*Sympathetically.*) You cry over him without letting him know?

Mother: Cry tears? No. For my children I cry tears.

Step 3: Prescribing Enmeshment

The group discussed the futility of persuading mother to allow any of her children to be unhappy. Worrying over her children was an important life job. Rachel knew this and kept her mother involved with her by continually giving her something to worry about.

Rather than trying to diffuse this intense involvement, we decided to prescribe the family's enmeshment—but in a way that would involve father in the transaction. We added a task that shifted some of mother's involvement with her children toward her husband. Our purpose in doing this was to test the parents' readiness to bridge the gap in their relationship left by Rachel's departure.

Peggy: It is the group's conviction that I am asking the impossible by asking a mother with a heart as tender as Helen's to allow her children to suffer. (*As an aside, I say, "There are a lot of Jewish mothers out there." Mother waves in recognition.*) It is equally impossible for Rachel to break her mother's heart. We, therefore, recommend that Rachel call every day and tell her mother about her unhappiness. Mother should then share this with Sam, who should then comfort her. (*Mother cries, father reacts negatively.*)

Father: I don't want that kind of scene. I don't want her to call every day and make Helen unhappy and I don't want her to confide in me. I don't see anybody getting better from a thing like that.

Peggy: You won't do that for your wife and Rachel?

Father: (*Laughs.*) It's like a prescription.
Peggy: That's exactly what it is—a doctor's prescription.
Father: That's terrible, that's very bitter tasting.
Mother: Why is it so hard to comfort me?
Father: Helen, the whole idea doesn't—
Mother: Why, honey? The only thing that's changed is the comfort, because she does call every day and unburden herself and I do listen.
Father: (*Surprised.*) You do call every day?
Mother: And I don't share it with you because I get the . . . (*She indicates with her thumb a downward movement.*) The only difference would be you would put your arm around me. (*She caresses him.*)
Clare: It would be nice if you were on mummy's side a little bit.
Father: I'm not not on her side.
Peggy: (*Earnestly.*) Sam, this is very important. Can you do that for Rachel—and for your wife?
Father: Sure I can do it.

Rachel did call her mother every day as requested, but mother became bored with her complaints, stopped trying to cheer her up and give her advice, and finally told her she would have to solve her problems herself.

After this session, the parents took a month vacation, cutting the bond with Rachel more decisively. Threatened by this separation, Rachel moved back to their home where she felt isolated and lonely without her old job of mediator. She fell into a morose state and complained endlessly about her feelings of unhappiness and failure.

There is a myth in our profession that if parents get together and free the child from the position of mediator, the child will automatically spring forth mature, well adjusted, and symptom-free. This rarely happens since the child's social development has been retarded through his/her preoccupation with the parents' problems. The child usually goes through a period of feeling a loss of identity as he/she relinquishes this very important family position.

Our next task was to help Rachel find a different position for herself. But this could not be done in the same way the family had tried, through encouragement and helpful advice, since she only rebelled against this. We decided instead to use her rebellious streak in the service of change and to define her unhappiness and failure as her way of differentiating herself from her family, which placed such a high premium on happiness and success. We decided to enlist her sisters in helping her to accomplish this task. Rachel had never felt supported by them in her attempts to establish her autonomy, as the sisters often took the side of the parents in haranguing and pushing her. The support she received from them in this new alliance proved to be enormously beneficial.

STAGE VI
ENLISTING THE SIBLING SUBSYSTEM

Step 1: Forming a Coalition with the Sisters

The sisters were more than happy to continue to meet without the parents and quickly joined me in my position that Rachel needed to keep rebelling in order to establish her independence. In the following session, I continually reframed Rachel's complaints within this framework.

Rachel: I feel sapped at this point.

Peggy: Well, your parents certainly wouldn't approve of that.

Rachel: No. I have to keep going.

Peggy: That's right, and by being completely sapped you're saying no to them, which takes a lot of guts.

Sandy: (*Wistfully.*) That's really true.

Rachel: But I have no self-respect.

Peggy: Do your parents want you to have self-respect?

Rachel: I think so.

Peggy: And you're saying you don't have self-respect. You say your parents want you to be happy and you're saying, "I'm unhappy."

Rachel: My parents want me to gain weight.

Peggy: And you're staying thin.

Rachel: I've gained five pounds and I'm very upset about it.

Peggy: I can understand that because you feel you're losing ground with them, that you're doing something they'd like you to do, which makes you feel a nonperson.

Rachel: I should move to Kalamazoo, get the hell out of New York, and not even think of pleasing my parents.

Sandy: (*Now in full support.*) Listen to what Peggy is saying. You are living your life to displease them.

Rachel: I want to please myself.

Peggy: Well, you are because you're displeasing them. The most important thing in your life right now is to say no to your parents, and you've found many ways of doing that.

Rachel: I want to please me.

Peggy: Well, you are because you're displeasing them.

The session ended with the group suggesting that Rachel enlist the sisters' help in the planned rebellion, saying it was too much of a burden for her to think up these elaborate schemes herself. The sisters eagerly agreed, with Sandy stating that it would be good training for her.

Step 2: Differentiating from the Sisters

We failed to anticipate that Rachel would sense her sisters' help at pressuring her to change, since it was being given within the context of therapy. Before forming an alliance with them, she made it clear that she had to first rebel against their expectations of her progress in therapy. She did this by remaining depressed and making veiled suicide threats. I defined these threats as her way of differentiating herself from her sisters' expectations.

Clare: I feel angry. What Rachel is doing is hostility, talking about killing herself. Besides the fact I love her, I'm angry at her for doing it to me.

Rachel: Then maybe I'll just make believe things are okay.

Clare: Why can't I say what I feel?

Rachel: Maybe I have to work it out away from my family. There are too many expectations and pressures.

Clare: Who puts expectations on you?

Rachel: You all do. You all expect me to deal with my problems in a certain way.

Peggy: (*Supporting her attempt to differentiate from her sisters.*) I think that's true. You do expect her to deal with her problems in a particular way and Rachel is saying no to all of you. Not only no to her parents but to her sisters.

Rachel: I don't think so—maybe if I were getting pleasure out of it, I could think so.

Peggy:	I know you're not getting pleasure out of it, that's not the purpose.
Rachel:	What is the purpose?
Peggy:	The purpose is to establish who you are, and that you are the one who says no to expectations.
Clare:	You really calm down when we get upset, don't you?
Sandy:	I noticed that last time. As soon as we get upset, you sit back. Maybe this is what you want. Maybe we have to prove we're so concerned, or maybe you want to shake us up.
Rachel:	I'm not doing it to be dramatic.
Clare:	Look at you. Five minutes ago you were crying and saying how miserable you were.
Rachel:	(*Coolly.*) It doesn't take that much to make me go one way or the other. I don't know what it takes.
Clare:	(*Heatedly.*) Bullshit! (*They argue.*)
Peggy:	(*Defining this again as Rachel's way of rebelling against her sisters.*) I can understand why you're feeling better now, because you've just said no to your sisters and their expectations of you. I think you need to just keep doing that, Rachel, and to find other ways of doing it.
Rachel:	I really don't get this whole thing.

I then enlisted the sisters in trying to think of more constructive ways for Rachel to rebel and asked about some of the ways they had successfully rebelled. Clare listed her rebellious acts as going out with married men, dating non-Jewish boys, letting her parents know when she was having sex, not joining B'nai B'rith, and so on. Rachel joined in listing her accomplishments, such as going without a bra, wearing pantyhose without panties, raising her voice in public. Sandy suddenly burst out with, "I enjoy talking about these things. It makes me feel good." The tense atmosphere changed to one of camaraderie and laughter as they banded together in discussing acts of "disloyalty."

Some questions might be raised as to the advisability of encouraging sisters to band together to form a coalition against parental control. The fact that the sisters were all adults rather than young children who are financially, physically, and emotionally dependent on their parents was a determining factor in this intervention. We would refrain from doing this with younger children with whom obedience to parental control is age appropriate.

Rachel's rebellious acts had always been accompanied by enormous guilt, and she therefore failed in each endeavor to become independent. By bringing her rebelliousness out into the open, planning it, condoning it, and scheduling it with the help of her sisters, we stripped off its more toxic aspects. Note that she then chose to rebel in relatively benign ways rather than those destructive to her health and well-being.

The parents returned from their vacation, and I telephoned to let them know we had not forgotten about them but had found the sessions with the sisters so helpful to Rachel we wanted to continue them for a while longer. I assured them they would be involved later on.

In the following sessions, I pushed the sibling alliance further and suggested Sandy teach Rachel how to become self-indulgent since Rachel emulated her father by being rigidly self-denying and frugal. Sandy coached her by instructing her to buy things she would never think of buying, such as expensive perfume, luxurious underwear, silk suits, jewelry, expensive cosmetics, and so on. I warned Rachel against indulging in food, however, and cautioned her against gaining too much weight. I set the limit at what Sandy weighed, nine pounds heavier, and thus, while seeming to restrain her, I actually encouraged her to gain. As they continued to discuss different modes of self-indulgence, some of the suggestions became outrageous, and I joined them in their frivolity and laughter.

The group interrupted to restrain me and to point out that the kind of rebellion I was suggesting was too enjoyable. I agreed with them that it was too soon to stop pushing the unhappiness prescription and I returned with the following message:

Peggy: (*Looking contrite.*) I have been reprimanded by my group.

Sandy: (*With dismay.*) Again, Peggy? You're doing badly.

Peggy: Yes, but I can see their point. They feel I got swept away in talking about things that would make Rachel happy, like being self-indulgent, buying expensive perfume, underwear, indulging in sex, because, Rachel, that would make you happy. And your parents would know you were happy.

Sandy: That makes sense to me. Does it to you, Rachel?

Rachel: It doesn't make sense to me. How does it make sense to you?

Sandy: Because if you're happy, Mummy will do what she did to me. She'll make you want to puke. She'll make more fuss over that than she does over you now. If you're unhappy on your job, you can quit, and that will make them unhappy. As the job goes on, you make a list of all the things that you can complain about, so even if you have some happy moments, don't talk about those. Go home and tell them about all the lousy things that happened to you today, and make their evening miserable, and that will make you miserable too.

Peggy: Good, good, very good.

At the end of the session the sisters gave the first indication of how they saw me in relation to the group. Although I had consistently told Rachel she must remain unhappy, they perceived me as being on Rachel's side. They picked up the second level of the paradoxical message.

Sandy: You have children, don't you Peggy?

Peggy: Yes. I have a son, 17, and a daughter, 21.

Sandy: Is your daughter why you keep on wanting Rachel to be happy? Do you identify a little? The group keeps reprimanding you for being too soft-hearted.

Peggy: I don't know. I'll think about that. It's hard for me to tell Rachel to be unhappy. (*To Rachel.*) Do you know that? (*I reach out a hand and touch her.*) It's hard for me to tell you to be unhappy—but I know they're right. When I think about it and I'm objective, I know that's what you must do.

Sandy: I guess that's what's good about having a group. They keep you objective.

Peggy: That's right.

STAGE VII
SAYING NO TO THERAPY

Step 1: Pushing the Prescription to the Breaking Point

This next session was the most crucial session in therapy, marking the turning point of a lasting change. Before Rachel could become a truly independent woman, she had to be able to say no to therapy and to the absurd task we had given her of keeping herself miserable. She had been conscientiously trying to follow it, but she was becoming more and more dissatisfied with living with her parents and remaining unhappy. During this session, I pushed the prescription to the point where Rachel said no to therapy.

Peggy: (*To Rachel.*) Well, Rachel, are you being unhappy, covering up what is pleasurable? How well are you doing that?

Rachel: I'm trying to cover up whatever's pleasurable.

Peggy: Good. How well are you doing in that?

Rachel: I'm trying to say no to all my mother's suggestions, and I hate it there. (*She cries.*)
Peggy: You're supposed to hate it there. Of course you hate it there.
Rachel: I feel so out of it there, I really can't stand it.
Peggy: You're going to be unhappy as long as you're at home.
Rachel: So why do I have to be there? I don't want to be there. I have this chance to sublease this apartment and I think I'm going to do it, if it works out.
Sandy: They're telling you to do something and if you're planning to rent an apartment in April you're just not listening again. And just like mother's going to have to be unhappy for a while until things get better, maybe you're going to have to be unhappy for a while.
Rachel: Why can't I get out of there? I want out.
Sandy: Well, you can't. So it's just too bad.

Rachel moans and groans and ends up looking imploringly at me with big, wet eyes, asking, "Why can't I sublease the place for just six months?"

Peggy: The harder it is for you now, the better.
Rachel: I don't understand it, and I can't go on like this.
Peggy: You won't understand it right now.

The sisters supported me and Rachel argued, finally screaming, "I can't stand it, and why do I have to force myself to be there?"

Peggy: (*Kindly but firmly, like a doctor administering medicine.*) For the time being, the worse it is, the better it will be. The worse it is now and the more unhappy you are, the better it is. So have your sisters been helping you with that?
Rachel: With being unhappy? No.
Sandy: We were supposed to—if she felt guilty doing something, she would call us.
Clare: She hasn't been calling me.
Peggy: How come you haven't been calling your sisters?
Rachel: Sometimes I don't feel like it because I'm frustrated and I don't like this. I feel like evaluating the situation and how to make things better, and instead I'm told to make things worse, and I can't stand that. I can't go against my instincts any longer.
Peggy: For the time being, Rachel, you have to make things worse.
Rachel: Well, I can't, Peggy. I want to go out and get a better job and I want to make myself happy. I can't make myself get a bad job and I can't make myself more unhappy.
Sandy: Is it necessary for her to stay with her present job to make her more unhappy?
Peggy: She should make herself unhappy in every way possible.
Sandy: Why?
Peggy: Because only in that way is she going to be able to find herself.
Clare: She is making my parents so dissatisfied with her they both stood there and smiled at me like dummies, they were so happy to see me. They never did this before. I looked so good in comparison with Rachel.
Peggy: Don't you appreciate what she's doing for you?
Clare: Yes. I felt I didn't deserve it.
Peggy: She's giving you a gift.
Clare: I guess so, so I shouldn't be mad. I feel guilty when I get mad at Rachel. This is my baby sister.
Peggy: No. Anything you can do to help Rachel be unhappy is fine.
Clare: Rachel is so self-involved right now.

Peggy: But she needs to be self-involved in her unhappiness. She should be totally pre-occupied with it.

Rachel: (*Crying.*) I can't deal with people on that basis. This totally isolates me from the entire world. It's a ridiculous request to make. How am I supposed to relate to friends when I'm unhappy? Who the hell wants to be with me?

Peggy: (*Sympathetically.*) I know this is hard.

Rachel: This is crazy! Not hard—crazy! This means you're asking me to exist alone, to lock myself in my parents' basement and exist alone, because no one is going to want to be with me and I don't want to be with myself when I'm like this. It doesn't give me any reason for doing anything—any purpose for wanting to exist. It's making my existence so much more miserable.

Step 2: Escalating the Therapeutic Triangle

Peggy: Let me talk to my group a minute. Maybe they will allow you to do something that will relieve you a little bit. You seem to get into trouble, though, every time I relent . . .

The group decided not to relent but to take a position of consternation in relation to Rachel's rumbling of rebelliousness.

Peggy: The group says it sounds like you're not only saying no to your mother but you're getting ready to say no to me, and they are quite appalled. Are you saying no to me?

Rachel: (*Hesitates, and then blurts out.*) Yes, I am. (*Changes her mind.*) Not to you, to the group. (*She is not quite brave enough to risk alienating me, but she feels it's safe to take a position against the group since she knows I have sometimes disagreed with them.*) I'm fed up. I don't know what to do. My human instincts tell me to do something to make things happier, and you people are telling me to be unhappy, and I don't know how to relate to other people on that basis.

Peggy: (*Acting puzzled.*) That was the way you were relating to them for quite a while. Can't you just go back to that? Or stay there?

Rachel: No, I can't. I can't sit around and complain.

Peggy: But you have been doing that, so it's hard for me to understand what would be intolerable about it now, since you were doing that for quite a while. What's different about it now?

Rachel: Because I see it differently now. I see the world is not interested in me and my problems and it's not appropriate.

I dismissed myself to talk to the group, thinking it might be time for me to take a position in favor of change. It is decided I should first explore what Rachel would do if she were allowed to change.

Rachel: I don't know. All I know is I've really been trying the past few weeks to do what you told me to do and really work at it between sessions, and Peggy, I can't stand it! And I can't stand living with my parents. I'm regressing.

Peggy: (*Pursuing the question of change.*) What would happen if you said no to them and me? What would you do?

Rachel: I'd try to do what the rest of the world does—break away from home, become an adult, get a job, find my own place to live, find my own circle of friends.

Peggy: (*Challenging her to prove herself.*) But that's just what we're afraid of, Rachel. You know the consequences of that. You know what's happened every time you've attempted to do that. The results have been disastrous for you. You've felt you couldn't do it, felt like a failure, something has always gone wrong, you've felt lonely, isolated, that you were going crazy, the noises bothered you—it was a disaster, and we're trying to save you from that.

The group called me out and we decided it was time for me to side with Rachel against the group and push for change. When given her freedom to go forward, Rachel hesitated. The medicine I had been prescribing, despite its bad taste, was a comfort to her, giving her a sense of security. The sisters also registered some apprehension as to Rachel's ability to assume responsibility for her own happiness.

Step 3: Opposing the Group

I entered the room and asked Rachel to support my opposition to the group.

Peggy: Rachel, you want to help me say no to the group? I just had a big fight with them. I can't budge them. Let's you and me say no to the group.

Rachel: (*Tearfully.*) I was afraid when you went out there I was going to hear my sentence for the week.

Peggy: Are you ready to say no to them with me?

Rachel: What do they say?

Peggy: They're adamant. I cannot budge them. They say absolutely you should stay at home. You should be unhappy, should not make your life any better, should stay miserable, isolated, complain, not look for a job.

Rachel: Forget that. Forget that right there.

Peggy: (*Extending her hand.*) Thanks, thanks. I told them you had suffered enough, been unhappy enough, said no to Mother enough, and enough is enough. And you have the right, if you feel you can do something different, to try. And I want to say, "Go ahead."

Rachel: With what?

Peggy: With whatever you want to do. Whatever you want to do to make yourself happy, and we will know whether or not I'm right or the group is right.

Rachel now had a choice of siding with me by changing or letting the group win a victory by remaining the same.

Rachel: How about saying no to my parents?

Peggy: I think you've had enough of that.

Clare: Can't she say no when she wants to say no?

Peggy: Oh, that's fine; if you want to say no or if you want to say yes, feel free at this point to do whatever you want to do.

Rachel: (*Stunned at this sudden shift and not knowing how to respond.*) Are you sincere?

Peggy: I am.

Rachel: (*Apprehensively.*) What do they feel I'm going to gain from doing things their way? Because, Peggy, the only thing is that when I'm unsure and don't know what I'm doing I can say, "Well, my therapist told me to do this, so it must be what I'm supposed to do." So I just don't know.

Clare: You're taking all the supports away from Rachel by saying do whatever you want to do.

Peggy: You mean you feel the group is right?

Clare: I would say it's all right to say, "Do whatever you want to do" in certain directions, but I think you're pulling all the props out from under her by putting all the responsibility on Rachel. I feel she's not ready.

Peggy: What do you think, Sandy?

Sandy: I'm a little bit afraid for her.
Peggy: Do you think the group's right, too?
Sandy: I think they are too extreme.
Peggy: Maybe I just had a reaction against them.
Sandy: I think gradually. I look back on her life as being too much at one time and see her doing the same thing again. She'll have too many demands on her and expectations will be too great.
Peggy: Actually, then, the two of you are taking a position between me and the group.
Rachel: I'm also taking a position between the two.

Step 4: Supporting Autonomy

I then took the position that Rachel had the right to decide on her own how fast she should change.

Peggy: I think you're right. My position is extreme. I lost my head and got angry. I admire the fact that you were able to say no to the group and also to me just now, and to stop me from going too far. I think your judgment will guide you now as to how much pleasure and progress you allow yourself.

Her task had been changed from being unhappy and saying no to deciding on how rapidly to say yes. Thus, she was placed in charge of her own change.

STAGE VIII
SOLIDIFYING CHANGE

Step 1: Anticipating and Rehearsing a Regression

Having defied the therapists, Rachel took a giant step toward independence and in the following session described her new life. The group reminded me to schedule a regression in order to solidify change.

Clare and Sandy arrived for the session without Rachel, who was late for the first time having gone for a job interview. Sandy burst out with: "She's so happy. She's always happy. I've been under pressure lately, I've had a lot on my mind, and there's Rachel off being so happy, and I'm saying to myself, 'Goddammit, enough of this already with the smile.'"

Peggy: That must be quite an adjustment for you.
Clare: Even my mother and father commented on how happy Rachel is. I'm giving my parents problems now, so it takes the pressure off Rachel.
Peggy: That's terrific. What kind of problems?

Rachel entered, elegantly dressed and looking radiant.

Rachel: (Glowingly.) I'm having such a good time, Peggy. I can't believe it. I bought myself this silk suit. (Proudly shows off an elegant and stylish suit.) A hundred and fourteen bucks. I want to start being really good to myself.
Peggy: (Cautiously.) I'm afraid to be too enthusiastic because of my group.
Rachel: I'm afraid to be too enthusiastic too. I'm so happy I began to be afraid it wouldn't last. I don't want to be devastated. I haven't been this happy in years.
Peggy: What's making you so happy?

Rachel spoke excitedly about her new life. She was working on a magazine, getting published, meeting famous people, and doing something for the first time in her life that she really enjoyed. She had a chance to sublet an apartment for six months and was thinking about taking it. She felt she was making less frantic decisions, but looked apprehensively toward the mirror as she said, "I know the group won't like my moving." I said maybe they would change their minds now. She spoke about a new interesting man she was dating who looked like Woody Allen. I asked if her parents would approve of him and she said she was afraid they would. She discussed her problem of saying no to men for fear of hurting their feelings, and I asked her sisters to help her with this since they had had more experience. As I joined them in a humorous and intimate conversation, the group interrupted with a knock on the door and called me out to say they would like to take a position counter to the merriment and begin instead to worry about a regression. Passover was coming up and would probably create tension and conflict as it had last year. Also, Rachel was planning to move again and we could anticipate a recurrence of the former problems.

Peggy: The group is critical of me again. They feel we're having too good a time. (*The sisters boo.*) They are worried about what is going to happen on Passover or if you attempt to move again.

Rachel said she had already told her mother that she was not going to go to Seder on Passover. I asked her to anticipate her parents' reactions so she could be prepared for the worst. How might they draw her back into the fight between them? How could she deal with her guilt? How would she keep from siding with one against the other? What would happen to father at the dinners when she wasn't there to side with him against mother's family? Rachel replied, "I'll just have to give up that quest to please him." We went over all the possibilities carefully and Rachel said she was confident she could handle them.

Before the session ended I came back with one last warning from the group against premature optimism.

Peggy: The group is not as optimistic as we are. They anticipate you will get depressed again, and this will probably occur around Passover or if you move. They recommend, therefore, that you deliberately allow yourself to get depressed on those two occasions.

Rachel: What if I'm not?

Peggy: Try to feel that way. Try to go back to the way you were feeling or—(*Loud groans and laughter from everyone.*) You don't have to go all the way back.

Rachel: You don't know what you're asking. I want to be able to deal with these times.

Peggy: Then practice them.

Rachel: Okay.

We decided it was time now to involve the parents again as we anticipated they would have a reaction to the new Rachel.

The whole family was convened for this session. Rachel looked stunning with a new hairstyle, new clothes, new makeup, and a radiant expression on her face. She began the interview with:

Rachel: I'm great. I've never been greater.

Peggy: Tell me about it.

Rachel: Number one—I'm in love.

Peggy: In love? Not with a man? (*Laughter.*)

Rachel: Yes, with a man—with a really nice man.

Peggy: Jewish?

Rachel: (*Chagrined.*) Yes. That's his only drawback, but he didn't want a Jewish woman either, so we decided we'd overlook it. We don't have those attributes we were trying to avoid.

Peggy: Well, at least it's equal.

Father: Maybe you'll both convert. (*Much laughter.*)

Rachel: He's the one who looks like Woody Allen. Things are working out nicely. He's very kind and sensitive. Lots of fun. He loves me, and I'm living in Manhattan doing publicity work and I have a lot of promising job prospects.

Both parents expressed their pleasure over the changes in Rachel and only once attempted to use her new romance as a focal point for an old argument between the two of them.

Step 2: Redefining the Marital Relationship

It was quite clear now that the parents would never have a tranquil relationship but would probably go on fighting for the rest of their days. The important thing was that Rachel was no longer involved in their battles. She managed to stay out of this one and I described the parents' relationship as a profound and lasting bond between two stalwart, equally matched opponents who had strong and differing points of view and felt free to express them on every subject. Since it was their way of making love, they certainly didn't need any interference from anyone outside. Father, surprisingly, agreed, saying, "After all is said and done, we are meant for each other." And mother conceded that there must be something they enjoyed about fighting since they were always doing it.

An appointment was made for one month later, and I stated this would give us time to see if Rachel could stay out of her parents' love making. If she felt her parents needed a third party, she should call one of her sisters and ask them to be the third member. The sisters vociferously declined.

STAGE IX
PRESCRIBING A FAREWELL RITUAL

In a presession discussion we decided that if Rachel had managed to maintain her gains, we would ceremonialize her leave taking by prescribing a farewell ritual.

The family reported things *were* going well and the parents declared it was a relief to have Rachel out of the home as it was more peaceful. The session was spent giving the family credit for the changes that had been made, anticipating future trouble spots, and making some suggestions as to how to avoid them. The session ended with my suggesting they plan a farewell party to celebrate Rachel's becoming a woman and leaving home, and that father should propose a toast to send her on her way. They responded positively and Sandy suggested they have a broomstick for Rachel to jump over, as in Jewish weddings, symbolizing the beginning of a new life.

FOLLOW-UP

A one-, two-, and three-year follow-up revealed Rachel still in good spirits, living alone in her own apartment and loving it, excited about her new career, and dating several different men. The parents were still making love in their characteristic way, but the three sisters were staying out of it.

Editors' Introduction

This case illustrates an eclectic approach and one way in which meditation can be used as a tool in psychotherapy. Deane Shapiro teaches meditation, a technique often associated with contemplative approaches to personal growth, in the context of a behavioral approach to therapy that also addresses client insight and the importance of interpersonal relationships in understanding this client's depression and insomnia.

Shapiro uses the case to point out the parallels between meditation and hypnosis, another technique used in many different schools of psychotherapy. While Shapiro presents meditation to this particular client in the context of self-management, transpersonal and humanistic psychologists are likely to frame the experience in terms of personal growth and transcendence. Although the theoretical explanations for the efficacy of the technique may vary across orientations, instruction in the actual practice of meditation is fairly consistent across practitioners.

This case describes a common clinical scenario: a motivated client who presents with multiple concerns including the desire to minimize or eliminate the use of psychotropic medication. The client's problems include insomnia, a lack of assertion skills, excessive self-criticism, poor stress management skills, and vocational problems. The sense of mastery associated with the development of skill in meditation appears to have generalized and had a positive influence on many of these concerns. The case reminds us that few clients, few problems, and few approaches to therapy are as tidy as our theories suggest.

12 | MEDITATION AND PSYCHOTHERAPY: A CASE STUDY

Deane H. Shapiro, Jr.

THE ORIENTATION OF THE THERAPIST

I remember being asked my religious orientation in a religious studies class at Stanford. I wrote: a Jewish existentialist with Zen Buddhist inclinations. My clinical orientation is similarly complex. It is behavioral, insofar as that implies belief in the importance of carefully evaluating the efficacy of my clinical work (rather than adherence to a specific body of techniques). It is also behavioral in that it involves an emphasis on action-oriented therapy, a setting of goals with the client, the collection of data, working on change—behavioral or cognitive—i.e. new ways of acting, thinking, feeling about the world and oneself. It is insight-oriented insofar as that means that a client's understanding of his/her behavior, thoughts, actions, habit patterns is important, rather than *a priori* assuming historical insight into psychosexual stages is needed. It is relationship oriented—I believe trust, empathy, and understanding provide a critical context for therapeutic change. However, I do not believe, in general, that relationship is sufficient, and do not believe it should be the focus of therapy, except as it facilitates changes the client is trying to make outside of the therapeutic context. Finally, it is religious, spiritual, transpersonal, insofar as this means I am committed to my own personal growth and work, believe in working toward developing myself toward the farther reaches of my potential, desire to find a core connection between myself and others, and have experienced feelings of unity and oneness with nature, myself, and others. It does not mean I believe all clients should experience this; that there is only one path to its experience; or that it is an *a priori,* true reality, but rather one which I believe to be true, part of my path of heart: a belief system that, for now, *works* to nourish and sustain me.

Thus my orientation is really a combination of personal, clinical, and religious elements. Interestingly, at the risk of being an overly "general" armchair philosopher, it appears to me that for many, there is a large overlap between the psychological and religious. Scientists and psychotherapists have, for many in our culture, become a type of guru: priests of a technological and secular age.

To label my orientation, we could say I am an applied pragmatic behaviorist who believes in relationship, insight, and spiritual growth, all with appropriate reservations!

THE THERAPIST'S BELIEF IN THE EFFICACY OF THE STRATEGY

I believe meditation to be a useful self-regulation strategy for certain clients with certain clinical problems. I do not believe meditation to be any more (or less) effective than other self-regulation strategies for a client who wishes some type of stress-management strategy. My decision to use it (rather than other strategies) would depend upon the client's belief system, values, and expectations. Further, I do not feel a particular need to call a cognitive focusing strategy "meditation" if a client has a resistance to that term either because of prior religious training, or dislike of its "mystical" association. I am also not convinced, at the level of actual behavior, how different meditation is from other cognitive strategies. As Ted Barber noted,

> The overlap between self-hypnosis and meditation is tremendous. In fact, it seems to me that the variability within self-hypnosis and meditation is almost as large as the variability between these procedures. There seems to me to be so many parallels that it appears possible to at least conceptualize self-hypnosis as one type of meditation, or vice versa, meditation as one type of self-hypnosis.

It should be noted, however, that for me we are talking here only about meditation as a self-regulation strategy, and its use for clients who wish some form of training for a stress-related problem.

THE CLIENT AND PRESENTING PROBLEM

James Sidney, an Australian male in his mid-thirties, was a short, rather unassuming individual, with a kind and sensitive face. When he introduced himself to me, he shook my hand, but didn't directly make eye contact. Although he had a pronounced accent, his speech was clear and lucid, but his voice was often so soft that I could not hear his words. When we sat down, he said, "I have a problem with insomnia, and wondered if you could teach me meditation." He said he knew of my clinical interest in meditation, and on the recommendation of a mutual colleague on the East Coast, presented himself to me to learn an approach to meditation that was not immersed in "cultic" paraphernalia: incense, pictures of gurus, candles, etc.

I told him that yes, I would be glad to teach him meditation and work with him on the issue of insomnia. As one way of doing this, I told him it would be helpful for me to get to know him a bit better and to learn what he had heard about and expected from meditation.

Clinical Note

I have three goals in obtaining this information. First, before teaching a technique to a client, it is important to gather information about the client's expectations, hopes, motivation for learning a particular technique. Second, I interact with this information in a way which attempts to build a trusting relationship between us. I believes this relationship provides an important context for the teaching of technique and skill training. Without the trust, the teaching of any technique, whether meditation or a behavioral strategy, is more difficult. Third, I want to obtain some initial background information about the client, as well as a broader profile of what other issues may currently be going on in this client's life that may be relevant to therapy.

Overview of Therapy Duration

This client was seen for ten months. The first six months we met once a week; the next two months, once every other week, and then I saw him twice at three-week intervals. There was a six-month, written follow-up. The sessions were face to face in the office and involved homework assignments and data collection outside the office.

CLIENT EXPECTATIONS

The client noted he had heard and read in the newspaper about the scientific experiments showing meditation's effectiveness for stress and felt it would be helpful for him. He said that he was not particularly interested in the "spiritual mumbo-jumbo" that went along with the technique. He noted that although raised a Catholic. he had had no formal religious affiliation for several years. "I consider myself more interested in down-to-earth human concerns than metaphysical issues."

CLIENT BACKGROUND

The client noted he used to sleep about eight or nine hours a night, but that a couple of years ago, for no reason he was aware of, he began to wake up during the night. He began to awaken with increasing frequency per night during the next six months, and finally decided to go into therapy. He noted that he was in therapy for the next six months, and that the therapy focused almost exclusively on trying to understand his dreams. The therapist indicated that the sleep disturbance was only a "symptom." After six months of dream analysis and no improvement, and even some deterioration in sleep, he left therapy. The therapist told him he was not giving the process long enough, and was only leaving now out of fear of confronting the really deep, true material.

The client then began taking Valium (5–10 mg. nightly) and had been doing so for the year prior to our first meeting. He came in now because the insomnia problem seemed quite bad, he felt tired and tense at night from fear of not going to sleep; and during the day from lack of sleep. He also had read and been told that it was not good for him to continue to use Valium every night.

Over the next few therapy sessions, I learned the following information. In addition to the issue of insomnia (Concern Number 1), he was quite shy and unassertive. He noted that he had almost no contact with either his own or the opposite sex. Further, it was hard for him to be assertive, particularly with his family. He had two brothers, and both parents were living. He felt quite pushed around, "bullied" by the older brother, and ignored and not attended to by the father. The mother was somewhat distant and he had never really felt too close to her. The issue of shyness and assertiveness became Concern Number 2. The client also noted he was quite self-critical, frequently noting in the session how poorly he did almost everything (Concern Number 3); felt stress a high proportion of the time during the day (Concern Number 4), and finally that he was an administrative assistant in business, currently out of work and having difficulty finding a new job, partly because of a poor recommendation from his previous employer (Concern Number 5).

CLIENT MOTIVATION

The client felt his general weariness and stress from lack of sleep had reached "crisis proportions" and something needed to be done. He noted he was quite willing to learn and practice the technique of meditation.

The client initially appeared highly motivated to me and this was borne out in the course of therapy. Initial concurrent evidence of this motivation and ability to adhere to self-regulation practice was a special diet he was put on by his physician for a phosphorous imbalance. He had to be extremely careful about his eating behavior and monitor closely his intake. He followed this diet meticulously.

During therapy he maintained accurate and complete records of the homework assignments of areas monitored, practiced meditation exactly as instructed, and put a great deal of personal effort and energy into each problem we worked on.

BASELINE DATA

Because of the behavioral part of my orientation, I felt it important to have the client gather data (i.e., monitor) in diary and/or chart form, on each of the areas of concern: i.e., the frequency, nature, duration of the target behaviors. This baseline data for each of the areas of concern is discussed below.

Concern Number One: Sleep Behavior

As noted, the client stated that he used to sleep seven to eight hours a night, believed he currently was getting only three to four hours of sleep per night, if that; and felt he needed at least six to seven hours. To assess current sleep patterns we monitored length of night, amount of time asleep, number of times awoke, length of time awake, and whether or not he took Valium that night.

From a two-week baseline we found that this client on an average was sleeping a mean of 5.8 hours, was waking about 4.14 times, and was up 1.53 hours (i.e., twenty-seven minutes per time). The kinds of things that awoke him were: (a) anticipation of a noisy neighbor coming in; (b) actual noise from a neighbor (e.g., jogging upstairs, loud music); (c) a bad dream; (d) no actual incident. We also noted that Saturday nights were particularly difficult, partly because of the general noise in his apartment complex. During each week of the two-week baseline, the client took Valium on six of seven nights.

Concern Number Two: Companionship/Assertiveness Skills

The client was asked to monitor the amount of his social interactions not related to job searching. The first week, he noted that his only companionship was a hitchhiker to whom he had given a ride. The next week, it was his brother on the phone, the one he felt nagged him too much—about his health, about not having a job. When asked how he responded, he said he didn't say anything to the brother about the nagging. We discussed the client's fear of being pushed around, being taken advantage of and used both by his family and by potential acquaintances.

The client also noted that he really didn't want to have people back to his apartment because others might think it was sterile and unattractive, "just because it is neat, clean, and totally bare." He said he didn't feel any need to fix it up and artificially put "his stamp on it." He also noted that he seemed to have a response of ignoring (or pretending to ignore) insults or put-downs of other people and then all of a sudden to "snap" (his word) and become aggressive and verbally angry.

Concern Number Three: Positive and Negative Self-Thoughts

The first week of monitoring positive and negative thoughts, the client noted that his thoughts were primarily negative and that every time he had a positive thought (e.g., my piano playing sounds good), he followed it with a negative statement (e.g., who cares?).

Concern Number Four: Stress/Relaxation Experiences

A fourth area of monitoring was stress—times when he felt stress (antecedents, behaviors, consequences). He felt he was always pushing himself—what's going to happen next; how will I cope with tomorrow? Stress for him included physical symptoms of tight jaws, back, and shoulders. Mentally, he would block everyone out and ignore them. Stress frequently occurred for him when he felt there was too much to do with too little time. We also looked at times when he felt relaxed: when he was walking alone and sometimes when reading.

Concern Number Five: Job

The final area of monitoring was to look at behaviors he engaged in that led him toward finding a new job and how that process felt to him.

INTERVENTIONS

Thus, after the first few weeks, a more complete picture of this person began to emerge, and we began to work together to set goals in each of the areas of concern and develop appropriate intervention strategies to help him meet these goals.

Meditation

In structuring a treatment intervention, I try to relate the client's concern to the research literature, to see what interventions have and have not been effective with this type of problem. To my knowledge there is only one study in the clinical literature on meditation and insomnia (Concern Number One). Although there are methodological problems with the study (measuring sleep onset and sleep duration), meditation was shown to be as effective as progressive relaxation in treating insomnia, and both were more effective than a non-treatment control. Further, as there are problems with drug dependence and as the client requested to learn meditation, it seemed to be the treatment of choice for the sleep problem. Further, it was hoped, with appropriate cueing and practice, that the relaxation aspect of meditation would generalize to other high-stress times in this client's life (Concern Number Four: Stress).

Clinical Note: Client Background Information

Before actually teaching meditation, the therapist should have made a careful assessment of the client's feelings, hopes, and expectations. Why did the client come into therapy? What is his/her concern? Is the client willing to take responsibility for that concern? How committed is the client (i.e., how motivated to change)? What is the client's vision of what might (can) happen if he or she does try to change? Does the client fear failure? Why? What are ways the client might sabotage his or her own efforts to change? Does the client fear success? Why? What are the client's reactions to "meditation"? Is there a fear of it, e.g., as mystical? Why? Does the client fear being controlled or losing control? Is there an attraction to meditation? Why? Is the client motivated by the idea of learning to yield and let go of thoughts? A cognitive avoidance? Or a hope for growth? Is the client willing to trust him or herself with an essentially non-analytical technique?

After this assessment, the therapist should determine whether meditation is indicated or contraindicated.

Characteristics of This Client That May Be Helpful for Meditation

First, the client requested meditation. Second, the research literature suggests its effectiveness for insomnia and stress management. Third, the client's anxiety was primarily cognitive. The client was highly motivated and once he made a decision would stick to it and therefore would probably score high in internal locus of control, and also fit a personality profile of inward-directed, relatively neutral affect (one which correlates with success in meditation).

Potential Contraindications

The client seemed shy and of low affect. Meditation as a sole strategy might merely reinforce that behavior pattern. Further the client was a "perfectionist" and might apply these same standards to the technique, perhaps being too self-critical.

If an individual has negative association to the term "meditation," I feel no need to try to convince the client that it is an effective strategy and that the client should change his or her beliefs. Rather, as noted earlier, I would rather change the label— e.g., calling it a relaxation technique, a cognitive (attention) focusing strategy, etc.[*]

Assuming the client does want to learn meditation, what do I then tell them in terms of outcome results and practice?

Clinical Note: "Demand" Characteristics Outcome Results and Practice

Because I believe it therapeutically beneficial to create positive expectancies, I often find it useful to share in lay terms these results. In this particular case I noted, "I think your choice of meditation for dealing with insomnia and general stress is a good one, for it has in fact been found to be effective for these types of concerns."

However, I also feel it important to state that meditation is not a magical panacea, and that the effects from meditation are a result of practice. I ask if the client is willing to give it a chance to work. "Normally, you should begin to feel a significant reduction in stress and anxiety within four to ten weeks. Are you willing to practice the technique on a regular basis for at least that period of time?" If the answer is yes, I spend some time talking about, planning when, and visualizing where the person might have an opportunity to practice on a daily basis. If the answer is equivocal, I spend some time on this issue, again stressing the importance of practice and talking with the client about how much effort they are willing to expend to deal with their concern. Before teaching a strategy, I do try to get some form of commitment from the client.

Relationship Issues

By this time there should also be at least the initial development of trust and rapport between the therapist and client. As noted, the therapist should be aware that techniques appear to be more effective if offered within a context of trust and support. Because exploring one's self, with any strategy, can be frightening, the therapist's gentleness and encouragement in this process are crucial.

---

[*]Earlier, before I would screen clients for their reactions to meditation, I had an interesting experience teaching meditation as part of a relaxation group in a psychiatric ward at the V.A. Hospital. A patient leaped up and ran out of the room shouting, "You're trying to steal my mind with Eastern witchcraft."

Selection of a Meditation Technique

The research literature on this point is not yet very helpful. For example, we do not yet know whether individuals with certain strong perceptual representational systems (e.g., visual, auditory, tactile, etc.) would be better off with an object of meditation which either is or is not in that same representational system (e.g., should an "auditory" person utilize a mantra or a mandala?). The biofeedback literature indicates that relaxation is facilitated if the feedback is in the non-preferred mode: i.e., biofeedback is more effective for an auditory person receiving visual feedback than for an auditory person receiving auditory feedback. However, Davidson and Schwartz suggest that an object of concentration in the same mode as the problem is preferred. If a person has too many thoughts, he or she should attend to a verbal focus such as a mantra, koan, etc. Further, there is some question about whether individuals would be better off learning concentrative versus mindfulness meditation, or both; and if both, in which sequence. The classical literature says first concentration, then mindfulness.

Instructions

This client was initially instructed in breath meditation, including counting one through ten, and asked to practice twice a day, twenty minutes each session. Why breath meditation? There is no empirically valid rationale for choosing this particular meditation technique over any other. Personally, it is the one I was taught in the Orient, and clinically, it is the one with which I am most experienced. At this point, there seems no clear-cut reason not to utilize the meditation technique with which a clinician feels most comfortable.

I generally spend part of two or three sessions instructing clients and having them practice the technique in the office. There are particular signs of "correct" practice I look for, and particular areas of the "teaching" that I believe important to emphasize.

One question often raised is when, in relation to the therapy session, should the person meditate? Carrington and Ephron have described having individuals meditate right before a treatment session so that whatever material may surface would be available for that therapeutic session. I have a meditation room next to my office where individuals can meditate prior to the session, for reasons similar to Carrington and Ephron's, as well as after the session, as a way of attempting to make sure that anything which is dealt with in the therapy session, which may be painful, might just be observed for a certain period of time during the meditation session without undue analysis. Meditation sessions before and after, even though brief, seem to serve also as a helpful transition, both preceding therapy and following therapy before returning to the "real world."

Why a Tape?

In addition to the verbal instructions and practice in the office, I also often give clients a tape to utilize at home. The tape follows the instructions in the office and provides a time frame of twenty minutes. I do this as a way of facilitating practice at home. There are two potential advantages to the tape. (1) The tape repeats the office instructions, and thus provides clients an opportunity to re-check in case they feel they have forgotten or are not practicing correctly. This helps avoid the statement the following week of "I didn't remember exactly how to do it so thought I would wait till our next appointment." (2) The tape is structured with a successive approximation to silence. The first part contains dialogue of instruction followed by a thirtysecond silence, then re-instructions to keep focused on breathing, followed by a ninety-second silence; then briefer re-instructions, followed by a ten minute silence. Many people find this gradual approach to silence more comforting than just abruptly sitting down and counting breaths. Some people, however, find the instructions a disruptive, external intrusion. Therefore, in my instruction to the use of the tape. I note that some people find the tape helpful to facilitate their practice, by keeping them from having to worry about time boundaries, etc. I ask them to try it and if they find it helpful initially, to continue to use it. I note, however, that once they feel comfortable they can practice on their own schedule and time, using the tape only as a checkup when and if they feel it appropriate.

James's Experiences During Meditation

A general description follows of the issues that occurred during the nine months of meditation practice and how they were dealt with.

First Month

After the first week of practice, James noted tension in his face that he had not realized was there and also how hard it was for him to be attentive and relaxed. In the morning he felt his heart beat slowly and heavily, but not in the evening—then he got restless. He noted that the tape kept him sitting. This points out one of the potential initial issues in working with a client in meditation: that initially a certain discipline is necessary. Generally, he said, by the end of the tape, even though he was not aware of the process by which it happened, he felt more relaxed and refreshed. He noted, "It's easier with the tape than without it." Without it, he said, he felt too time-conscious.

Several times in the first month he noted that he felt "energetic" during meditation-a positive contrast to the lethargy he often felt during the day. The nature of the thoughts that occurred were generally of a "planning ahead" nature, such as people he had talked to or he was planning to talk to. Nice images included flowers, trees, mountains, birds. Sometimes he said he felt sad, lonely, and withdrawn.

Clinical Note

The above comments raise several important issues. First, what should you instruct a client to do with thoughts—either positive ones or aversive ones? I agree with the recommendation of Glueck and Stroebel that when ideas that seem important to the therapeutic session come up during meditation, the meditator is to treat them like any other thought and return to the meditation focus or "anchor."

In other words, the client is instructed to merely observe the thought, notice any feelings associated with it, watch it and when he or she is ready, to return the focus to the breathing. In the therapy session, we then would spend time discussing issues or insights resulting from meditation. For example, the client's strong awareness of his/her feelings of loneliness became part of the incentive and motivation for him to decide to risk practicing social skills. The positive images gave us helpful information about useful competing responses to the aversive, fearful images in the evening of not being able to fall asleep.

It should be noted that Easterners say we should let go of thoughts when we meditate. They criticize the Western approach of thinking about thoughts and say that many Westerners believe they are meditating when in fact they are only performing therapy on themselves. My feeling is that a balance is needed. During meditation I believe, as noted, that it is best to let thoughts go. In meditation as a clinical self-regulation strategy, we can learn to see what issues come into awareness, feel how salient they are (i.e., how attached we are to them); watch them with equanimity, and then let them go. However, I believe that after meditation, in therapy, the talking about, discussing, analyzing the issues, antecedents, consequences, etc., is important to facilitate change. The East would say let it all go. The West would say analyze it when it comes up. I think. sequentially, both approaches are possible and useful.

A second important issue is the "anxiety about anxiety" that often can occur when people initially meditate. They become aware of how tense they are (e.g., face tension for this client), how restless they are, and how inattentive their minds are. Here the therapist's reassurance that "this is part of the process" is important.

Third, it should be noted that there is a certain discipline needed for the practice of meditation. For this client the tape helped, i.e., kept him sitting, so that by the end he felt more relaxed.

Next Four Months

These were generally positive sessions for the client in which he experimented with a variety of cognitive strategies—self instructions, imagery, etc. The client noted that the best way for him to let go of thoughts was an image of a window in his mind's eye. He meditated on one side of the window in the room (in his mind); outside the window was a pasture with cows. He opened the window and let the thoughts fly out to pasture to graze with the cows, or let the thoughts "drift away" like kites without a string.

He also said he generally looked forward to the meditation practice, felt it refreshing, that it gave some structure to his days, and to him, a sense of competence. He learned about his thought process, realizing which thoughts he felt were more important (i.e., he was more attached to) because these thoughts had a higher emotional charge and it was harder to let them go.

Sixth to Ninth Month

At the start of the sixth month of meditation he said he was attaining deeper levels of meditation; that he liked it, in general, and yet he was noticing more thoughts and he felt he was more distracted than when he had initially begun. After six months of meditating, we shifted from counting one through ten to just counting one after each out-breath. He said he did not like this as much as there was too little structure, and so we returned to counting one through ten. He noticed, however, that there was still a constant stream of thought and he was becoming angry at himself for this, feeling a failure every time a thought occurred.

We discussed the importance of acceptance. I re-emphasized that "if thoughts come, that's okay, if they do not, that's okay, too." I tried to get the client to view meditation as a process of acceptance of what is and help him become aware of how he was bringing "old" behavior patterns to the practice, and applying "perfectionist" (goal-oriented, accomplishment-oriented) standards to meditation. We explained how this could, in fact, just be a way of setting himself up for failure. The image he liked was one which recognized the discipline it takes to practice meditation while trying to stay calm: "A fighter who meditates acceptingly." After two more months, he noted that he was fighting the meditation less and becoming more accepting of where he was with the process. He still noted that at times he felt inundated by his mind: "I can only turn it off . . . so seldom, it feels keyed-up, planning, worrying, finding chores to do." During the positive times he said his hands felt warm and good. They turned into furry, soft, heavy paws.

At this point I suggested he choose his own length of meditation. If he felt distracted and not able to meditate well, not to force it. It was all right to just stop after a few minutes. Again, it was a process of acceptance, not a goal of "reaching the end of the tape." He found this helpful, and sometimes he meditated more, sometimes less, "Not to fight it, to give up if thoughts get away from me."

Clinical Note

It is important to note the issue of balance involved here. Initially, I believe a certain discipline is necessary to give a self-control strategy like meditation a chance. However, we need to be careful that the discipline does not turn into a compulsive rigidity: "I must practice twenty minutes or I'm a failure," etc. The therapist needs to be sensitive to when to encourage the discipline, and when to encourage the letting go of "rigid" standards, e.g., you "should," "it is 'better' if you can practice twenty minutes twice a day." Further, as noted, the therapist can utilize this information to explore with clients their psychological patterns and styles as an aid to therapeutic learning.

Non-Meditation Interventions, by Concern Areas

Let us now turn to each of the five specific concerns of this client and note how other interventions, in addition to meditation, were utilized to help him accomplish his goals.

Concern Number One: Insomnia

The client's general insomnia-related goals, on coming into therapy, were to lose his dread of going to sleep at night, increase sleep to at least six to seven hours per night, stop taking Valium, and as a by-product, feel more relaxed and rested during the working day.

After the two-week baseline, the client realized he was getting much more sleep than he had thought. This self-observation in and of itself, therefore, became an intervention, and helped the client to feel more confident about his sleep problems. A second intervention was my telling the client, "When you are lying in bed, either initially or after awakening, you should remember that resting quietly is as good as sleeping. So don't worry about being awake. Just let yourself lie there and relax." The client noted that it really helped him to say this statement. (This cognitive restructuring was a strategy taught to me by my father when I was a child!) As the client noted, "I am practicing relaxing and meditating, and I'm getting pretty good at it. I'm not dreading going to sleep as much. It's good to know I'm getting an adequate amount of sleep."

In addition to the regular meditation practice twice a day, the client used the focused breathing and counting as a general relaxation strategy while lying in bed beginning to go to sleep. Besides meditation, the baseline observation, and the cognitive restructuring strategy, this client also used humming, listening to an ocean record, and pep-talks (self-instructions) to deal with the anxiety and fear associated with sleep and the racing future-planning thoughts that would keep him tense and lying awake.

Another sleep-related issue the client had which we monitored during the initial few weeks was the amount of Valium that he took. The first two weeks he went one night each week without it; the third week, two nights; the fourth week, three nights. The fourth week of three nights without Valium was quite difficult for the client and in the following few weeks he resumed taking it every night. However, since the client was sleeping between five and six hours per night and felt comfortable with this, the sleep issue faded into the background and, with only minor spot checking (weeks six through ten, week fourteen), we turned to the other areas of concern.

At week twenty-one, we returned to the sleep issue, particularly in relation to Valium consumption. The client was feeling quite confident about his sleep patterns and wanted to work on stopping the Valium. We decided to take a "successive approximation approach," beginning by not taking it two nights of the week.

While going off Valium he gave himself the following self-instructions, "I am practicing relaxing, meditating, so I'm getting pretty good at this. I am not taking that much

Valium anyway; don't force it; let it go. If I can't get to sleep right away, it's not a big thing. Practice and be gentle on yourself as you try something new."

Weeks twenty-one through thirty-one involved working on decreasing the number of evenings in which Valium was taken. He gradually tapered off Valium, until in the last two weeks, he took it only twice.

This felt like a comfortable level to the client—to take it if he needed it, or felt in trouble, but to first practice the strategies mentioned above.

Interestingly, the sleep data revealed that often the client slept as well with or without Valium. These data charts helped him realize that in many ways the Valium was merely a "psychological" aid, one which in fact did not seem to help him on a regular basis—many nights he would sleep better (i.e., more sleep time, less awakenings, less time up per awakening) without Valium than with it. However, we agreed that sometimes, when needed, there was certainly no problem with taking it.

In summary, for this client in the area of concern about sleep, the following observations are in order. The actual amount of sleep per night, on the average, did not change throughout the course of therapy, ranging from a low of $z = 4.8$ hours in week twenty-six, to a high of $x = 6.28$ hours in week five. If anything, there is a slight, though non-significant downward trend in the data, indicating slightly less sleep per week. However, the client reported feeling quite pleased about this area of concern, noting that his fear of going to sleep had lessened, his ability to stay relaxed when he woke up during the night improved, and he was able to substantially reduce his Valium intake.

Concern Number Two: Assertive-Companionship

After several sessions of not dealing directly with this issue because it was too anxiety provoking, we began to talk about companionship and meeting other people. The client got in touch with the "dread" of meeting other people, the fear of being taken advantage of, the fear of getting into hassles with other people, and not wanting to snap, and yet not wanting to be passive either. Yet, he acknowledged that he did have a desire to meet new people. Therefore, we made lists of places where there would be the opportunity of meeting new people. He refused to go to bars, so we came up with the YMCA, a dance-movement class, and a singing and music appreciation class. After exploring several options, he did join a music appreciation class. There he noted that he had a "freedom reflex," i.e., if somebody approached him, his "gut response" was to hide, to feel trapped, and to abruptly end the conversation.

Over the course of the music class, he was able to approach and initiate conversation with several people of both sexes. In addition, he was able to stand up in front of the group and sing, a risk-taking behavior he had not believed possible.

Another issue he raised was his feeling that all the people he seemed to meet were merely acquaintances (superficial). He also realized how lonely, depressed, and withdrawn he felt and decided it was worth the risk to try to meet other people.

Our goals for companionship were twofold: 1) to increase the number of people (quantity) from the baseline of zero to three or four, and 2) a later goal was added of increasing the depth of intimate experience.

We made weekly tasks, beginning with inviting one acquaintance to lunch. We made a list of current acquaintances—there were three—and several times in the office we role-played asking each of them out to lunch. After three months he had gone out with each several times and felt comfortable about it. However, he felt the conversations were still too superficial, so we began, at least "loosely," to operationalize what was meant by a "more intimate conversation."

It should be noted that at the same time I agreed to work cooperatively with this client on the goal of developing "deeper" relationships I also requested that we spend part of our sessions acknowledging the enormous progress that had been made over base-line in even asking people to lunch!

The client felt, by the end of therapy, that he was able to improve the depth of sharing with two of his "acquaintances," and felt genuine intimacy was occurring with greater frequency in their conversations.

Toward the end of the therapy session he noted that in general he felt more natural being with people, although he still had a gut feeling that he did not contact people very well and the would not really be interested in getting to know him. He admitted that although he could do it, he still did not enjoy taking the initiative and felt it an enormous strain on him. The reason he was willing to take the risk is that he balanced strain against the fear and the dislike of the isolation. He also noted that he did feel *more* confident and more able to non-defensively take criticism than before.

Finally, on the issue of assertiveness, he confronted his parents and expressed his feelings of hurt and not feeling cared for; and was able to ask his brother tactfully not to nag him about his health problems, his job, or lack thereof, and to explore other areas to communicate about. Although he noted relapses, a falling back into "my old docile, trying-to-please self," he generally was able to behave much more assertively, both with his family, and at work, to "not be afraid to say what I feel."

Concern Number Three: Positive and Negative Self-Statements

This was a theme that ran throughout this client's life. His critical, perfectionistic standards got in his way whether trying to learn to meditate, meet new people, or perform a job correctly. Here we worked on increasing positive self-thoughts, in particular, and on "sprucing up" his appearance and environment.

He agreed to "fix up the apartment" for himself—a candle, a couple of green plants, flowers, a Sierra Club calendar. He also decided to take more pride in his appearance: new clothes, getting his hair cut stylishly, grooming himself. He noted, "I am beginning to feel more confident more often although it is so hard for me to justify 'pampering' myself. Am I really worth it?" We worked on catching the "critical" self and using these statements as cues for positive ones. We made a list of the positive qualities he had: intelligence, sense of humor, thoughtfulness, musical ability, a good sense of rhythm. Homework for a while was at least one positive thought per day more than the number of critical thoughts.

He also realized a need to be gentler on himself—not to be always pushing for meeting new people. Sometimes it was all right to feel comfortable being alone, a self-retreat or a self-nurturance; to walk, to swing, to play the piano, or to read. Or, as we discussed earlier with meditation, not needing to have *a perfectly* "empty" mind.

Concern Number Four: Stress/Relaxation

First, we worked on generalizing the relaxation from formal meditation to other times throughout the day. We did this by recognizing antecedents to stress, and also by using the behavior of stress as a cue for relaxation (focused breathing, coping self-instructions, and imagery).

Concern Number Five: Job

He did get a job in May after eight months of conscientious searching. It included several different simultaneous demands: phoning, typing, filing. His perfectionist side rebelled. We worked on generalizing the "accepting" attitude of meditation, and stress-management strategies of focused breathing, coping self-instructions, etc. At work he found it easier to set limits on what he could accomplish by being more assertive with others and more accepting of his own limits. He found that people did not reject him when he did set the limits.

DID MEDITATION AND THERAPY WORK EFFECTIVELY FOR THIS CLIENT?

The client noted at the end of therapy that he was smiling more, seeing more colors in the world, holding his head higher, hearing the wind, taking the time to look at things. A six-month follow-up revealed that the client still felt good about his sleeping patterns; used Valium only infrequently (once every two or three weeks); continued to see the friends he had made on a weekly or more frequent basis; practiced meditation at least once, and generally twice a day; and felt much less stress throughout the day.

Why?

He attributed this success both to meditation and to his excitement at working on the companionship area. Yet I could also, with a certain justification, add the issue of dealing assertively with his familial relationship, increased pride in his appearance, and finding a job. Meditation did seem a useful and powerful therapeutic tool for this client. However, we must recognize it as one technique among many. On an applied clinical and empirical level, we do not really know much more than that.

The client learned the skill of being able to observe thoughts, watch them with relative equanimity and eventually let them go. In this way, high-affect issues were diffused. This is a mechanism involved in many therapeutic approaches. For example, the task of the therapist, as Freud noted in his *Studies in Hysteria,* is to help the patient assume objectivity to his own dilemma. This was done by making the patient into an intellectual collaborator, and by showing the patient that he had nothing to fear by revealing the true memories. And Rogers noted that by fulfilling certain conditions of interpersonal warmth and acceptance, the therapist creates an interpersonal situation in which material may come into the client's awareness and in which "the client can see his own attitudes, confusions, ambivalences and perceptions accurately expressed by another, but stripped away of their complications of emotion. This allows the client to see himself objectively, to see that these feelings are accepted and are acceptable, and paves the way for acceptance into the self of all these clients. The therapist helps the client to see that the client is a person who is competent to direct himself and who can experience all of himself without guilt." From a behavioral perspective, classical systematic desensitization involves having a person observe, in a relaxed way, issues that normally cause distress. This results in extinction of the maladaptive affective charge associated with the fear or phobia.

Similarly, meditation helped give this client a perceptual clarity on events in his life, and with a lessened affect. This may have allowed him to face so many aspects of himself as quickly as he did. Emphasis on meditation therapy is on detachment (objective assessment) and not a manipulation of the environment. This increased equanimity may have helped in the decrease of negative thoughts (Concern Three); the reduction of stress (Concern Four); and the ability to deal more calmly and acceptingly with the number of job-related inputs. This affect-reduction and acceptance might also been helpful in giving the client the inner strength to be more assertive with others. Further, meditation in many ways seemed to help give this client a sense of mastery and control, a sense of increased self-esteem at his success. It also afforded him a "portable" relaxation technique to help him cope with his "generalized anxiety," and a technique he could use any place at any time.

But I believe meditation was only part of the reason for the therapeutic success. Another part was that the client, feeling more confident, was willing to have his affect *raised* and to take risks. He was willing to be assertive with his family, take the initiative to invite people to lunch or to talk with them. The social-skill and assertive-skill training also seemed a critical element in this case. Further, the baseline data and goal-setting seemed to help with his perfectionist style. It showed him the progress he had made so that he was literally forced to acknowledge improvement, even though his preference would have been to ignore (forget) improvement and only focus on the next mountain. Finally, the client himself was very highly motivated, the therapeutic relationship was an accepting one, and the therapist seemed to be both trusted and respected.

SUMMARY CLINICAL NOTES

In this case there were several areas of concern, individual strands of this person's life. They were not all tackled simultaneously. Sometimes more time in a session would be spent on one issue, sometimes another. However, all of the areas of concern together were important in the fabric of this person's life, and to have had the focus of therapy exclusively on only one would, I feel, have done a therapeutic injustice to this individual.

The following points, illustrated by the case of James, need to be kept in mind when using meditation as a self-regulation strategy with a client.

The client initially presented a problem area of insomnia and requested meditation; however, meditation was not offered as a technique until the context of his life was better understood and his reasons (expectations) for wanting to learn it were made clear. Clinicians need to gather such contextual information to insure that they understand the full scope of the problem and that there are not reasons why meditation might be contraindicated. Second, meditation was not taught as a unimodal strategy for insomnia, but one technique among many. Third, meditation was taught within a therapeutic context of trust. Fourth, additional techniques, which seemed useful for other areas of this person's life (ranging from assertiveness training to role-playing social skills) were also utilized. I do not believe that meditation alone would have been sufficiently therapeutic for this client. Clinicians need to be careful in matching therapeutic interventions individually and as appropriate to the presenting concerns. Finally, careful evaluation and assessment seem important to determine whether the technique-therapy is having its desired effect. If not, why not? What changes can be made? The above comments are standard operating procedures for all good therapists. If meditation is to be considered as a therapeutic treatment, the same guidelines apply.

Editors' Introduction

Although some therapists still adhere dogmatically to the theoretical model in which they were trained, a rapidly increasing number of therapists simply identify themselves as eclectic. In short, they do what works, and when what they are doing doesn't work, they try something else.

Larry Beutler coauthored the chapter on integrative psychotherapy for Current Psychotherapies. *He is a master therapist and one of the world's leading psychotherapy researchers. In the following case, he demonstrates the application of systematic treatment selection (STS), an eclectic methodology for therapy in which patients are thoughtfully and scientifically matched with a variety of specific therapeutic approaches. Beutler applies STS to a deeply troubled client with a serious addiction to heroin and cocaine and concomitant marital and financial problems.*

This case study illustrates the way in which behaviorally oriented therapists still use and benefit from psychological tests, such as the MMPI-2, and the ways in which these assessments can be used to guide treatment. It shows how homework assignments can benefit clients and demonstrates the utility of medication as an adjunctive treatment. Most important, it demonstrates the apparently seamless integration of diagnosis with assessment of stages of change, coping style, resistance level, and the patient's personal preferences.

Will you be comfortable with an approach to treatment like the one outlined by Larry Beutler, or will you be more likely to identify with a particular school of therapy? Is it reasonable to assume that any given theoretical approach can be applied to every patient who walks in the door? If psychologists are licensed to prescribe medications—like the antidepressants prescribed for this patient—will you make psychopharmacology a part of your practice?

13 | INTEGRATIVE THERAPY WITH MR. F. H.

Larry E. Beutler

Our approach to psychotherapy is broadly characterized as integrative and specifically labeled *systematic treatment selection,* or STS. Concisely put, we attempt to customize psychological treatments and therapeutic relationships to the specific and varied needs of individual patients, as defined by a multitude of diagnostic and particularly nondiagnostic considerations. We do so by drawing on effective methods across theoretical schools (integrative), by matching those methods to particular cases on the basis of empirically supported principles (treatment selection), and by adhering to an explicit and orderly (systematic) model.

Systematic treatment selection is a flexible system whose principles have identified a number of dimensions on which patients and treatments and relationships may be matched and customized. The actual number of dimensions that have received research support for their ability to optimize treatment outcomes surpasses that which can easily be applied by a clinician operating in the absence of a computer-assistant program. Such programs exist (e.g., www.systematictreatmentselection.com), but for convenience of the current illustration, we have selected some of the more common dimensions used in treatment planning and have applied them to the current case.

Systematic treatment selection (Beutler & Clarkin, 1990; Beutler, Clarkin, & Bongar, 2000) embraces two basic assumptions: (a) no treatment methods work well on all patients, and (b) most treatment methods work well on some patients. The effects of most (if not all) treatments range from very positive to at least mildly negative depending on the patient observed. STS seeks to identify which patients will respond positively to various mixes of interventions from different treatment models.

Contemporary efforts to construct research-informed guidelines do not address the commonalities among treatments, preferring instead to think of each treatment as a discrete and identifiable entity that can be applied to all patients who are assigned a given diagnosis. However, the presence of a shared diagnosis occludes the presence of important differences among patients. Thus, the appropriateness of any given treatment depends both on the pattern of methods used and the fit of these methods to both the diagnostic and nondiagnostic characteristics of the patient.

In contrast to the broad-grain approach of fitting a treatment solely to a patient's diagnosis, STS seeks to identify multiple patient dimensions that best fit with corresponding treatment strategies and a therapist's particular relationship style. Rather than identifying treatments purely in terms of global theories (e.g., cognitive therapy, psychoanalytic therapy, interpersonal therapy) or specific techniques that comprise it (e.g., interpretation, thought records, evidence analysis), STS is constructed around research-informed principles of behavior change. These guiding theorems of change and relationship cut across theoretical orientations and can be applied by individual therapists from different perspectives (Beutler et al., 2000).

The principles and applications of STS were developed through a four-step process (Beutler et al., 2000). The first step was a series of literature reviews to identify predictors and moderators of therapeutic change. The second step was to collapse and combine these variables into a smaller set of clusters, each of which identified a particular fit or match between patient qualities and treatment strategies that reliably relate to change. Our third step was to develop means for measuring the patient qualities and treatment strategies that emerged from the prior steps. The fourth step was to test hypotheses extracted from the reviews of literature, all of which bore on the question of what factors accounted for optimal therapeutic change.

In the following case, we apply some of the resulting STS dimensions to planning and conducting psychotherapy with Mr. F. H. He was a patient experiencing comorbid depression and substance abuse who was seen in a randomized controlled trial of the efficacy of STS predictions (Beutler et al., 2003).

CASE DESCRIPTION

Mr. F. H. is a 39-year-old Caucasian man with 14 years of education, married for about 3 years, and with no children. F. H. has just started a home-based business with his wife, after having changed several jobs in the last few years. He decided to consult a psychologist because he was undergoing severe financial problems due to his drug abuse (he had incurred a considerable debt by borrowing money to pay for his drugs) and his wife was threatening to leave him if he did not find a definitive solution to his addiction. He also reported symptoms of anxiety, feeling sometimes "overwhelmed by a lack of motivation," and talked about having "no desire to do anything," describing some severe episodes of depression. Now he is "tired of lying to himself and to others."

INITIAL INTERVIEW

F. H. appeared 15 minutes late for the first interview. His language was logical and coherent, even if sometimes distracted. He claimed slight memory impairment because of the drug use, and therefore, he was vague and found it difficult to remember some dates and events. The following information was extracted from the initial interview and administration of standardized intake procedures, which included the MMPI-2, STS Clinician Rating Form, and Beck Depression Inventory.

The client was taking both heroin, approximately one-quarter gram three or more times a week, and cocaine, approximately one-half gram almost every day. He reported using them together or alternatively and stated that he was able to stay clean from one drug or the other just for a few days. He was trying to self-titrate the doses, but he felt that he "cannot go any lower." He had been treated twice for drug abuse, one treatment consisting of detoxification only, but he was not able to remember the specific dates of such treatments. F. H. tried numerous "30-day" outpatient programs but never methadone because "it's just synthetic heroin, but with a third of the power. If I want that, I can just take less dope." He attended several AA and NA meetings, expressing a preference for the first. None had produced more than transitory relief from his addiction.

F. H. reported difficulties in various cognitive functions, such as concentration and decision making. He was experiencing frequent loss of appetite and insomnia, leading him recently to spend an entire week without sleeping. Everything went from bad to worse after visiting his stepbrother. Nonetheless, he "didn't feel like going to a shrink" before the visit, and he tried to "get into a better mood" by consuming more drugs and alcohol.

Mr. F. H. was raised by his natural parents until the age of 14, when they divorced and he stayed with his mother. She remarried soon after the divorce; meanwhile, his father disappeared, and the client has never known if he is dead or alive. F. H. reported that his father was an alcoholic, and his mother possessed a "paranoid phobic" personality. He always suspected she was a prostitute, but he was not sure about this attribution. She committed suicide 16 years prior to this interview and only a couple of months after the patient had a terrible car accident. F. H. stated that she physically abused him and his brothers. He does not remember his father abusing him, but he was hurt for all the times the father ignored what the mother was doing to his brothers and him.

Mr. F. H. started drinking when he was a teenager, and he has continued to abuse alcohol since then. Sixteen years before entering treatment on the current occasion, and in reaction to both the physical problems that followed his car accident and the nearly concomitant suicide of his mother, the patient started using heroin to "get out from the physical and emotional pain." In a short period, he developed an addiction to heroin, and he started consuming regular amounts of cocaine as well. After 6 years of drug abuse, he was arrested for the first and only time, charged with drug possession. Following this event, he entered or was committed by the court to several 30-day outpatient treatment programs. He successfully stopped using drugs and remained "clean" for a period of 4 years, during which time he started seeing a psychiatrist. He was dissatisfied and left treatment without further benefit.

Seven months ago, F. H. went to visit J., the older stepbrother he had not seen for a long period. While there, his stepbrother helped F. H. remember some physical and emotional abuses they had both experienced in childhood at the hands of their parents, especially their mother. When he came back home, F. H. felt depressed and began having suicidal thoughts. He subsequently slashed his wrists in an attempt to kill himself. At the time of this evaluation, however, he reported no suicidal ideation. He did report continuing depression and anxiety and indicated that this had been relatively constant for a period of more than 6 months. He reported a recurrent fear that he might "go crazy."

F. H. has many friends among drug abusers but only "two good pals" who were not drug-related. These two friends and his wife were the only persons he could trust. One of these friends was a physician who had sometimes helped him by prescribing drugs during the patient's efforts to withdraw.

CASE FORMULATION

Most psychotherapies can be represented by mapping the therapist's actions against several dimensions (Beutler & Clarkin, 1990; Beutler et al, 2000; Castonguay & Beutler, 2006), including the following: (a) variations in intensity of treatment, (b) variations in the focus on insight versus behavior and skill change, (c) variations in the level of directiveness used, and (d) variations in the way that patient affect is managed. STS proposes that each of these variations in therapy implementation tends to be most suitable for a patient who has a particular and corresponding quality of personal or situational attribute. In other words, different folks need different strokes. Patient characteristics and environments serve as powerful indicators (and contraindicators) of different treatments. Below we present a sampling of five patient characteristics commonly used by integrative psychotherapists. These patient characteristics or variables guide us in identifying a beneficial "fit" between patient and treatment. As noted earlier, integrative therapists are not confined to these five considerations in making treatment decisions. The dimensions applied here serve to illustrate the process of clinical assessment and treatment matching in integrative psychotherapies.

I. Diagnosis and Functional Impairment

A patient's *diagnosis and level of impairment* serve as the basis for the assignment of an appropriate level of care. A thorough assessment of functional impairment includes a consideration of the patient's problem complexity (comorbidity and personality disorder), chronicity, and the available social support system. Level of impairment is considered a determiner of treatment intensity, which can be varied by increased length, the use of multiple formats, and increased frequency. Concomitantly, complexity—a condition indexed by comorbidity and related to level of impairment—is an indicator for the use of multiperson or family-based interventions.

F. H. displayed moderate impairment as indicated by his chronic history of multidrug abuse and alcohol abuse, both combined now with a diagnosis of depression and a previous suicide attempt. Additionally, his MMPI-2 Social Introversion (*Si*) and Paranoia (*Pa*) scales were elevated, indicating his feelings of alienation from others. Thus, current levels of social support were considered weak, and his problem was characterized as complex because it was impacting negatively on numerous areas of functioning, and at the time he sought treatment, he was in danger of losing both his job and his marriage. MMPI-2 scores and various indicators of work and family disturbance also suggested above average difficulties. Accordingly, the intake clinician gave F. H. a global assessment of functioning (GAF; American Psychiatric Association, 2000) rating of 56, indicating moderate disturbance in functioning.

Based on the conclusion of moderate impairment, treatment was scheduled at an intensity of twice a week, at least for the beginning 4 to 6 weeks of the therapy. Because of his low level of social support, high level of problem complexity, and sense of alienation from others, two of the early sessions were scheduled for work with his wife and him together. Some later sessions were also planned to include work with his wife (as it turned out, a total of 7 of the 15 sessions of treatment were with his wife). After an initial 4 to 6 weeks of treatment, if the patient had been adequately stabilized and symptoms had been addressed (e.g., the drug abuse noticeably declined, he was less depressed and anxious), then he may be able to decrease the frequency of the sessions to one a week supplemented by phone calls and emergency sessions if needed.

The primary goal of therapy and the initial focus of treatment were on reducing the risk posed by self-destructive behaviors (substance abuse and suicidal behavior). The principal means of accomplishing these aims was through increasing level of felt support from his wife. The need to provide a protective environment was given serious consideration and remained an option throughout treatment, even though it was eventually decided that frequent outpatient visits would be adequate to the patient's needs.

Mr. F. H.'s level of functioning also suggested that the therapist assign and monitor his attendance at NA and/or AA meetings on a regular, perhaps daily, basis. His wife agreed to play an active role in helping him monitor these activities. Antidepressant medication was considered as an eventual adjunct to psychotherapy (specifically, an antidepressant that may also help reduce the patient's symptoms of general anxiety). In the long run, the recommendation encouraged the patient to employ psychological change procedures as a first-line treatment before applying biochemical agents, in an effort to help maintain the patient's focus on developing a chemical-free lifestyle.

In the service of achieving chemical-free living, the patient also was encouraged to decrease his use of substances based on a realistic schedule of substance use reduction/ titration. A medical specialist in substance abuse was consulted with respect to the titration schedule, and a physical exam was conducted that cleared the patient for gradual withdrawal from drugs. Additionally, the patient and his wife were provided with educational material describing the possible withdrawal effects and specific behaviors (e.g., exercise, diet, vitamin supplements, sleep hygiene, stress management) that have proved helpful in reducing the negative aspects of the withdrawal process.

Because of the chronicity and complexity of the patient's problems, the STS model recommended long-term outpatient care. The frequency of treatment was adjusted as the patient succeeded in reducing drug use, but the therapist was encouraged to expect periods in which the patient's symptoms would become stimulated or activated, necessitating temporary increases in treatment frequency. During these times, work with the patient and his wife as a couple was also increased to both support his changes and to enhance the level of pleasure available in his relationship.

2. Stage of Change

The stages represent a person's readiness to change, defined as a period of time as well as a set of tasks needed for movement to the next stage. People progress across six stages: precontemplation, contemplation, preparation, action, maintenance, and sometimes termination.

Mr. F. H.'s substance abuse history is that of a chronic contemplator who occasionally enters the action stage for a few successful months or years but then returns to contemplation. People can remain stuck in the contemplation stage for long periods (i.e., years and even decades). But F. H. is now preparing to enter the action stage, largely at the insistence of his wife and due to his financial problems.

The patient's stage of change is an indicator for both treatment methods and relationship stances. As someone in the preparation or early action stage, F. H. is most likely to prosper from methods traditionally associated with the existential, cognitive, and interpersonal therapies. As he enters the later action stage and progresses to maintenance, then behavioral and exposure methods are probably most useful. Each therapy system has a place, a differential place, in the "big picture" of behavior change.

The therapist's relational stance is also matched to the patient's stage of change. The research and clinical consensus on the therapist's stance at different stages can be characterized as follows (Prochaska & Norcross, 2002). With precontemplators, the therapist stance is often like that of a nurturing parent joining with the resistant youngster who is both drawn to and repelled by the prospects of becoming more independent. With contemplators, the therapist role is akin to a Socratic teacher who encourages clients to achieve their own insights and ideas into their condition. With clients who are preparing for action, the stance is more like that of an experienced coach who has been through many crucial matches and can provide a fine game plan or can review the person's own action plan. With clients who are progressing into maintenance, the integrative psychotherapist becomes more of a consultant who is available to provide expert advice and support when action is not progressing as smoothly as expected.

3. Coping Style

An assessment of the patient's coping style informs the focus of treatment, encouraging the therapist to select methods that vary along a continuum from insight-focus to behavior-change-focus. In this, there are aspects of patient coping style that correlate with one's stage of readiness to change. Thus, coping style serves as a partial cross-check on the treatment decisions that arise from assessing a patient's stage of (or readiness to) change.

For example, externalizing and impulsive behaviors (i.e., coping styles) indicate the value of problem and behaviorally focused methods, much as does the action stage of change readiness, whereas internalizing and restraining behaviors indicate the value of insight and emotional awareness, in a similar manner as indicated by a contemplative stage of change.

F. H. presented with a mixed pattern of internalizing and externalizing symptoms. He had a history of acting out (externalizing) through drug use and substance abuse. A history of suicidal acts accompanied by the self-reported claim of "interpersonal conflict" suggested the presence of impulsiveness, which accompanied a correlated pattern of self-blame emotional restriction. The MMPI-2 also confirmed the presence of mixed personality features, including both internalizing and externalizing behaviors. Specifically, F. H. produced elevations on several internalizing scales, like the Depression (*D*), the Social Introversion (*Si*), and the Anxiety (*Pt*) scales, but also elevations on two externalizing scales, the Impulse (*Pd*) scale and Paranoia (*Pa*) scale.

The symptoms that placed this patient at risk for continued drug use and for suicidal behavior were given priority and served as the initial focus of psychotherapy. Because he presented with both externalizing and internalizing coping patterns, short-term work focused directly on developing impulse control, while long-term goals included achieving insight into his motivations and awareness of his unmet emotional needs. This decision was consistent with that associated with the assessment of his contemplative and early action stage of change.

Initially, work with the patient and his wife aimed at identifying drug and suicide risk behaviors and at establishing a sense of emotional caring and support that could help him weather these occasions. Later, as the patient began individual treatment, the focus shifted more to the achievement of understanding and insight. The following exchange, which took place during his fourth session (two sessions after the two sessions in which he was seen with his wife), shows how the therapist tried to facilitate insight and personal and emotional awareness by teaching the patient (notice the focus on understanding and feeling identification):

T: When you take a lower dose, and you believe that nothing is happening and that you need to have another "hit," how do you feel?

FH: I don't know—helpless, I guess is the word.

T: Because that's actually what you are likely to feel when you are at the detox program. You are not going to get the feeling that you have to have your stuff to help you feel more powerful!

FH: That's true.

T: What do you think? What do you tell yourself, when you are in that spot? Something like, "the stuff is not working, I've gotta get more!"

FH: I don't know. Maybe.

T: Let's assume that this is the feeling and thought you have—of being helpless and needing something to pull you out of it. How does that sound?

FH: It's uncomfortable—I feel lost. I hate it.

T: It feels like you don't have any options at that point?

FH: It does! Yeah! Actually, I feel that way about a lot of things right now! I feel like my options are very limited, I feel helpless, and I don't like what I see. What I've been left with.

T: So, even though you feel helpless and don't like that, maybe there are some options, but you just don't like them!

FH: Probably. Yeah, you're right!

T: This is important because the more you can get an understanding of how those feelings make you do things, before going to the detox program, the easiest it will be for you.

4. Resistance Level

An assessment of the patient's level of resistance informs the selection of the therapist's level of directiveness. High resistance is taken as an indicator for the use of procedures that deemphasize therapist control, and vice versa. Resistance is defined as the degree of patient opposition to perceived efforts on the part of the therapist to control the patient's behavior. Managing resistance by the selection of methods that are either nondirective or directive and skillfully adapting to changes in resistance levels will minimize the occurrence of negative interactions in therapy and enhance the development and maintenance of the therapeutic alliance.

At the beginning of treatment, and in his wife's presence, the patient expressed a strong desire to quit his drug abuse, and his motivation seemed to be quite high—good signs with respect to treatment compliance. Based on quantitative assessments early in treatment, F. H. scored just above average on a measure of resistance (Dowd Trait Reactance Scale; Dowd, Milne, & Wise, 1991), but he scored below the average on the MMPI-2 Readiness for Treatment scale (*TRT*). Taken together, these scores suggested that F. H. manifested low average resistance, therefore indicating the use of therapist-directed procedures.

For example, early in treatment, the therapist offered a directive homework task:

FH: Change apartments, go to work, talk to my doctor, detox. I should make a list! I keep making lists, but every time my priorities change.

T: Maybe you should make a short list and a long list. The long list is what you have to do in the next couple of weeks or so; the short list is what you have to do today.

T: Keep it simple. Just one thing at a time; commit to one thing each day. You have to say to yourself: "Today I'm definitely gonna do this for me!" Can you do that?

FH: Yeah.

T: So, what can it be today?

FH: Well, calling the detox program!

T: Okay. So next time you can tell me how it went and what's your next choice.

The patient's homework assignment was reviewed and monitored in each session. The patient's cooperation and compliance confirmed for the therapist that the client possessed a relatively low level of resistance. Thus, the patient continued to benefit from the structure and guidance provided by the symptom-focused strategies employed. Nonetheless, the therapist remained vigilant to any signs of increase in resistance level (e.g., patient is often late for therapy, patient becomes argumentative, homework is not completed) throughout the course of therapy and adjusted directiveness levels accordingly.

5. Patient Preferences

When ethically and clinically appropriate, we accommodate a client's preferences in psychotherapy. These preferences may be heavily influenced by clients' sociodemographics—gender, ethnicity, sexual orientation, for example—as well as their attachment styles and previous experiences in psychotherapy. These preferences may refer to the person of the therapist (age, gender, religion, ethnicity/race), therapeutic relationship (how warm or tepid, how active or passive, etc.), therapy methods (preference for or against homework, dream analysis, two-chair dialogues), or treatment formats (refusing group therapy or medication).

In this case, F. H. was interested in some work in couples therapy to improve the quality of the relationship with his wife and to lower her level of frustration with his many failed efforts to overcome his addictions. Thus, two early sessions included his wife. As she became more hopeful, we shifted more to an individual focus. This shift could only occur, however, when the patient was comfortable with the clinician, the therapeutic relationship, and the treatment plan offered. What was important to him was his level of emotional arousal in the therapy session. In psychotherapy, patients usually seek treatment to reduce the intensity of painful emotional states; however, if emotional arousal levels are too low, patients may lose their incentive to continue the therapy, and they may fail to persist in making positive changes in their lives. Conversely, when anxiety is high, the patient may be too distressed to approach treatment in a planned and receptive manner.

An examination of the patient's treatment history revealed that F. H. usually entered treatment in an acute state of anxiety that dissipated rapidly, after which he had little motivation for change. Based on this assessment, it was decided to employ a modest amount of confrontation to maintain the patient's anxiety and, hence, his motivation for change. F. H. preferred this strategy: one in which the therapist would take an active role in keeping him engaged in the therapeutic work, would not allow him to terminate prematurely, and would present him with new challenges every session or two.

A decrease in F. H.'s anxiety through the development of a supportive structure, the improvement in his relationship with his wife, and a safe psychotherapy environment were used to enhance the development of the therapeutic alliance—a necessity for continued involvement and successful treatment. The integrative therapist provided phone and pager numbers to the patient and encouraged him to contact the therapist anytime he felt the need to do so.

The following exchange, which occurred in session nine, illustrates the therapist's efforts to manage and control the patient's discomfort.

FH: I'm doing better. My work, my behavior, my being with other people, the sensation of being sober and clean instead of drug motivated.

T: When you say that you are doing better, I don't think that you completely believe that, but . . .

FH: I believe that I'm going in the right direction and I have more desire to get clean and sober. But, like you said, it's not entirely true.

T: What is really better right now?

FH: I have that desire and, at the moment, I'm off the coke, and right now it just disgusts me! You know, I disgust me! When I think about using it . . . I just wanna be out of that!

FH: Yes, physical and psychological.

T: Both. And your body is telling your brain: take more, use more, you need it! Our mind and our body tell us a lot of things. But we don't have necessarily to obey.

It is notable, from an integrative perspective, that one must balance and integrate the level of confrontation that produces arousal and the focus of treatment—in this case, the focus on insight and awareness of feelings.

T: These experiences have been really, really dramatic.

FH: You know, the drugs don't scare me one tenth as much as the idea of some of these stuff reoccurring.

T: The drugs have been an escape from those memories.

FH: I guess so. I don't remember the time when I was home.

T: Unconsciously, they have always been there.

FH: Sure. I would say that I didn't think about that until the day I talked to my stepbrother.

T: I think it's gonna take time to process all those memories.

COURSE OF TREATMENT

After the first four sessions, two of which had included his wife, F. H. and the therapist were able to start working on the establishment of self-awareness and insight, complemented by homework assignments that targeted specific behaviors such as drug abuse, impulse control, and the development of healthy interaction skills. At this point, the therapy was tailored to track the patient's drug use, drug cravings, and his unique pattern of depressogenic events, thoughts, and behaviors. Considering the client's low resistance, his preferences for guidance, and early action stage, the therapist used primarily directive interventions that combined insight and action goals. These included homework, the psychoeducation, scheduling of healthy (nondrug use) activities, and goal deadlines.

After 15 sessions, fewer than the scheduled 20 sessions of therapy, F. H. was able to begin a methadone detox program and attend NA meetings on a regular basis. By the end of this time, F. H. was abstinent from all drugs and was able to establish new social networks and increase his social contact within nondrug-using contexts. He successfully moved from his previous residence, and he started a new job in a new environment, the combination of which required that he terminate psychotherapy. In the final termination sessions, F. H. reported improvements in his marital relationship, and he had managed to eliminate his financial problems through careful counseling and skills gained in budget management and couples therapy. All these changes gave the therapist the opportunity to partially shift his attention to F. H.'s lifelong threatening memories and his history of losses and abandonment, very likely the primary causes of his depression and suicide attempt.

At follow-up 6 months after treatment, F. H. reported that he was "on the right track." He was abstinent from heroin and cocaine. He was not depressed. He acknowledged the therapist as an important and trustful figure. And impressively, he was ready to slowly discuss and face what he experienced in childhood.

SUMMARY

Systematic treatment selection, broadly integrative in nature, fits the treatment to the patient on the basis of research-based principles of change. This approach stands in contrast to many pure-form or brand-name systems of psychotherapy that tend to fit the patient to their particular treatment on the basis of preferred theory or personal bias.

STS fits the treatment to the individual patient and his or her singular situation on a host of interacting, empirically informed principles. The patient's functional impairment, for example, is used to set the treatment intensity. In the spirit of basing psychotherapy on principles rather than recipes, the way in which therapy is intensified will necessarily vary from patient to patient. In our case example, the therapist chose to vary the frequency of sessions, but one could add treatments, extend treatment, or do some combination of these things. The resistance level, another example, is used to select the therapist directiveness. The directiveness defines the therapist's role as either teacher and authority or collaborator and student. On one hand, the therapist may assume the role of authority as in behavioral or psychodynamic therapies, and on the other, he or she may assume a reflective and questioning role, much like that used by cognitive and client-centered therapists. In the case presented, the therapist adopted a largely teaching and guiding role with the patient, recognizing the patient's relatively low resistance. In many cases, of course, the therapist will adopt both strategies in a seamless and responsive manner.

Different folks require different strokes. The five client characteristics, as illustrated in the case of F. H., serve as reliable markers to systematically tailor treatment to the individual patient, problem, and context. Although these client characteristics are likely to evolve as research progresses, they are based on extensive reviews and meta-analyses of the treatment literature. These client characteristics, including but not limited to diagnosis, can be applied independently of a specific theoretical orientation. All of this is to say that psychotherapy has progressed to the point where clinically relevant and readily assessable patient characteristics can inform specific treatment plans and thereby enhance the effectiveness and efficiency of our clinical work (Norcross & Beutler, 2008).

REFERENCES

American Psychiatric Association. (2000). *Diagnostic and statistical manual of mental disorders* (4th ed., text revision). Washington, DC: Author.

Beutler, L. E., & Clarkin, J. (1990). *Systematic treatment selection: Toward targeted therapeutic interventions.* New York: Brunner/Mazel.

Beutler, L. E., Clarkin, J. F., & Bongar, B. (2000). *Guidelines for the systematic treatment of the depressed patient.* New York: Oxford University Press.

Beutler, L. E., & Harwood, T. M. (2000). *Prescriptive psychotherapy: A practical guide to systematic treatment selection.* New York: Oxford University Press.

Beutler, L. E., & Harwood, T. M. (2002). What is and can be attributed to the therapeutic relationship? *Journal of Contemporary Psychotherapy, 32,* 25–33.

Beutler, L. E., Moleiro, C., Malik, M., Harwood, T. M., Romanelli, R., Gallagher-Thompson, D., & Thompson, L. (2003). A comparison of the Dodo, EST, and ATI indicators among co-morbid stimulant dependent, depressed patients. *Clinical Psychology & Psychotherapy, 10,* 69–85.

Castonguay, L. G., & Beutler, L. E. (Eds.). (2006). *Principles of therapeutic change that work.* New York: Oxford University Press.

Dowd, E. T., Milne, C. R., & Wise, S. L. (1991). The Therapeutic Reactance Scale: A measure of psychological reactance. *Journal of Counseling and Development, 69,* 541–545.

Norcross, J. C., & Beutler, L. E. (2008). Integrative psychotherapies. In R. J. Corsini & D. Wedding (Eds.), *Current psychotherapies* (8th ed.). Belmont, CA: Brooks/Cole.

Prochaska, J. O., & Norcross, J. C. (2002). Stages of change. In J. C. Norcross (Ed.), *Psychotherapy relationships that work* (pp. 303–313). New York: Oxford University Press.

Index